Barry Jones is a lecturer in politics at the ersity of Reading. He was the founding tary of the British International Studies ciation and convenor of the SSRC-orted International Relations Theory up. With B. Buzan, he is co-editor of *nge and the Study of International Rela-s: The Evaded Dimension*, and he has llshed articles in *British Journal of Inter-onal Studies* and *Review of International dies*.

Perspectives on
Political Economy

Perspectives on Political Economy

Edited by
R. J. Barry Jones

St. Martin's Press, New York

© 1983 R.J. Barry Jones

Library of Congress Cataloging in Publication Data

Perspectives on Political Economy.

   Based on seminars given in the Dept. of Politics of the
University of Reading during 1981.
   Includes index.
   Contents: Political Economy/R.J. Barry Jones —
The Political Economy of the Public Sector/Charles Rowley —
Critical Political Economy/Andrew Gamble — (etc).
   1. Economics — addresses, essays, lectures.
2. Economic Policy — addresses, essays, lectures.
3. International Economic Relations — addresses, essays,
lectures. I. Jones, R.J. Barry.

HB34.P426 1983   330   82-24027
ISBN 0-312-60258-8

For my parents, for whom 'political economy' has been a matter of more than academic interest.

Contents

Preface

Perspectives on Political Economy grew out of series of seminars on 'political economy' organized by myself for the Department of Politics, University of Reading, during the spring and autumn of 1981. The success of the seminars owed much to the quality of the papers presented and the continuing interest of my departmental colleagues and of visitors from elsewhere. The quality of the contents of this volume again owes much to the ability of the contributors, many of whom have responded with patience and sympathy to editorial comments.

The warmest appreciation is due to Paul Whiteley, of the Department of Politics, University of Bristol, who not only contributed a most interesting paper to the seminar series but also provided invaluable advice and assistance during its preparatory phase.

Particular thanks must also be extended to Professor Peter Campbell, and the Department of Politics at Reading, for the generous support accorded to the seminar series and the subsequent preparation of this volume. It is no more than the literal truth that this venture would have proceeded no further than mere inclination had not such invaluable assistance and encouragement been forthcoming.

R. J. Barry Jones
Reading
August, 1982

PART I

INTRODUCTORY

1 Political Economy: Contrasts, Commonalities, Criteria and Contributions

R. J. BARRY JONES

THE PERSPECTIVES: CONTRASTS AND COMMONALITIES

The recent resurgence of interest in political economy reflects a crisis of control and conception: the control of economic developments in the real world, and the conceptions upon which both policy-makers and analysts based their approach to such developments. The crisis has thrown into sharp relief the serious shortcomings of some, hitherto popular, analytical perspectives, while emphasizing the renewed relevance of debates and approaches that had once seemed to be no more than historical curiosities.

The 1970s witnessed a number of dramatic developments that inflicted a fatal blow upon a number of post-World War II intellectual orthodoxies. The 'oil diplomacy' of the Arab members of OPEC (Organization of Petroleum Exporting Countries) during 1973 and 1974 shattered the cosy presumption that 'economics are economics and politics are politics' in the international arena. The desperate efforts of governments around the world to combat the pernicious combination of economic stagnation and rising inflation, during the latter 1970s, then painfully demonstrated that the problem of macroeconomic management have not finally been laid to rest by the advent of Keynesianism. Nor too, it was now all too apparent, had issues of economic policy been firmly relegated to some technical 'back room' and withdrawn from the political spotlight. Finally, continuous attempts to combat inflation *and* to live with deep economic recession have prompted such international acrimony (squabbles between the EEC and the USA; squabbles between the USA and Japan; squabbles between the EEC and Japan) as to bury any illusions that the domestic and the international are, or can be, insulated from one another.

Such developments could not but expose the overwhelming deficiencies of established approaches to economics that were based upon grossly simplifying, yet technically convenient, assumptions about reality and that, in related manner, largely took politics as 'given'.[1] Indeed an approach that defined its subject matter as the 'allocation of scarce resources' would seem to have little to offer a world confronted by the problem of how to mobilize, and place back into employment, a palpable overabundance of under-used resources!

Matters of such moment also revealed the limited nature of the contribution made by those who had sought to develop highly formal, or economics-like, theories of political and governmental behaviour. Contributions there most certainly have been from this quarter, particularly on collective action, public choice, and governmental manipulations of economic activity,[2] as there have been from policy-orientated conventional economics and its welfare economics offshoot. Neither approach, however, constitutes the stuff of which a serious response to the profound contemporary crisis is likely to be made.

While exposing the limitations of much that had held the centre of the intellectual stage, the crisis of the 1970s also evoked a renewed concern with the fundamentals of economic life and its relationship with government and politics: a renewed concern that inevitably revived interest in, and disputation between, 'older' approaches to political economy. It is the content of this renewed clash between contending political economies that forms the backdrop to much of the content of this volume and that, indeed, frequently surfaces in individual discussions.

Where economic life is surrounded by controversy and uncertainty, the basic issues of political economy propel themselves to the forefront of attention. At one level, the central issues are those concerning the relationship between the state, or its government, and the economy: what that relationship *is*, both generally and in particular cases; and, most critically, what that relationship *ought* to be. Redefined, in perhaps slightly more profound terms, the issues are those of the nature of the economic domain,[3] the general patterns of relationships that characteristically develop between the 'economic' and the 'political'; and, again, the nature of the relationship that ought to exist between these two realms.

The basic character of the modern economy is viewed quite differently by the major, contending schools of political economy. The *ultra-liberal* (as represented, herein, by Charles

Rowley)—an extreme development, if not final retrenchment of, the general 'liberal' approach—identifies a competitive economy which, if left to its own devices, promises individual freedom and stability combined with the efficient use of productive resources and the greatest satisfaction of consumers' wants and needs.[4]

In opposing this benign vision, *Marxists* (as here presented by Andrew Gamble) perceive a capitalist economy, founded upon exploitation and class antagonism, which is self-propelled towards inevitable collapse and replacement by a socialist order.[5]

A third 'school' has begun to crystallize in recent years: *national political economy*, to adopt Andrew Gamble's term, or its corollary *neo-mercantilism* (reflected in a number of contributions in this volume). This perspective entertains a somewhat more mixed vision of contemporary economic reality. States and governments are seen to be inevitably involved in their economies, albeit an involvement of varying quality, intensity and consequence. Perfect competition is held to be largely a neo-classical fantasy in an economic world which is highly structured by differential distributions of power and influence.[6] The operation of an uncontrolled and undirected free-enterprise system is, moreover, seen to be somewhat uncertain: empirical confusion being the characteristic result, rather than the nirvana of the liberals and neo-classicists, or the inevitable collapse of the Marxists.

The contending perspectives on political economy also offer markedly differing views of the state-economy, politics-economics relationship. The ultra-liberal approach identifies a politically and bureaucratically propelled over-extension of governmental influence on and intervention in economic life. Economic inefficiencies and undue constraints upon individual freedom result from such governmental encroachment. Both efficiency and freedom may be restored only, it is claimed, if the burgeoning Leviathan of the modern state can be halted and forced into retreat, possibly by a restrictive constitution.

In sharp contrast to the ultra-liberal, the Marxist sees political phenomena as primarily a reflection of developments in the economic infrastructure. The strength of the modern state thus reflects the need of a maturing capitalist system to control the consequences of sharpening internal contradictions, intensifying crisis and general disintegration. Only when capitalism has been replaced by socialism will the need for a strong state begin to recede and progress be possible towards the final dissolution of the formal state apparatus by the eventual communist society.

The national political economy/neo-mercantilist disposition sees a close and intense relationship between the political and the economic: a relationship that is held to be both characteristic of, and wholly legitimate within, the modern world. While the state is no mere creature of the economy, its activity remains vital to the success of a nation's industry and commerce and, hence, to the well-being of its citizens.

In considering recent economic difficulties, and those of the less successful industrial nations in particular, the three major approaches to 'political economy' thus offer markedly different diagnoses. To the ultra-liberal the problem has been that of too much government. The Marxist, on a divergent tack, views the growing role of the government as inevitable and ultimately futile. To the national political economist or analytical neo-mercantilist, the ills of many advanced economies reflect too little, or misdirected, government involvement in national economic development.

Studies of political economy have conventionally drawn an implicit distinction between domestic and international matters. The contemporary crisis, however, clearly demonstrates the danger inherent in such an unwarranted division of attention and conception. The combination of domestic, comparative and international perspectives within this volume helps to illustrate the importance of an approach to political economy that, by being neither parochial nor constrained by an illegitimate intra/international divide, can illuminate the complexities of the contemporary global economy. Many and diverse are the connections between developments in the domestic economy and in foreign economies, the behaviour of multinational corporations, global markets, and, in an aggregative manner, developments in the international system; and many and taxing are their consequences for policy-makers and analysts alike. Certainly, a worthwhile political economy must possess the capacity to apprehend these dimensions of reality and subject them to informed and informing analysis.

The contrasts between the contending political economies

are thus reasonably clear. Their commonalities centre upon a number of concerns, practical and intellectual, which they share and which reduce to questions about the empirical problems that lie behind the contemporary crisis of recession and governmental inadequacy, and the intellectual difficulties of analysing such problems. Central to such questions have been the core issues of the basic nature of the modern economy and the relationship that exists, or ought to exist, between it and government.

CRITERIA FOR EVALUATION

While the battlelines between the contending perspectives upon political economy are well charted, it is no longer a simple and straightforward matter to adjudicate between them. Empirical developments have undermined many earlier confidences in the field of political economy, while intellectual debates elsewhere have opened up uncertainties about the criteria for evaluating theories about the 'real' world.[7]

A number of difficulties affect the relationship between theory and 'reality'. The very act of observation and description is, in important respects, governed by the ideas that the observer already entertains about the subject matter (what, really, is an 'inch', and why should we be interested in it?). The expression of theories about human activity may, furthermore, prompt the human subjects to modify their behaviour. Finally, and by no means least, the subject matter may be so complex and dynamic as to defy capture by any one neat, internally coherent and intellectually (or emotionally) attractive conceptualization. Certainly the days are long past when it was possible to rest content upon the view that human affairs could be studied 'scientifically' by applying the simple formula, 'observe, hypothesize and test'.

Once the safe shores of simple, albeit naïve, empiricism are abandoned there is, however, a serious danger of losing clear criteria for selection between alternative perspectives: of surrendering to an 'anything goes' mentality in which prejudice and emotional appeal are the ultimate arbiters of choice. Some explicit criteria of discrimination and choice must, therefore, be salvaged from the wreck of simple empiricism if analytical anarchy is not to prevail. Unfortunately any such criteria, once the alternative anchorages of pure positivism or philosophical idealism are abandoned, will be less than watertight and many assume a more or less arbitrary appearance.

If perspectives upon the political economy are to be judged one against another, some criteria are clear contenders for adoption. General suspicion can clearly be directed towards overly reductionist, or even monocausal, 'explanations' of central phenomena (a point worth considering in connection with the ultra-liberals' supposed 'explanation' of government's expanding role).

Beyond clear oversimplification, however, judgement remains problematical. Where special knowledge of particular phenomena is not the primary concern, a perspective will generally be more satisfactory the greater its analytical power.

The power of an approach, perspective or theory rests, initially, upon the range of phenomena that can be accommodated. 'Power', secondly, reflects the wide range of questions that can be asked about the subject matter under investigation and that can be provided with reasonably satisfactory answers. The ability to handle basic changes in, or alternative states of, the empirical referent is a further major indicator of this second facet of analytical power.

An analytical perspective's power with regard to its empirical referent clearly entails some measure of veracity and responsiveness. No perspective, however broad its coverage, will be worth much if its assertions about empirical reality are palpably false or if it clearly ignores features that are of obvious salience. These criteria relating to empirical evidence rule out much that might otherwise make some claim to acceptability.

The difficulty, that empirical evidence is itself 'theory governed' in its accumulation can be met, in part, by the argument that while a bias may exist in theory-directed observations such bias may be somewhat less than clear distortion. Where the selectivity of a perspective has resulted in the exclusion of potentially pertinent information it remains possible for it to be considered, subsequently, by the researcher who has been sensitized to it, and to its relevance, by exposure to appropriate theories and perspectives. Analysts are not, in short, condemned to the exclusive employment of but one perspective now and for all time.

The criterion of empirical veracity, and the accommodation

of pertinent information, becomes problematical only where a dominant intellectual perspective is systematically distorting in the view that it provides of reality (say a belief in a flat earth by a geographically immobile individual), or a perspective that calls upon forces or phenomena that are not superficially apparent or not directly observable in empirical 'reality'.[8]

Further, and equally interesting, criteria for assessing the power and utility of a perspective are, firstly, its capacity to accommodate other perspectives, or their better features, and, secondly, its ability to comprehend its own genesis (incorporate a suitable sociology of knowledge). Perspectives that can deal with other perspectives only as aberrations, *ad hoc* contributions or as matters to be discretely ignored are clearly inferior to those that can account for, or embrace much that derives from, other approaches. Again, perspectives that are sensitive to the social, economic and political conditions in which they emerged and which, in part, they reflect will appeal more to those of a healthily sceptical turn of mind than those of that pretend to objective truth, immaculately conceived and delivered.

THE CONTRIBUTIONS

It is for the reader to decide how far each of the major contending approaches to political economy satisfies the evaluative criteria suggested in this brief introduction or, indeed, the extent to which these criteria are, themselves, valid. Whatever the reader's ultimate judgement, the contributions to this volume offer an introduction to the major perspectives and some of their more significant implications.

Charles Rowley and Andrew Gamble summarize the contending positions in the ultra-liberal v. Marxist debate. Rowley offers a systematic account of the liberal critique of modern, 'big' government and an extensive public sector. The wish of such 'liberals' is to see the government's power to tax and to spend constrained, probably by a restrictive constitution. Much is made of the inherent uncertainty of reality, an uncertainty that liberals believe necessitates the flexibility of private enterprise and individual decision-making and, hence, of minimal government (despite the fact that it is this very same uncertainty that can be used to justify extensive governmental activity designed to secure its control and minimization).

Andrew Gamble, prefaces his account of the Marxist approach to critical political economy with a critique of the liberal perspective. He then surveys the bases of the Marxist approach and some of its more important recent developments, with their attendant controversies—particularly those regarding the labour theory of value and the role of the state.

The contributions of David McKay, Wyn Grant and Colin Crouch all fall, broadly, within the national political economy perspective. McKay reviews a range of contrasting perspectives upon economic policy and national economic performance that, while being of general pertinence, purport to explain Britain's recent, relatively poor, economic record. McKay concludes that the most promising perspectives are those that highlight those peculiar historical conditions that have contributed to a British political tradition of avoiding real, positive involvement in economic life and development, despite the availability of these capacities for such involvement that have been so dramatically demonstrated by experience in two world wars.

Wyn Grant develops much of McKay's message in his consideration, first of what political scientists might contribute to a 'hybrid' political economy and, second, the important lessons that can be drawn from an examination of other nations' approaches to industrial policy. Grant draws particular attention to Eire and its Industrial Development Authority, with its capacity for selective encouragement of desired types of incoming investment and industry.

Colin Crouch explores the general relationship between state activity, politico-economic traditions, domestic economic configurations (centralization of wage bargaining, etc.) and the creation of those socio-economic policies promoting harmony and, potentially, long-term prosperity. Comparative statistical evidence of the past experience of advanced industrial societies establishes a general, positive relationship between such factors.

International political economy constitutes, in many respects, an extension of, rather than a contrast to, domestic and comparative political economy. Distinct, but largely complementary, contributions are made in the discussions offered by R. J. Barry Jones, Susan Strange and Roger Tooze.

Jones surveys the major, established approaches to the global political economy—liberal, Marxist, neo-mercantilist, and (although rather less cogent) structuralist—and suggests some of the foundations upon which a more effective, albeit somewhat synthetic, approach might be based.

Strange argues vigorously for the consideration of values *and* structures in any study of international political economy. She then proceeds to argue that *risk*—its nature, prevalence and management—is a major feature of the contemporary global political economy that ought to be accorded a central place in its study and analysis.

Tooze, finally, offers a brief but cogent argument for a discriminating approach to the study of the international or, more properly, the global political economy based upon its division into *sectors* and, within each sector, analysis that reflects its specific patterns, processes and characteristics.

A number of points emerge quite clearly from these contributions. First, that many of the established perspectives leave serious questions unanswered. Can the world ever be as the ultra-liberals hope and have modern conditions really developed for the narrow set of reasons identified in their analysis? Furthermore, do such ultra-liberals have anything real to say about the confusion that unrestrained free enterprise can create or the appalling costs that it can impose upon humanity and the environment, as revealed in the recent exposures of the activities of the asbestos industry?

Elsewhere, what kinds of criteria of verification do the Marxists actually rest their case upon and to what time scales does their analysis actually relate? Finally, what level of theoretical precision and rigour can be achieved by the national political economists and neo-mercantilists and, hence, with what confidence can governments implement their policy recommendations?

Such uncertainties aside, however, it is clear that any useful and realistic approach to the modern political economy must accommodate both 'political' and 'economic' dimensions equally. Equally clear is that such an approach must address itself to the *structured contexts* within which economic developments take place, both intra- and inter-national, as well as the *processes* characteristic of such developments.

A suitable approach to the study of the political economy might also be modest in its claims and flexible in its analytical foundations. Discrimination would be a further hallmark of an approach that would be of real use to policy-makers, for the complexities and demands of the contemporary world make such discrimination essential. Developments need not always be seen in simple terms of black and white: industrial support does not have to be across the board, as Wyn Grant's discussion of Eire's case illustrates; protection does not have to be absolute or entail an automatic and total retreat from all forms of 'free' international commerce. Capitalist economies might, furthermore, merely bumble along for a considerable time without achieving great vitality or total collapse.

Many are the tasks that remain to be completed in the development of political economy. Many initial steps have, however, been taken and are illustrated in various of the contributions to this volume. To the extent that they satisfy the criteria suggested in this introduction, the perspectives surveyed may be deemed valuable and worthy of further development. And such development is most certainly a serious and urgent matter. On the last occasion that political economy—both practical and analytical—was in such disarray the world experienced mass unemployment and misery, Hitler and Tojo, and, ultimately, a world war that left millions dead and endowed the world with the legacy of Hiroshima and Nagasaki. Economic malfunctions may not 'cause' dramatic political developments in any simple or direct manner but they may certainly hurry them along. The development of a more effective political economy may, therefore, be considerably more than a matter of mere academic interest.

NOTES AND REFERENCES

1. For accounts of such traditional political economy see Y. P. Venieris and F. D. Sebold, *Macroeconomic Models and Policy* (New York, Wiley, 1977); and K. Hartley, *Problems of Economic Policy* (London, Allen & Unwin, 1977).
2. See some of the references made by Charles Rowley and R. J. Barry Jones in their contributions to this volume. See also N. Frohlich and J. A. Oppenheimer, *Modern Political Economy* (Englewood Cliffs, Prentice-Hall, 1978); P. Whiteley (ed.), *Models of Political Economy* (London and Beverly Hills, Sage, 1980); Bruno S. Frey, *Modern Political Economy* (London, Martin Robertson, 1978); D. C. Mueller, *Public*

Choice (Cambridge, Cambridge University Press, 1979); and M. Laver, *The Politics of Private Desires* (Harmondsworth, Penguin Books, 1981).
3. See T. W. Hutchinson, *Knowledge and Ignorance in Economics* (Oxford, Basil Blackwell, 1977).
4. See also C. K. Rowley and A. T. Peacock, *Welfare Economics: A Liberal Restatement* (London, Martin Robertson, 1975); James M. Buchanan *et al.*, *The Politics of Economics*, IEA Readings 18 (London, IEA, 1978); the seminal F. A. Hayek, *The Road to Serfdom* (London, Routledge & Kegan Paul, 1944); and Milton Friedman, *Free to Choose* (London, Secker & Warburg, 1980).
5. See A. Gamble and P. Walton, *Capitalism in Crisis: Inflation and the State* (London, Macmillan, 1976); P. Walton and A. Gamble, *From Alienation to Surplus Value* (London, Sheed & Ward, 1972); D. McLellan, *Marx* (London, Fontana, 1975); A. Walker, *Marx: His Theory and its Context* (London, Longman, 1978); M. C. Howard and J. E. King, *The Political Economy of Marx* (Burnt Mill, Longman, 1975); A. Bose, *Marxian and Post-Marxian Political Economy* (Harmondsworth, Penguin Books, 1975).
6. See, amongst others, A. S. Eichner, *A Guide to Post-Keynesian Economics* (London, Macmillan, 1979); W. J. Samuels, *The Economy as a System of Power*, 2 vols (New Brunswick, Transaction Books, 1979); and Joan Robinson, *Contributions to Modern Economics* (Oxford, Basil Blackwell, 1978).
7. See the arguments of R. Little in 'Ideology and change', and J. Maclean, 'Marxist epistemology, explanations of "change" and the study of international relations', pp. 30–45 and 46–67 respectively in Barry Buzan and R. J. Barry Jones, (eds), *Change and the Study of International Relations: The Evaded Dimension* (London, Frances Pinter, 1981).
8. See Maclean, *op. cit.*

PART II

CONTRASTS: LIBERAL v. MARXIST PERSPECTIVES

2 The Political Economy of the Public Sector

CHARLES K. ROWLEY

INTRODUCTION

Without doubt a central issue in the economic debate on the public sector from the early 1970s has been the public sector borrowing requirement (PSBR) which has now achieved pre-eminence in most of the relevant economics literature. Such pre-eminence of the PSBR as the single economic indicator of the public sector policy stance of governments, nevertheless, is a fairly recent phenomenon. For, as Peacock and Shaw [28] clearly demonstrate, for a lengthy period following the Napoleonic Wars, attention was focused on the size of the National Debt, whilst, towards the end of the nineteenth century, the 'Pre-Keynes Treasury view' emphasized the desirability of budget balance, at least 'above the line', and therefore the avoidance of budget deficits even under conditions of recession. As is now widely recognized, the adoption by governments of Keynesian economic policies placed considerable emphasis on attaining high levels of employment/output 'equilibria' essentially by manipulation of the budget either into surplus or (much more commonly) into 'above the line' deficit. During the early postwar phase of Keynesian policy (especially in the United Kingdom) there was some emphasis upon utilizing tax rates (elastic with respect to incomes) as automatic stabilizers, thereby reducing the importance of discretionary fiscal interventions. However, as inflation increasingly became a characteristic of the macro-economic system the phenomenon of 'fiscal drag' emerged and the notion of automatic stabilization of employment and real output lost credibility. Governments, encouraged by the apparent existence of a 'Phillips-curve' trade-off between inflation and unemployment displayed an increased enthusiasm from the mid-1960s until the mid-1970s to manipulate the public sector as a major instrument in macro-economic control.

The revival, from the mid-1970s onwards, of the quantity theory of money, combined with increasing concern that fiscal deficits crowded out private capital formation, induced a more critical attitude within successive governments towards fiscal policy and a much closer monitoring of the public sector. As a consequence, the PSBR assumed central significance as a measure of the macro-economic achievements of government.

THE PSBR AND THE PUBLIC SECTOR: THE INCOMPATIBILITY OF DEFINITIONS

The nature of the PSBR itself, as currently defined, requires a wide definition of the public sector for reasons of internal consistency, encompassing the central government, the local authorities and the public corporations (including nationalized industries). The central government encompasses all organizations and funds financially accountable to Parliament and subject to a formal supply vote. There is an element of arbitrariness in this definition, with some organizations financially dependent upon government but possessing access to alternative financial sources classified as falling within the private sector. In such cases, the provision of financial support by government is to be treated as a transfer to the private sector for accounting purposes. But, in reality, such organizations comprise part of the public sector. For the central government's borrowing requirement most certainly is the excess of all its outlays over its receipts.

The local authorities encompass all bodies dealing with local government administration and taxation except for certain services (notably the water boards) which are classified as public corporations. Together, the central government and local authority sectors comprise the general government borrowing requirement as the excess of central plus local government outlays over the combined sum of central and local government fiscal receipts, netting out transactions between both sectors.

The public corporations encompass the nationalized undertakings, together with other trading bodies, such as the Civil Aviation Authority, Telecom, the Post Office, the BBC and the National Enterprise Board. Such bodies often are provided with some financial autonomy from government, with their own borrowing powers and ability to hold financial reserves. Where such reserves are held in government bonds, they affect the overall funding of the public sector. But organizations in which the government has a major shareholding are usually excluded. Any subsidies to such companies are recorded as

Table 2.1: Growth of the public sector borrowing requirement

Period	PSBR as % of GDP
1970/71	1.5
1971/72	1.8
1972/73	3.8
1973/74	6.0
1974/75	9.1
1975/76	9.6
1976/77	6.7
1977/78	3.8
1978/79	5.5
1979/80	5.0
1980/81	6.0

Source: Peacock and Shaw, *The Public Sector Borrowing Requirement*, p. 9.

transfers to the private sector, whilst surpluses are frequently used to purchase public sector debt whilst appearing formally as equivalent to a tax on expenditure. Once again, a significant problem of definitional compatibility arises.

Thus, as Peacock and Shaw [28] indicate, the PSBR is a very wide concept, with public borrowing utilized not only to finance current and capital expenditure undertaken by the public sector but also lending to the private sector and overseas. As such, it has fluctuated quite widely as a percentage of gross domestic product over the period 1970 to 1980, whilst overall it has remained very considerably higher than the percentage inherited by the 1970 Conservative Government. Table 2.1 illustrates this.

THE PUBLIC SECTOR: A MACRO-ECONOMIC PERSPECTIVE

One important measure of the relative size of the public sector within an economy is the ratio of general government expenditure (excluding transfers to the rest of the world) to the gross domestic product of that economy. This measure is inclusive of transfers (most notably of social security payments) and for this reason may be viewed as exaggerating the relevance of public sector *output.* Nevertheless, it remains an important indicator of the extent to which governments control the macro-economy and of course it is of paramount importance (given taxation policies) for the PSBR indicator.

General government expenditure, so defined, has proved to be an increasing function of GDP (with minor oscillations) throughout the postwar period both for the United Kingdom in particular and for the OECD countries more generally. The ratio has continued to increase, indeed, throughout the period of the so-called monetarism of the majority Conservative administration in the United Kingdom (1979–81). Relevant statistics for the United Kingdom reflecting the overall period 1950 to 1981 are outlined in Table 2.2. Moreover, the very high

Table 2.2: Government expenditure as a ratio of GDP in the UK 1950-81

Period	Government expenditure as % of GDP
1950	30.2
1960	30.8
1970	35.5
1976	52.0
1977	43.6
1980/81	47.0

Sources: National Accounts and *Economic Progress Report*, March 1982.

ratios of government expenditure to GDP recorded since 1970 are not expected to abate significantly—even on the Conservative Government's own forecasts—over its remaining period of present office. Table 2.3 illustrates this. A comparison between Table 2.2 and 2.3 clearly indicates the close similarities, especially taking account of corresponding business cycles, between post-1970 governments in their overall treatment of public expenditure as a percentage of gross domestic product, irrespective of political positions adopted for attracting votes at the election hustings.

A second important measure of the relative size of the public sector (at least in principle) is that of value added by government-owned enterprises. However, since government services, as

Table 2.3: The government's forecast of UK public sector
performance, 1981/82-1984/85

Period	Government expenditure as % of GDP	PSBR as % of GDP
1981/82	53	5
1982/83	47	4
1983/84	45	3
1984/85	44	2

Source: Economic Progress Report, No. 143, March 1982.

analysed for expenditure purposes, are not traded, such a
measure in practice cannot be obtained. For the most part,
measures based upon input expenditures have to be utilized,
with the caveat that such measures almost certainly under-
state the relative size of the public sector. Given the measurement and definitional problems concerned (not least the volume
v. relative price effect debate) no attempt is made in this
paper either to chart the temporal progress of public sector
'proper' importance, or even to estimate its present size relative
to gross domestic product. Instead, a few potentially relevant
orders of magnitude are advanced cautiously.

One such measure, which eliminates the contentious issue of
transfers and subsidies, is that of government consumption as
a ratio to gross domestic product at factor cost. In volume
terms, this ratio has fluctuated only slightly between 1960 and
1980 with a mean value of 23 per cent. In value terms, however,
relative price effects (in part a consequence of relative wage
increases and in part of the inability to evaluate productivity
gains in the public sector) have implied a significant expansion
from 17.8 per cent in 1960 to 23.6 per cent in 1980 in the
relevant ratio. Moreover, these relationships reflect a significant decline in government fixed investment since 1974, implying some relative increase in government current consumption
relative to GDP even in volume terms.

A weakness of the above measures of public sector impact is
the exclusion of the trading public corporations from the overall relationship. Only by reference to employment and earnings
statistics is it possible meaningfully to combine the trading and

Table 2.4: Employment and the wage bill in the UK public sector
relative to national aggregates

Sector	Public sector employment as % of total labour force			Public sector wages and salaries as % of total income from employment		
	1970	1975	1979	1970	1975	1979
Central govt.	7.76	9.0	9.3	9.5	10.7	10.2
Local auth.	10.4	12.0	12.3	9.7	12.1	10.8
Total public sector	26.3	29.2	29.8	29.3	34.0	32.4

Source: R. W. R. Price, *Public Expenditure* in Cohen, ed., *Agenda for Britain 2: Macro Policy*, p. 78.

the non-trading components into an overall public sector measure. With a strong caution concerning the validity of such measures, the relevant statistics are outlined in Table 2.4.

Once again there is some evidence of the presence of Baumol's law, with public sector incomes generally relatively higher than public sector employment by reference to the relevant national aggregate. Interestingly, this is not the case with the local authority sector where the reverse relationship obtains.

Interestingly, and no doubt because of the definitional and measurement problems involved, the Economic Progress Report May 1982, entitled *The Public Sector for the Public* nowhere attempts to define or to measure in detail the size of the public sector. Instead, it modestly concludes: 'The public sector accounts for a significant part of the UK economy: in 1981, about 30 per cent of total gross domestic product (GDP) was in the public sector (including central government, local authorities and public corporations).' If this is so, the first two years of the Conservative Government produced no decline in this important ratio. For reasons to be outlined later, it is doubtful if any long-term decline will occur in the ratio in the absence of significant constitutional reform.

THE PUBLIC SECTOR: A MICRO-ECONOMIC PERSPECTIVE

Utilitarian economists would argue, for the most part, that the provision by government of goods and services should be confined to areas dominated by pronounced characteristics of publicness (i.e. to commodities which are non-exclusive and/or non-excludable in consumption). For, if commodities are non-exclusive in consumption, once provided, the consumption by one person implies no diminution in the consumption opportunities. With opportunity cost thus zero, price optimally also should be zero. But private markets cannot function on such a basis. If commodities are non-excludable in consumption, equally private markets cannot exist since economic man will not pay a price, however optimal, for a commodity that he can obtain for free. For such reasons, even the most anarchistic of utilitarians envisage a provision role for government, albeit one much more restricted than actually exists in any modern economy.

Marxist economists (of 'Old Left' vintage), in contrast, envisage a much more extensive role for government in the provision of commodities—in the limit to encompass all the means of production and distribution—as a device for eliminating the capitalist 'exploitation' of the surplus 'created' by labour and of avoiding the 'alienation' which is viewed as being endemic in the capitalist system of production. Once again, in practice, such a complete system does not exist even in economies that profess to follow the teachings of Marx and his successors. Even in its partial form, as for example exists in the USSR and in Poland, it has not always proved to exhilarate the population that endures it.

Marxist economists (of 'New Left' vintage) disenchanted both by capitalist and by bureaucratic methods of resource allocation find solutions in the workers' co-operative and in the labour-controlled organization of production and distribution. Such systems are not encountered commonly nor do they exist for long in economies that freely tolerate any autonomously viable and legal method of resource allocation. Although they are prescribed organizations in certain dictatorships, most notably Yugoslavia, they are not universal to such economies nor are they universally endorsed by the peoples subjected to such dictatorships. Nevertheless, organization forms such as these are virtually all that is left to those who abhor capitalist *and* bureaucratic methods of resource allocation and yet who hold back from the potential output losses of anarchy.

Liberals bring yet another perspective to the debate on the relevant role of the public sector. By emphasizing the importance of liberty rather than of economic efficiency, their normative viewpoints diverge not infrequently from those of the utilitarians, and diverge consistently and sharply from those of the Marxists of whatever vintage. By emphasizing the real-world pressures that impinge upon politics and by underlining the relevance of self-seeking both of politicians and of bureaucrats, as well as of households and firms, liberals paint a very different portrait of the mixed economy and draw forth, from such positive evaluation, normative conclusions of constitutional significance. It is this approach to the public sector and its role which is outlined and evaluated in this chapter.

At this stage, however, it is instructive to centre attention upon the utilitarian, public good-based case for the existence of government as producer within an essentially market economy and to assess, from the specific viewpoint of the United Kingdom, just how far public sector provision of commodities has strayed from the dictates of that ideology. For, as clearly will be established, the United Kingdom public sector is involved only to a minority extent in the provision of commodities with marked publicness characteristics.

To this end, it is fortunate that Arthur Seldon [33] provided just such a relevant breakdown of the United Kingdom public sector on the basis of the *National Income Blue Book, 1974* though his analysis included subsidies and other transfer payments. Reworking his statistics, ignoring subsidy and other transfer payments, the following overall picture emerges within the 1974 context.

(i) *Public goods where privatization or public sector charges essentially are uneconomic.* This category encompasses military defence, civil defence, external relations such as embassies, missions, EEC, etc., Parliament, the law courts, prisons, public health, land drainage and coast protection, finance and tax collection and a limited range of other government services. In 1974 the public provision of such commodities accounted for some 21 per cent of public expenditure here defined (and only for 15 per cent of total government expenditure).

(ii) *Public goods with some separable benefits where partial privatization or charging is economic.* This category encompasses central and local government and public corporation current and capital expenditure, roads and public lighting, research, parks, pleasure grounds, etc., a range of local government services not elsewhere specified, police, fire services, records and registration, and surveys. In 1974 the public provision of such commodities accounted for some 20 per cent of public expenditure here defined (and only for 14 per cent of total government expenditure).

(iii) *Commodities with substantially or wholly separable benefits where full privatization or charging is economic.* This category encompasses education, health, personal social services, school milk, meals and welfare foods, employment service, libraries, museums and art galleries, housing, water, sewage and refuse disposal, and transport and communications. In 1974 the public provision of such commodities accounted for some 59 per cent of public expenditure here defined (and for some 40 per cent of total government expenditure).

Thus, at least by reference to 1974 statistics, over 60 per cent of the public sector might be privatized (in some cases with limited fiscal intervention) by reference to standard utilitarian economics. The very limited privatization programme of the present Conservative administration has barely scratched the tip of this formidable public sector iceberg.

THE PUBLIC SECTOR: A PUBLIC CHOICE PERSPECTIVE

Many economists of neoclassical, utilitarian persuasion present policy recommendations in the light of apparent market failure as if such recommendations will be implemented efficiently by a government which is impartial, far-sighted and itself motivated by utilitarian ideals. In so doing they tend to ignore the harsh reality that public sectors in all advanced democracies do not conform in their composition to the dictates of conventional welfare economics. Specifically, the public sector encompasses major areas of activity which are characterized not at all by elements of publicness and yet, in some instances (notably research), tolerate the private provision of commodities with marked elements of publicness. In large measure, a developing recognition of this gap between policy recommendations and political action motivated the study of public choice [4, 11, 30] or, as it is sometimes referred to, of the economics of politics.

Once it is recognized that the political process itself is a marketplace in which policies and votes are traded by agents motivated essentially by self-interest, the public sector perspective shifts significantly, and a much more satisfactory understanding of its growth and composition emerges, as subsequent sections of this chapter will attempt to demonstrate. For it will not always be the case that vote-seeking governments pressured by well organized interest groups, reliant to a considerable extent upon bureaux that are pursuing their own objectives, will seek to implement policies that satisfy the conditions of Pareto-efficiency, even when the appropriate policy is clearly defined. Moreover, once uncertainty is recognized and positive search costs are incorporated into the analysis, it may not be self-evident as to just which public sector decisions should be effected even by reference to the criteria of welfare economics.

Essentially, there are two major approaches to the analysis of public choice which are increasingly utilized at the present time. The first approach, more abstract in its nature and less effective in its overall contribution, is the spatial analysis of political parties and of their response to vote pressures. First presented by Downs [11] in 1957, and subsequently extended and developed by Hinich, Ordeshook and others, the spatial approach centres attention upon the existence, uniqueness and stability of political equilibrium under specified voter preference conditions, spatial dimensions and willingness to vote. Depending upon the assumptions employed (notably that the voter preference distribution is unimodal and that two parties compete for a pluralistic majority) a unique equilibrium is found to exist at the median or (where abstentions are potentially high) at the mean of the vote preference distribution. The two positions of equilibrium will differ unless the voter preference distribution is symmetric. Where asymmetry is marked, the difference may be substantial, making the abstention factor highly significant. Spatial analysis has encountered very considerable difficulties in defining the relevant issue space(s), in specifying the relevant model and in testing the implications of the model. Until these problems are surmounted (if ever) the approach must remain a 'curiosum' albeit one with potentially a highly important scientific possibility. The second approach is more institutional in nature [6, 8, 10, 32], focusing attention still on the importance of votes for the utility of political parties and their members and emphasizing the relevance of self-seeking behaviour as an important (though not the only) characteristic of individuals in society, be they in households, in private enterprises, or within the public sector. Although this emphasis upon self-seeking behaviour is viewed by some critics as placing an altogether too pessimistic impress upon human nature it is to be emphasized that the self-interest assumption essentially is an 'as if' assumption, designed to generate predictions which are testable. Even where it proves highly successful, in no sense necessarily does it rule out the presence of benevolence or indeed of malevolence within society.

This approach pays much more detailed attention to the actual institutions engaged in public sector activity within specific economies. To the extent that such institutions differ from economy to economy and within each economy over time, the institutional approach inevitably is less general than the spatial alternative and its predictions tend to be more specific. But, certainly, it is much more realistic in its assumptions and it is able to take account of non-voting determinants of governmental behaviour such as rent-seeking pressures, migration and even the threat of revolution or *coup d'état*. It is this approach which is utilized here as a method of analysing public sector behaviour and as an aid in presenting potentially promising constitutional adjustments.

THE PUBLIC SECTOR: A LIBERAL PERSPECTIVE

There is no single clearly defined view of liberty and hence no single clearly defined liberal perspective concerning the public sector of an advanced mixed economy. Indeed, as will be argued here, pluralism in approach is one highly ranked liberal priority, albeit within certain well defined constraints. This section outlines the more important characteristics of the liberal viewpoint, indicates areas of legitimate controversy within liberal thought, and makes clear the more important differences between liberal, utilitarian and Marxist philosophies as a basis for subsequent analysis of the political economy of the public sector.

Perhaps a useful starting point for this discussion (and one which does underline differences within the liberal camp) is a categorical rejection of a recent liberal statement on the practical impact of this philosophy upon the postwar economics profession within the Western world. Robert Sugden, in introducing his important text entitled *The Political Economy of Public Choice* [38] asserts: 'Most of what has been written in recent years in the field of welfare economics and social choice theory has been based on value judgements that are, in a broad sense liberal' (p. 10).

In reality, most recent contributions to welfare economics are Paretian rather than liberal in emphasis and, as Sen [34] has demonstrated so decisively, Paretian welfare economics may run counter to liberal ethics under conditions which demonstrably abound in modern interventionist societies. Moreover, even where no such direct conflict exists, Paretian welfare economics, by its concentration upon problems of market failure and by its explicit or implicit support for the notion of perfect government, has contributed not a little during the postwar period to the destruction of the liberal order in Western society. Yet further, the contributions of economists working in the field of social choice, masquerading in utilitarian guise, have encouraged the notion (as Sugden himself has recognized) [37] of the 'dictatorial social decision-maker' which is totalitarian in nature and which is ends- rather than process-orientated in the best traditions of Marxist and Fascist dogmas. The fact that Liberalism remains 'one of the main strands in the history of political and economic thought in Western Europe and the English-speaking world' is due in large part to the enduring contributions of great philosophers of the past, notably Locke [22], Hume [19] and Mill [26], and to a lesser extent to the minority contributions of a small number of eminent political economists of the present, notably Lachmann, Machlup and Hayek. It owes nothing whatsoever to the writings of Arrow [1], Bergson, Samuelson and (even until recently) of Sen, writers all who would be viewed by many as conservative rather than radical contributors to modern political economy.

As a means of defining the liberal approach to political

economy, in all its diversity, the following important and closely interrelated strands of the philosophy serve as a useful guide:

The notion of negative freedom

Liberalism in the sense employed in this chapter is concerned with freedom rather than with choice, though as Jones and Sugden [20] have recently re-emphasized, the two concepts are frequently if erroneously conflated by the casual observer. Freedom is defined in this context as the absence of coercion of some individuals by others and a person 'is unfree to the extent that he is prevented from doing something by the actions or plans of another person'. In an essential sense, this notion of freedom is negative, as Hayek [15], *inter alia*, has clearly indicated:

It is often objected that our concept of liberty is merely negative. This is true in the sense that peace is also a negative concept or that security or quiet or the absence of any particular impediment or evil is negative. It is to this class of concepts that liberty belongs: it describes the absence of a particular obstacle—coercion by other men. It becomes positive only through what we make of it. It does not assure us of any particular opportunities, but leaves it to us to decide what use we shall make of the circumstances in which we find ourselves.

In this sense, a person may be entirely free and yet may be endowed with minimal or zero opportunities of choice. Such, for example, is the situation of a non-swimming individual who freely ventures forth across a tidal causeway only at the midpoint of his journey to find himself cut off by the rising tidal waters. Such also may be the situation of an individual located in an economy completely absent of human coercion who, having gambled away his total wealth, has no effective choice within the economic marketplace. Thus it is that a society may increase the freedom of its citizens whilst reducing the latters' effective economic choices, as arguably occurred in India once released from the British Empire. Equally a society may reduce the freedom of its citizens whilst increasing the latters' effective economic choices, as was arguably the successful objective of the Peacock Throne in pre-Khomeini Iran.

Of course, this concept of negative freedom, if extended to its limit, collapses along with all other concepts under the pressure of philosophic debate. For, in reality, it is a relative and not an absolute concept and, as such, only one pillar in the liberal structure. Jones and Sugden [20] lucidly expose some of the areas of indeterminateness in the following passage:

Do obstacles count as restraints on freedom if they are man-made but unintended? Can impersonal economic and social forces, such as trade-cycles and price changes, count as man-made restraints? Do general 'laws, which apply to everyone equally' count? Can someone be made unfree by someone else's omitting to perform an action, or can he only be made unfree by another person's positive act? Can rightful human actions limit freedom, or only wrongful ones? (p. 51).

Liberals undoubtedly would respond differentially to these searching questions and with good cause. For any systematic and unanimous response itself would suggest more the Orwellian nightmare than the pluralism of a free society. Some answers to some of these questions may be derived once the remaining pillars of liberalism have been outlined. In the meantime, perhaps the clearest understanding of negative freedom is to be obtained by contrasting it with what arguably has proved to be its greatest enemy, the concept of positive freedom, or effective economic choice, as wielded by the advocates of social and economic intervention. For to many of those who advocate positive freedom there is a direct association between extended economic choice and the power for some to intrude upon the negative freedoms of others. Such has always been the message of dictators and their regimes, from Mussolini, Hitler and Galtieri at the one extreme to Lenin, Stalin and Brezhnev at at the other. It is unfortunate indeed that misuse of the concept of freedom, in phrases such as 'freedom from want' and 'freedom from disease', with the implication of the necessity of effective power, has resulted in a serious misunderstanding of one of the most important legacies of eighteenth-century English political philosophy. Thus Isaiah Berlin [2]:

The freedom which consists in being one's own master, and the freedom which consists in not being prevented from choosing as I do by other men, may, on the face of it, seem concepts at no great logical distance from each other—no more than negative and positive ways of saying much the same thing. Yet the 'positive' and 'negative' notions of freedom historically developed in divergent directions not always by logically reputable steps, until, in the end, they came into direct conflict with each other.

The notion of negative freedom, as here outlined, clearly distinguishes liberalism from all totalitarian philosophies, the most notable of which is Marxist–Leninism at least in its most frequently expounded form for the phase of socialism prior to the eventual withering away of the state as a political, social and economic vehicle of change. Almost equally, however, the concept distinguishes liberalism from utilitarian/Paretian welfare economics which has proved to be massively interventionist in its postwar emphasis, as well as from Keynesian and post-Keynesian contributions which have paved the way for macro-economic interventions malignant to the liberal order in all but a small minority of Western democracies.

The importance of individual choice

Liberals from Mill onwards have emphasized the importance of individuals within society making their own choices within the constraint of the feasible choice set with which they are confronted. Essentially, there are two interrelated but non-utilitarian reasons which underpin liberal support for individual choice, and which are not unrelated to the above-mentioned notion of negative freedom.

The first and by far the most important of these concerns the role of choice-making in the intellectual and moral development of the individual—the notion that individuals only develop their human capacities to the full when they are required to make choices between available alternatives and to assume personal responsibility for such choices as are effected. On this issue, Mill [26] was exceptionally eloquent, as the following passage indicates:

He who lets the whole world, or his own portion of it choose his plan of life for him, has no need of any other faculty than the ape-like one of imitation. He who chooses to plan for himself employs all his faculties. He must use observation to see, reasoning and judgement to foresee, activity to gain materials for decision, discrimination to decide and, when he has decided, firmness and self-control to hold to his deliberate decision . . . It is possible that he might be guided on some good path, and kept out of harm's way, without any of these things. But what will be his comparative worth as a human being? It really is of importance, not only what men do, but also what manner of men they are that do it.

Since liberals upon occasion are castigated for taking an unduly pessimistic view of human nature, it is important to underscore just how optimistic is this judgement. By emphasizing that the essence of humanity lies in the capacity to choose, and not even, or necessarily, in the ability to reason clearly at any point in time, liberals indicate their willingness—indeed their duty—to tolerate mistakes, idiosyncrasies and eccentricities in outcomes as consequences of freedom and, where relevant, as the price of individual development. Restrictions upon such choices, in the liberal order, are to be accepted only where such freedoms of choice run counter to each other, in which circumstances a prior ranking becomes essential if the liberal order is not to descend into anarchy. Even in such circumstances the liberal ethic must encourage the club principle (epitomized by political decentralization in the case of the public sector) so that like-minded individuals may freely exercise their choices in the process of individual development.

Viewed in this way, freedom of individual choice is not a means to some higher political or economic objective. It is an end in itself in that it forces individuals to confront the full responsibility for their own decisions and, thereby, to develop those capacities which essentially distinguish them from the rest of the animal kingdom. Thus liberals value individual choice quite independently from the end outcomes of such choice, even when such choices endanger the liberal order itself. This emphasis upon process rather than upon end states is a crucial characteristic in the distinction between the liberal and the utilitarian philosophy. Nozick [27] clearly underlines this issue in his reference to 'the meaningfulness of life', and in so doing powerfully erodes the case for paternalism that is so frequently encountered: 'A person's shaping his life in accordance with some overall plan is his way of giving meaning to his life; only a being with the capacity so to shape his life can have or strive for meaningful life.'

Such a view of individual choice is inimical to the Marxist position in which individuals are clearly subordinate to 'the state' which is defined organically as essentially distinct from the individuals of whom it is composed. The process orientation of the Marxist dialectic, of course, cannot be denied. But the process itself is deterministic, and is considered to be inevitable, whatever the apparent choices of individuals subjected to its outcome. What meaningfulness in the sense of Nozick is to be detected within the confines of the Marxist dialectic?

Equally, however, is the process orientation of liberalism inimical to Paretian welfare economics—a doctrine sufficiently ends-related to embrace equally the process of Buchanan [8] and of Lange-Lerner [13]. The distance between the two philosophies is perhaps nowhere better illustrated than in the following utilitarian message from Mirrlees [25].

If we reject the 'public good' argument for the public provision of medical care, housing, and education, as I think we must, we should not suppose that we have disposed of all possible arguments for their public provision. Indeed, we know well that the real argument is a paternal one, that individuals for one reason or another, make poor consumption decisions about these goods and services.

Let Mirrlees be transported from the cushioned environment of Nuffield College, Oxford and be consigned by the social decision-maker to a Toxteth council house, his children to St Saviour School, marked it would appear more by child violence than by classical scholarship, and his family to medicare facilities catering more for mainline heroin addiction than for the self-uninflicted infirm. Well might *he* ponder upon the meaningfulness of life and the utility of public provision? The second non-utilitarian liberal justification of individual choice is the belief that diversity itself is an important ingredient of a good society. Social, cultural and economic heterogeneity are viewed by modern liberals, as indeed they were by Mill, as desirable factors for any nation. Of course, logically, choice does not provide either a necessary or a sufficient condition for diversity of outcome. Nevertheless, in practice and in the long run the free play of individual choice is viewed by liberals as offering the most effective available framework for the diverse society.

As Jones and Sugden [20] correctly emphasize, this argument for individual choice is consequentialist in nature, but is not utilitarian. It is an ideal-regarding rather than a want-regarding argument. Of course, diversity also may promote utility as Mill himself certainly believed. But such 'remote utilitarianism' is of little relevance for Paretian welfare economics in the evaluation of existing economic arrangements. Certainly, it has no relevance for the Marxist philosophy.

The importance of the vote mechanism

Liberals writing in recent years have been especially critical of social choice theory, as it has developed following the seminal contribution by Arrow [1], on the ground that it represents an essentially dictatorial method of social decision-making, albeit a method which is grounded in utilitarian welfare economics and which does not bound the domain of individual preferences over social states within which the mechanism is presumed to operate. For liberals believe in the intrinsic value of a particular means of social decision-making—some form of majority voting by secret ballot—despite all the potential problems, notably of intransitivity, that such voting mechanisms bring with them.

A significant problem associated with majority voting concerns the precise method to be employed. In the absence of written constitutional rules—which themselves will be outlined and evaluated in a later section of this chapter—four methods of majority voting exist namely: (a) *first-past-the post*, (b) *the alternative vote*, (c) *the Borda count* and (d) *the committee procedure.*

Method (a) which is utilized for Parliamentary elections in the United Kingdom, places exclusive importance upon the highest ranking in each voter's ordering over feasible alternatives. This method tends to favour the winning party, over-representing their success as measured by the proportion of votes received and possibly involving a minority vote success. *Method (b)* operates in the first instance exactly like method (a). However, each voter records a strict ordering over candidates and, if no alternative has an absolute majority, the one with the least number of first preferences is eliminated and the votes of those concerned are reallocated to their second preference. This process continues until one candidate has an absolute majority, and more information is utilizable, where necessary, than in the case of method (a). *Method (c)* involves each voter in recording a strict ordering of the feasible set of candidates. If there are m candidates, the first preference receives $m - 1$ marks, the second $m - 2$, etc. Once again this is a voting system represented by a multiple-choice function. *Method (d)* is a knock-out system, using simple majority voting to determine each contest between a pair of candidates. Such a procedure may clearly be path-dependent unless there is one alternative which can beat every other alternative in pairwise comparison.

Liberals no doubt differ in their preferences for one or another of these competing methods, though methods (a) and (b) dominate in real-world national elections. My own preference, for reasons later to be discussed is for method (b) associated with some form of proportional representation. Of course, with elections periodic in nature, usually with competing parties offering a package of promises rather than a vote on each policy, and with voter memories subject to high rates of decay over time, the vote mechanism, though crucially important, remains only a limited defence against dictatorial government. Indeed, given the low level of probability of any single voter being decisive in specific elections (as low as 10^{-6} in American Presidential elections for example) it is difficult to explain why rational citizens make use of their vote at all.

The pervasion of uncertainty

To an entirely excessive extent the literature on social choice— concerning both the appropriate extent of the public sector and the mechanism for its control—is couched in deterministic terms with the overriding assumption that full information is available to some decision-maker in society concerning all individual preferences, and that social welfare can be maximized from such a full-information basis. This view of social choice is derived from a philosophic approach which has been denigrated by Friedrich Hayek [15, 16] as 'constructivist rationalism' which was first fully formulated by Descartes, developed and consolidated by Hobbes [18] and by Rousseau, in the notion of the 'social contract', and which found its first practical application in the French Revolution as the guillotines came down and blood splashed its way into the gutters of the Place de la Concorde.

Constructivist rationalists base their analysis on the notion that all relevant facts are known to some one mind and that it is possible to construct from such information the particulars of a desirable social order. Dominating this approach is the view that reason is paramount and that appropriate rules of social choice can be devised to encompass public sector decision-making in a manner fully compatible with the Paretian emphasis upon the primacy of individual preferences. Despite the fact that

Arrow's attempt to devise a set of 'desirable' rules for social choice was a failure (as the 'impossibility theorem' clearly underscores) his original contribution encouraged successive generations of social choice analysts to follow in his example and to develop even more complex systems, dependent upon ever more sophisticated information flows, for determining individual preferences over all feasible configurations of social choices.

In reality, of course, such social choice analysts suffer from what Hayek has designated as 'synoptic delusion', since social choice is characterized at best by low information flows and high-associated risk (subjectively perceived) or even, some would argue, by complete uncertainty in the sense of Knight (in which latter case it is not possible even to conceive of a probability distribution over future outcomes). Certainly, in practice, individual preferences over alternative social states are not easily divined by would-be social decision-makers. Information is a costly commodity and, in societies where individuals do not always register their preferences in market exchange, the existence of search costs will curtail the amount of information obtained, with social decision-makers imposing their own individual preferences to fill the void that otherwise would destroy the smooth calculus of social choice. Thus it is, not necessarily through evil design or corrupt influence, that the process of social choice encourages dictatorial decision-making by those who find themselves responsible for the implementation of policy within an extended public sector.

The importance of effective property rights for realizable expectations

Given the existence of uncertainty in a society composed of many individuals, each unaware for the most part of the preferences of their fellows, rules of conduct are required for the successful interaction of a specialized economy. Fundamental to the emergence of such rules of conduct is the existence of an effective system of property rights which defines for individuals strict rules of ownership, modification and transferability of property within the private domain. The role of the common law in providing the basis for realizable expectations and in establishing rules for the protection of all individuals from the seizure of their rights is seen by liberals to be of central

importance for the preservation of a liberal order and to be
a natural reaction to the impossibility of social decision-making
without dictatorship in an environment characterized by uncertainty. Thus Hayek [15]:

It will be one of our chief contentions that most of the rules of conduct
which govern our actions, and most of the institutions which arise out of
this regularity, are adaptations to the impossibility of anyone taking
conscious account of all the particular facts which enter into the order of
society.

Thus is it that rules of conduct regulating the behaviour of
individuals in terms of contractual commitments precede
society, even though they then do not take the form of property
rights formally endorsed by some kind of a constitutional
contract. These rules of conduct and the associated social
organizations which support them manifest themselves in a
regularity of action, in a matching of expectations with out-
turns. This order, which for the most part is self-generating,
has been designated by Hayek as a 'spontaneous order' capable
of encompassing circumstances beyond the comprehension of
any single individual mind. Although spontaneous orders may
well be illiberal—feudal England is testament enough to that—
liberals contend that certain characteristics of spontaneous
orders, most especially those which encourage the formulation
of realizable expectations in the absence of coercion, are
conducive to the maintenance of a liberal society.

In particular, it is argued that the general principles relevant
to the preservation of freedom, given uncertainty, form the
basis of the 'rule of law' and indeed are clearly discernible in
the evaluation of the common law. For the judge at common
law assists the development of spontaneous orders by concerning himself, in matters of intra-individual conflict, only with
the *ex ante* legitimate expectations of the parties in a transaction formed on the basis of established custom. In this
exercise, the judge is concerned not at all about the wider
'social' implications of his judgment. The rule of law requires
that all laws should conform to a set of principles. First they
must be prospective and never retrospective in their effect,
since the intention is always to influence future choices. Second,
laws must be known and certain, to the extent attainable, so
that individuals are in a position accurately to predict the

decisions of the courts. Third, *laws must apply with equal force to all individuals, including those who govern, without exception or discrimination.* It is this requirement in particular that serves to lower the probability that a liberal order will be overthrown by the coercive legislation of a passing government majority coalition.

The problem with representative government

Liberals are reared on suspicion of the coercive potential of all representative governments. Thus Mill [26]:

> The very principle of constitutional government requires it to be assumed that political power will be abused to promote the particular purposes of the holder; not because it always is so, but because such is the natural tendency of things, to guard against which is the especial use of free institutions.

They are also reared on the belief that individuals in government should be treated as if they are self-seeking and concerned little or not at all in the 'public interest' for its own sake, independently of the furtherance of their own specific self-seeking objectives. Thus, David Hume [19]:

> In constraining any system of government, and fixing the several checks and controls of the constitution, every man ought to be supposed a knave, and to have no other end, in all his actions, than private interest.

However well developed the spontaneous order, all but the most primitive of societies will engage in social choice, if only through government as referee, to ensure that the rules of the order are enforced effectively. Social choice, so limited, is referred to as the case of the 'minimal state'. In reality the minimal state is rarely found—indeed is never found in advanced economies. For the social organization of a spontaneous order is unlikely to capture all gains-from-trade, given the presence of public goods, externalities and other potential sources of market failure in the sense of the Paretian welfare calculus. In such circumstances, a collectivity, and an associated bureaucracy, typically emerges to facilitate the appropriate provision of collective commodities and to correct for deficiencies within the private sector. Thus is created the 'productive state' with social choice now encompassing more than the functions of the referee.

Even the 'productive state' does not denote the outer bound for social choice within societies characterized by constrained government. For concern over issues of primary distribution of rights extends the range of social choice to issues of redistribution, both in generalized purchasing power and, increasingly, in kind. In advanced economies the redistributive function may exceed both the functions of the minimal and of the productive state and become the primary source of government economic influence. Thus is created the 'welfare state' which is such a typical late twentieth-century form. But even the 'welfare state' is not the most extensive medium of social choice currently identifiable within the Western world. For, in certain countries, for example Sweden and the United Kingdom, there are no perceived limits to social choice, no constraints within which governments must restrain their expansionist designs. In such societies, the Leviathan of Thomas Hobbes [18] finds its practical manifestation. Such societies may be designated as being subject to 'the unbounded state'. Clearly, given the concern of liberals about the coercive threat from government, such threat is seen to increase as societies move along the spectrum from the minimal to the unbounded state, even though such governments remain subject to periodic electoral competition.

The problem of private market power

Liberals have traditionally been hostile to the development or maintenance of private power, be it in the product or in the factor markets. For such power constitutes a threat to individual freedom by offering the opportunity for certain individuals to impose their will arbitrarily upon others. Liberals are convinced by evidence to the effect that such power 'corrupts' and that individuals imbued with power over others tend to develop coercive and meddlesome behaviour patterns. It is primarily as a means of eliminating and dispersing such power —and of thereby providing freedom of choice in occupation and in consumption—that liberals advocate competitive capitalism as a principal method of organizing production [30]. It is also the explanation as to why most liberals rank freedom of choice in occupation and in consumption ahead of freedom of contract and coalition in the hierarchy of freedoms. Such liberals are prepared to argue for coercive measures such as antitrust and industrial relations laws designed to support the former over the latter freedoms.

Most especially, in this connection, are liberals opposed to the granting, via social choice, of exclusive rights either in occupation or in production, be it in the private or in the public sector. For sustained market power is typically based upon privileges accorded by government, which are usually protected from innovative competition. Indeed, some liberals would argue that real monopoly power, correctly defined, is *always* the creature of social choice—that market processes, unfettered, will always destroy established monopoly positions in a process of Schumpeterian 'creative-destruction'.

SOME IMPLICATIONS FOR MACRO-ECONOMIC POLICY

The popular notion of the macro-economic policy of government, fostered during the early postwar years of Keynesian dominance, was that of systematic budget manipulation in counter-cyclical fashion, with a surplus during the upturn and peak of the business cycle and with a deficit during the downturn and trough. Although taxation was viewed as an important element in such a process—and indeed was seen in part at least as an automatic stabilizer of aggregate output and employment—public expenditure (and with it the public sector even narrowly defined) was clearly expected to exert its own important impact via the consumption multiplier in the case of deficit or surplus, and of the balanced budget multiplier in the case of the balanced budget. During the past decade there has been a growing disillusionment, in virtually all western countries, concerning this Keynesian macro-economy policy prescription, not least because of the public choice implication of such policy discretion and of the implications of governments' reactions for the maintenance of a liberal society.

Four aspects of macro-economic policy require a detailed scrutiny in any liberal perspective on the political economy of the public sector, namely (i) the power to tax; (ii) the power to spend; (iii) the implications for budgetary policy; and (iv) inflation v. unemployment: the final macro-economic straw.

The power to tax

Within the liberal tradition is evident a deep-rooted concern about the tax-raising proclivities of unbounded government and the implications of this for liberal values. Thus, Mill: 'The interest of the government is to tax heavily: that of the community is to be as little taxed as the necessary expenses of good government permit.' [26]

For the ordinary citizen, the power to tax is the most familiar manifestation of the government's power to coerce. This power to tax involves the power to impose, on individuals and private institutions more generally, charges that can be met only by a transfer to government of economic resources, or financial claims to such resources—charges that carry with them effective enforcement powers under the very definition of the taxing power. In and of itself, the power to tax simply is the power to take. In the absence of effective constraints, this power might be fully utilized by a tax revenue-maximizing Leviathan, just as individuals unconstrained in the marketplace may well behave as self-seeking maximizers of private wealth. This monopoly state model of government thus is viewed as relevant not necessarily because it predicts how governments always, or even frequently, work but because there are inherent tendencies in the structure of government that push it towards such behaviour.

Of course, it can be counterargued that ordinary electoral processes will tend to check governments in their tax-raising endeavours. In essence, this is one major justification of democratically elected representative government. In an important recent text, however, by Brennan and Buchanan [6], this view has been questioned. The authors justify their fears concerning tax-raising discretionary power firstly by reference to evidence that voter preferences over taxation typically are not single-peaked. As is well known in such circumstances, majority rule generates cycles with the party most likely to win being the one which commences its policies last and which organizes appropriate transfers from some minority to a corresponding majority, appropriating any surplus to itself. In this way, important dimensions of monopoly government emerge out of simple majority rule. Even if all parties are constrained to announcing their tax policies simultaneously, Brennan and

Buchanan demonstrate (contrary to the claims of Anthony Downs [11]) that scope remains for genuinely monopolistic behaviour on the part of the non-cooperating parties. In addition, of course, cartelization on a single issue of policy cannot entirely be ruled out of consideration given the fewness of electoral competitors.

Such an expectation is enhanced once it is recognized that bureaucrats exercise genuinely discretionary power in the selection of support for implementation of policy proposals, in their case without any constraining threat of adverse effects from electoral defeat. By their very nature, bureaux tend to act as monopolists, whether in the supply of information to politicians or in the implementation of their preferred policies. Current theories of the motivation of such bureaux—which typically centre upon the motives of budget size maximization and/or growth maximization—in no sense moderate the liberal fear that governments will lean in the direction of high taxation policies.

Furthermore, the so-called 'taxpayers' revolt' which attracted widespread attention in the USA in 1978, following California's 'Proposition 13', 'Son' and 'Grandson of Proposition 13' reflects a deep-rooted public suspicion of the taxing behaviour of unconstrained representative government. First, the revolt emerged not from within the normal political process but from outside the system, against indifference and opposition from most of the political establishment. Second, the revolt took the form not of once-and-for-all tax and expenditure cuts but of explicit constitutional constraints designed to be operative over an indefinite future. The avowed intention was to constrain the size of government below the level that would prevail under normal electoral processes. There is no evidence that the electorate trusted the in-period political process to produce results in accord with the two-thirds or more majority electoral will.

The simplest model of Leviathan, then, presumes that governments maximize revenues from whatever sources of taxation are made available to them. In the absence even of constraints as to the uses to which revenues may be put, revenue may become equivalent to private income for certain governmental decision-makers. Certainly, 'revenue' becomes in part a proxy for 'surplus'. For example, if some proportion α of total revenues must be spent on specified public goods and services, then government surplus, S, the income available to government for discretionary use, is the excess of revenue collections over spending G: $S = R - G$, and since $G = \alpha R$, then $S = (1 - \alpha)R$. The taxpayer (unless himself a recipient of R) would prefer to have α set at unity. But even if initially this were the case, it seems unlikely that no slippage would occur. For social choice mechanisms, as we emphasized earlier, are characterized by extensive uncertainty and the agents of that process—politicians as well as bureaucrats—are viewed as searching actively for such rents as can be appropriated. To the extent that tax revenues cannot be appropriated directly but must be expended on public goods, it is predictable that those in government will minimize the tax burden upon themselves but otherwise maximize tax revenues expended upon public goods that they are best placed to expropriate. The best extant examples of such behaviour perhaps are to be found in Brussels (EEC) and in Washington DC (USA) where the combination of tax loopholes for public officials and contingent public goods are most lavishly in evidence. The dissemination of information concerning such behaviour may fail to induce curtailment especially during the early phase of the government's period of office.

Once it is recognized that governments finance expenditures on quasi-public and private commodities together with transfer payments the scope for additional rent expropriations is evident. In the guise of assistance to the poor, for example, governmental decision-makers may secure indirect transfer into their own welfare bureaucracy. In the UK, for example, the Manpower Services Commission has been one of the fastest growing bureaucracies. How far are its activities beneficial to the unemployed? How far to the bureaucrats themselves?

Not only does the unconstrained power to tax place in jeopardy the structure of property rights essential to a liberal society. It threatens in its practical implementations the very rule of law itself. For, as Hayek [15, 16] has argued, among others, implicit in the rule of law as above-defined is the notion that taxes (direct and indirect) should be proportional to income (or linear in their incidence). For progressive taxation offends against the notion that laws should be non-discriminatory. Yet, tax revenue maximization encourages the imposition of discriminatory taxes in the absence of tax-base constraints. In practice, few relevant constraints have survived the growing twentieth-century appetite of Leviathan. Even in the USA, the original constitutional requirement that taxes should be uniform in incidence was repealed in 1913 and, therefore, has failed to protect the taxpayer from progressive taxation. In Britain and Sweden no such constraints have ever existed. Until 1979 in Britain marginal tax rates on investment income peaked out at 98 per cent, and on earned income at 83 per cent. In Sweden even the 100 per cent barrier was destroyed as Leviathan sucked in the property rights of Swedish residents—as Ingmar Bergman's defection brought to international attention.

The power to spend

Yet worse is still to come. For the power to spend within the public sector is not now constrained entirely by the limits of taxation, as indeed was the case prior to the widespread acceptance by western governments of Keynes' vision during the postwar period.

During the early part of the twentieth century the growth of public expenditure, both in Britain and in the USA, was checked by two powerful constraints. The first such constraint was the unwritten rule that the budget should balance, implying that increased public expenditure must be financed via increased taxation. The second such constraint was adherence to the Gold Standard (subsequently the Gold Exchange Standard), which prevented any potentially reckless government from debauching the currency to finance profligate expenditure. The combination of these constraints encouraged successive governments to stand firm against the self-interest of public sector pressure groups and to limit public expenditure to a modest proportion of the gross national product. Thus a stable fiscal and monetary environment was provided, within which expectations might be realized and within which a spontaneous market system for the most part coordinated economic activity.

With the onset of the Great Depression and with the publication by J. M. Keynes of *The General Theory* [21], both during the 1930s, these important constraints were destroyed, leaving governments thereafter unfettered in their public-choice decisions. The Keynesian vision was that the economy in the absence of fiscal intervention was chronically inclined towards less than full-employment equilibrium with monetary instruments slow to make their mark. In consequence, governments should intervene fiscally to balance the economy, if necessary by unbalancing the budget. Such a view, it might be urged, has no trend implication for the rate of public expenditure which might expand during recessions and contract during the boom in an entirely offsetting manner. But, in practice, this has not proved to be the case. Massive overall budget deficits have piled up since 1945 (since 1960 in the USA) not only in Britain but in almost all countries employing Keynesian techniques of demand management. The explanation of this phenomenon is to be found in the lack of understanding by Keynes of the nature of the political system. His elitist contribution set in motion forces which yet may destroy not only liberty but democracy itself.

Democracy in deficit—an implication of budgetary policy

In practice, budgets are determined not via Harvey Road, Cambridge economics [9, 40] (the Keynesian vision) but rather by politicians and bureaucrats in response to signals within the political and governmental marketplace. Such signals are biased in the real world situation in favour of budget deficits, since attempts both to raise taxes (despite the Brennan/Buchanan [6] assertion) and to cut public expenditure in real terms will create identifiable losers among the electorate without providing a corresponding number of equally identifiable gainers. Voters for the most part appear to respond more immediately to the direct fiscal benefits of a deficit budget than to its longer-term adverse effects via low productivity investment, inflation, the crowding-out of higher productivity private investment and the reduction in occupational and consumption choices that monopoly provision implies. A majority vote system of representative government, therefore, may tend to induce an excessive use of deficit financing, to overexpand the public sector, and to erode individual liberty once the acceptance of the Keynesian paradigm has destroyed the implicit fiscal and monetary constitution, and with it the principle of the balanced budget.

The evidence of history supports this inference. In 1790 the total expenditure of the public authorities in Britain accounted approximately for 12 per cent of gross national product. In 1913, despite a substantial increase in government expenditure, the total accounted for exactly the same percentage. Since then, dramatic changes have occurred, with the ratio, widely defined, rising to 50 per cent in 1971/72, peaking at 60 per cent in 1975/76, then falling back, only to rise once again between 1979 and 1981 under the deficit financing influence of the present fiscally-profligate and GNP-destructive Conservative coalition administration.

Similar experiences are recorded in the USA, although the introduction of Keynesian macro-economics there was retarded until 1960 and was rejected at least on entry into office of the present Reagan administration. Between 1947 and 1960, there were seven years of surplus and seven years of deficit. With $32 billion of deficits and $31 billion of surpluses, the budget can be said roughly to have been balanced over this period of time, despite the impact of the Korean War. Since 1960, however, deficit-financing has become the norm, with only one year of budget surplus (1969) during a period of two decades, and with a total accumulated deficit by 1981 in excess of $400 billion. To those concerned to check the growth of Leviathan, to preserve the liberal order and to encourage spontaneous market forces, Keynes and his sycophants clearly have much to answer for.

Inflation v. unemployment: the final macro-economic straw

One reason for the worsening budget deficits over the period 1960 to 1980 was the widespread belief within governments that they were confronted with a stable trade-off between the annualized rates of price inflation and the rate of unemployment in their national economies. This view was fostered initially by the statistical contribution of A. W. Phillips published in August 1958 and based on British data for the period 1861 to 1957, and was swiftly seized upon by American Keynesian economists such as Samuelson and Solow [36] as providing the 'missing equation' in the Keynesian model. The macro-economic *débacle* induced by this viewpoint, with governments generating inflation by loose monetary policies associated with profligate fiscal deficits in essentially hopeless attempts to lower real wages, and thereby to generate output growth and to lower the rate of unemployment, has been recounted elsewhere. By the mid 1970s, most governments began to recognize that the trade-off was worsening to their political disadvantage and to accept not just that Friedman [32] had been correct essentially in his theory that the long-run Phillips curve was vertical, but even that Lucas [23] may well be correct in his 'rational expectations' theory that the macro-economic policies of government are rendered impotent by the anticipatory action of agents within the economy.

In much of western Europe (save for Italy and briefly for France) governments have attempted to move towards monetary and fiscal orthodoxy of pre-Keynesian vintage. The USA is facing problems with the Federal Reserve Bank pursuing monetary orthodoxy whilst the Executive attempts to sell a major fiscal deficit to Congress relying essentially upon 'supply side economics' as a mechanism for growth whilst improving the defence provisions of the USA. In all countries —but most especially in Britain—the general shift of emphasis has created social upheaval and some failure to satisfy fiscal targets, largely as a consequence of the micro-economics of the public sector, the central aspects of which are analysed in the following section of this chapter.

SOME IMPLICATIONS FOR MICRO-ECONOMIC POLICY

Neoclassical economics, utilizing the essential framework of Walras [14, 32], continues to emphasize a micro-economy within which markets simultaneously clear and adjust to under-lying real forces of demand and supply, in which competitive pressures tend to dominate, with factors of production receiving payments reflecting at the margin their contribution to the revenue of their enterprise, with long-run unemployment at the 'natural rate' which is dependent upon the essential institutional organization of the economy. In direct contrast, is the view, expressed most elegantly by Malinvaud [32, 39] of an economy in which markets do not clear in the sense of Walras but are characterized by quantity rationing and associated temporary equilibrium as a consequence of rigidity in the real wage structure in the face of market adjustment. In so far as the neoclassical viewpoint has lost ground to that of Malinvaud, the increasing relative size of the public sector essentially provides the explanation. For it is only within the public sector, given the high degree of worldwide competition in the product markets, that resistance to real market forces can successfully be sustained. In analysing the public sector's contribution to the micro-economic problem of inefficiency in resource allocation it is important to centre attention upon three issues, namely (i) the distinction between the trading and the non-trading public sector; (ii) the relevance of rent-seeking behaviour; and (iii) the impact of public choice.

The distinction between the trading and the non-trading public sector

The trading public sector consists essentially of the nationalized industries together with other publicly owned trading concerns taken out of the private sector to avoid impending bankruptcy. Such organizations are faced with financial targets (which at the minimum are at break-even levels), are subjected to Treasury test-rate-of-discount evaluations when applying for government investment finance and/or the market test when they are allowed/able to raise finance in the private capital market. In principle, therefore, such organizations should perform in ways not significantly different from their private enterprise equivalents.

In practice, however, significant differences do exist arguably with an adverse impact upon trading performance within the public sector. Firstly, the nationalized industries are statutory monopolies (more or less) protected from UK-based trading competition. Of course, they are not always protected from international competition (for example British Steel, British Airways, British Shipbuilding and the National Coal Board are not) nor are they always protected from competition from substitute commodities (for example, all of the above together with British Rail, the British Gas Corporation and the Electricity Council are not). Nor indeed does monopoly power automatically provide protection in the case of a declining industry, as Post Office and port experience has indicated. Nevertheless, in so far as residual monopoly power offers surpluses (or rents as henceforth they will be designated), the organizations concerned will be subject to rent-seeking activities which are rarely productive in their contribution.

Secondly, there is no equivalent to the private capital market as a monitor of public corporation performance. The capital market monitors the internal performance of the quoted public company principally via the asset valuation that share-trading provides. If that valuation falls significantly below its under-lying potential, as a consequence either of market or of technical inefficiency, the capital market provides a fulcrum either for shareholder revolt or for takeover, both of which will be designed to eliminate the defects within the organization. Moreover, by issuing stock options to senior management, shareholders enable such management to take a private gain from the future improved share valuation of the firm, thereby encouraging efficiency within the organization and reducing the impact of the divorce between ownership and control.

Thirdly, there is no formal equivalent to bankruptcy in the case of public sector trading, although a practical equivalent, in the sense of a political decision to cease trading, is available. However, such a solution, though threatened in the face of quite staggering deficits in the cases of British Rail, British Steel, British Airways, British Shipbuilders and British Leyland, has never been effected. Bankruptcies within the private sector have been manifold. Inevitably, differential incentives filter through to management and workers in such circumstances.

In such circumstances, it is not surprising that public expenditure upon the nationalized industries shows such low (or negative) return. For much of that expenditure is not investment at all but merely subsidies towards the labour bills of the corporations in question. In the case of such expenditure decisions, presumably, the test-rate-of-discount is conveniently ignored.

The non-trading public sector (henceforth designated as government bureaucracy) encompasses all those activities of central and local government characterized by the provision of an agreed total output in return for an agreed budget allocation and in which prices are zero or reflect only a trivial percentage of the unit cost of supply. Most important among such organizations in Britain are the National Health Service, Defence, Education, Social Services, and the central Whitehall Civil Service. In some cases, though by no means in all, bureaux supply commodities characterized by qualities of publicness. In most cases, the precise nature of 'output' is difficult to define and productivity changes, therefore, are difficult to evaluate.

Bureaux essentially are in a bilateral bargaining position with their sponsor department of government. Because of their privileged access to relevant cost-output information, and their ability to inflict output cuts in response to budget reductions upon the most vote-sensitive aspects of their activities, the relative bargaining position of many bureaux often is substantial. On the assumption that senior bureaucrats are concerned to maximize the size of their budget (as a proxy for all the specific utilities that they seek) Niskanen and others have predicted that bureaux provisions typically will be excessive by reference to conventional efficiency criteria and that bureaux will not be restricted to budgets that are minimally necessary for the output level that has been agreed. In such circumstances, rents will exist and rent-seeking behaviour is to be anticipated. Bureaux do not face either market competition or the threat of liquidation as constraints upon inefficient performance or upon successful rent-seeking invasions. Thus, any constraints imposed must emanate via the mechanism of public choice.

The relevance of rent-seeking behaviour

If rents exist within an organization, it is predictable that they will attract the attention of those who seek to privatize such rents, either in the form of direct transfers or in the form of unproductive expansion of the size of the management/shop-floor work-force [10]. Although such rent-seekers in principle can emerge from any section of society—and indeed may well do so in practice when rents exist within the private sector—the opportunities for those outside to penetrate public sector organizations without the consent of those already established therein are limited. For there are no private property rights to be expropriated and no capital market to invade. The managerial hierarchy is usually well defined and unions, typically operating closed shops, are extremely difficult to subvert or to replace. Only by working through the mechanism of public choice can outsiders invade directly such public sector rents as are available. Nevertheless, expenditures on such rent-seeking activity may be viewed essentially as a social waste.

In contrast, the existing management and labour unions within the public sector may possess very considerable scope for rent extractions in the form both of excessive or ill-judged capital expenditures, and of overmanning and, usually in direct association with these, in factor payments in excess of marginal revenue product. Such rent extractions, for the most part, must be treated as social waste, although socially beneficial by-products cannot be discounted entirely. Past experience within the United Kingdom (perhaps Concorde is the best example) suggests that the wastes involved, both in the trading and in the non-trading sectors, may be very large indeed. As one eminent economist, significantly involved in reviewing public expenditure proposals supported by government departments, recently remarked in a public address: 'Whenever I am confronted with a public sector investment proposal, my instinct is to see yet another white elephant with its trunk in the Treasury trough.'

Moreover, divisions occur inevitably within specific public sector organizations concerning the allocation of rents. In some cases, the division is between different tiers of management, in others between management and workers, in others between or within the unions themselves. In all cases, the result is a diversion from productive activity and involves rent destruction of a socially wasteful nature.

The impact of public choice

With market inefficiency, technical inefficiency, and successful rent-seeking clearly available within the public sector, for reasons outlined above, in the absence of political constraints public choice considerations assume supreme importance. Unfortunately, at the micro-economic level, such latter considerations tend to be the subject of temporal and issue-specific variability, with the inference that generalization is inappropriate and that predictive caution is at a premium. Specifically, it is assumed, following earlier analysis, that public sector decisions are viewed by governments as political commodities, to be manipulated as instruments in pursuit of maximum political support. Since the political marketplace, like all others, is subject to continuous adjustment, conditional predictions only can be made. Much must depend upon the preferences of voters, the relative power position of government v. its bureaucracy, the penetrative power of pressure groups over the issue of economic efficiency of public sector organizations and the constitution that constrains political freedoms.

For the most part, and as always with exceptions, the first thirty postwar years in Britain were characterized by the dominance of producer over consumer issues, most especially with respect to investment and employment within the public sector (save for a brief aberration during the period of office as Chancellor of the Exchequer of Roy Jenkins). In part, this was a legacy of Keynes and of Beveridge, with their emphasis upon the lexicographic priority of employment above all others as a political objective and their emphasis upon fiscal policy as the mechanism for its achievement. In part it corresponded with the preferences of median voters, many of whose occupation expectations were linked to the continuous expansion in real terms of public expenditure. In part it was manipulated by interest groups, both in management and in labour, who sensed the availability of newly developed economic rents.

In such an environment, as always with exceptions, the rent-seekers succeeded, at a relatively high cost in rent-seeking conflicts, in extracting the rents available, whilst thereby restricting the real value of services provided to consumers. In the case of the nationalized industries, low productivity was either funded by deficits (where market forces penetrated) or by monopoly pricing (when it did not). In the case of bureaucracies, increasing real expenditures for the most part were reflected by falling real outputs, as measured by the consumers of such commodities. Despite a battery of government auditing procedures—well documented elsewhere—the polity effectively lost control over the level of public expenditure in volume terms.

Since 1975, however, the public choice perspective has shifted, almost inevitably as a declining private sector (relatively) was called upon to shoulder mounting public sector deficits. Governments, both Labour and Conservative, have introduced much tighter controls over public expenditure (despite such aberrations as occurred when Sir Keith Joseph was let loose as Secretary of State for Industry) and rents within the public sector have been reduced even at a time of world recession unprecedented during the postwar period. Whether such policies will prevail over the longer term, not only in Britain but elsewhere through the Western world, cannot be predicted at the present time. At the time of writing this chapter, the situation is more hopeful in that respect than at any other since the termination of World War II.

TOWARDS A LIBERAL SOLUTION

Constraints in the original position

As governments expand and the domain of social choice grows beyond the limits of the 'minimal state', through the 'productive' and even the 'welfare' state and approaches the 'unbounded' extreme, as arguably is the case with late twentieth-century Britain, so the groundswell in favour of constitutional reform may be expected to make itself felt increasingly within the political process. There are two alternative ways of characterizing such constitutional reform, two paradigms of 'Leviathan in Chains'.

The first approach [8] conceptualizes 'society' in the preconstitutional situation characterized by the Hobbesian jungle in which predacity and defence compete with productive exchange in the allocation of resources, in which the strong successfully plunder the weak and in which life tends to be 'brutish and short'. In such circumstances, the gains-from-trade from 'minimal government' are high and a constitutional settlement designed to establish and to enforce property rights via 'government as a referee' is highly predictable. However, at such a constitutional assembly, it is argued, the potential growth of Leviathan to an unbounded state would be recognized and suitable constraints would be devised. It is the essence of this paradigm that the assembly gathers behind 'a veil of ignorance' which precludes each constituent from all knowledge of his endowments, life chances, indeed of his likely success position within the post-constitutional settlement. As developed by John Rawls [30], the constituents are seen to play the minimax strategy within an environment which cannot be seen necessarily as alien, with the (in my view unreasonable) inference that they all must be characterized by infinite risk-aversion in protecting themselves unanimously against 'worst outcomes'.

However, as adjusted by Brennan and Buchanan [6], the process of guarding against worst outcomes behind the veil may not imply necessarily infinite risk-aversion. For, as they model the situation, the government itself is viewed as potentially alien, thus requiring participants to play the minimax strategy even where infinite risk-aversion did not prevail. Moreover, in so far as asymmetry exists between relatively limited potential gains and quite dramatic potential losses—as would be the case for liberals if unbounded government really chose to exercise its authority—it makes sense to protect against worse outcomes even if governments on average are not conceived as universally alien bodies.

Thus is it via Rawls or, more plausibly, via Brennan and Buchanan, that the chaining in of government is legitimized via constitutional constraints within the universal, Wicksellian model of social choice. There is a sense indeed in which the written constitution of the USA may be viewed as the outcome of such a process, though the mechanism of its imposition was not that of universal constitutional assembly but rather that of the authoritarian resolution of the founding fathers.

However, the mechanism of the 'veil of ignorance' cannot be used to explain the process through which government, once unbounded, then allows itself to be reigned in. For, in such circumstances, the veil has already lifted, all the agents within the system are acquainted with their existing life chances and can be expected to take a view as to the likely impact upon such chances of specific patterns of constitutional reform. Most particularly, those politicians who find themselves in the majority coalition of a sovereign parliament, together with the bureaucracies that service and are serviced by such majorities, clearly are aware of the authority that is provided to them via an unbounded domain and an unrestricted range of social choice. By what route can such agents be expected to divest themselves of accumulated power and to put themselves into the chains of constitutional government? Two alternative such paths are clearly discernible.

The alternative paths towards constitutional constraint

The first path [11, 12] envisages the politicians essentially as the agents and the electorate as the principals of the political process. If the electoral preferences for reform effectively cluster around the median (or in some cases the mean) of the issue-space distribution, the spatial model, following Anthony Downs, will ensure that such reforms are adopted and are implemented by party coalitions that seek access to the machinery of government. To the extent that such an outcome then is avoided as a consequence of the fulltime enforcing of policies, or of the time-lags between elections, political participation in the form of pressure group and social movement activities, migration, even attempted *coup d'état* or revolution by those who find themselves coerced, may induce the enactment of constraints by reluctant government coalitions [4].

Such a path to constitutional reform depends, almost certainly to an unrealistic degree, upon the ability of the consumer-orientated electorate, possessed of a very varied understanding of the direct and indirect effects of constraining public sector growth via the mechanism of constitutional reform. Is it feasible that such an electorate will prove capable of identifying so complex an issue dimension without any leadership from the agents of the process or from the rent-seekers who thrive on the unbounded state? In itself, this path to constitutional reform looks unpromising.

In practice, however, two important stimuli may be expected to emanate from within the political process and to provide a potential fulcrum for an alternative path towards constitutional reform. The first is the frustration of political coalitions who find themselves in an enduring political minority and whose interests remain unprotected in the 'unbounded state'. The second is the growing recognition within the major political groups that unbounded government is a mixed blessing, both because one's rival itself can interfere boundlessly when in office, perhaps imposing costs upon oneself which cannot fully be recouped during one's own periods of unbounded authority, and because the absence of constraints paradoxically leaves government vulnerable to the ravages of rent-seeking pressure groups which exist to sustain and to extend membership advantages [31].

Under the combined pressure of such stimuli, constitutional reform may occur, even in the face of powerful vested interests, given the presence of highly skilled entrepreneurial talent of an appropriate kind at the crucial moment of constitutional decision when the issue dimension itself is delineated and the electorate appraised of its significance.

The constitution of liberty

Many learned texts have been written concerning the essential elements of a constitution of liberty [15, 16] should an electoral majority accept the values of this text and the latter's interpretation of the limitations of unbounded government. It is not the purpose of this chapter, nor is there sufficient space, to outline in detail the author's views on this issue, but rather to indicate the central features that any such constitution ought to embrace. These features are as follows:

(i) *Taxation powers should be constrained.* The optimal taxation literature [5] is replete with suggestions concerning both the optimal structure of commodity taxes (designed essentially so that the proportional change in demand should be the same for all commodities) and the optimal rates of income tax (designed to equalize the proportional change in the demand for leisure). But this literature takes no account of externality corrections in the case of commodities and it has been manipulated by egalitarian weightings and model specifications in the case of incomes following the 'disturbing' initial result by Mirrlees that marginal tax rates should fall as income levels increase, with top incomes charged at a marginal rate of only 20 per cent.

Brennan and Buchanan [6] concerned more to constrain the tax-raising powers of government than to optimize their structure, suggest that a shift to a limitation of the tax base (e.g. to money incomes) together with progression in the marginal rates chargeable against that base would be established in any pre-constitutional assembly gathered behind a veil of ignorance by risk-averse citizens who so would protect themselves against the tax appetite of their to-be-appointed government. Thus they claim all other arguments, based upon equity, would be rejected, at the pre-constitutional stage.

The liberal approach to tax reform [15, 16, 26, 30], based upon the values earlier outlined, differs sharply from the recommendations of either of these competing schools, although it does emphasize the importance of constitutional rules freely selected and not imposed. The liberal emphasis is upon equality before the law, with tax powers constrained to prevent the coercion of minorities by majorities, which otherwise is a predictable outcome of public choice. For example, the majority of households in Britain at the present time face a linear tax schedule on incomes (with constant marginal rates). The marginal rates are dramatically higher for the poor and for the rich, minorities highly susceptible to the median or mean income voter preference. In itself, perhaps, equality before the law does not require a linear tax schedule, since other commodity taxes, required perhaps for externality corrections, may be regressive (or indeed progressive) in their incidence and poverty may require negative tax rates over certain income ranges. Nevertheless, strict limits on the deviation from linearity are necessary if equality before the law is to be ensured, and an upper limit is required on the basic marginal rate involved if public sector growth is to be constrained. Such a constraint system, alterable only by a two-third majority referendum vote would assist significantly in reining in the tax-raising proclivities of in-period government. In the USA several constitutional amendments at state level now require two-third majorities for the enactment of new taxes, usually with escape clauses in times of war or national emergency.

(ii) *The budget should be balanced.* Clearly this is essential if relative public sector growth is to be constrained, given the public choice pressures upon in-period governments to engage in deficit financing. Such a constitutional requirement, however, involves delicate definitional issues. One element of a balanced budget constitution is the exclusion of certain items implied by the set of transactions of which the budget is a description, notably borrowing and money creation, except in times of war or other carefully defined external crisis when the constitution temporarily might be suspended. Further definitions are necessary, however, if sleight-of-hand manoeuvres by governments are to be prevented [40].

For example, in the case of federal systems of government—which includes the UK for fiscal purposes—it is always possible for the highest level of government to evade its fiscal responsibilities by placing upon the lower chambers expenditure requirements which are expected to win itself votes whilst leaving the vote-losing financing decisions as the responsibility of such lower chambers via rate levies and state or local taxes. Even in unitary systems of government, 'off-budget' expenditures are possible via legislation which requires citizens to expend privately upon themselves what the constitution prevents government from expending directly, though in this case the financing implications are more likely to be associated directly with the legislation of the government. To protect against either such manoeuvres, the fiscal constitution must be tightly drawn, especially when rival political factions occupy respectively the higher and the lower echelons of government.

Yet further definitions are essential concerning the precise time period over which the balanced-budget requirement is to be monitored. Since tax revenues fall due unevenly over the fiscal year, any period shorter than one year clearly is untenable. Yet, although expenditure decisions may span several years, and may have investment implications for decades more, to lengthen the fiscal time horizon beyond the year itself is to offer excessive fiscal discretion to the in-period politicians. The twelve-month balanced budget, therefore, is almost universally endorsed by those who favour fiscal constitutions of this kind. Two associated problems arise from the selection of such a time period.

The first concerns the treatment of fiscal decisions legislated in one such period but which affect expenditures in future fiscal years, for example legislation designed to index-link all public sector pensions. Clearly, a system of present-value accounting would be essential if vote-seeking governments were to be constrained from placing excessive public expenditure obligations upon those who succeed them into office.

The second concerns the treatment of expenditures which would classify as investment if effected within the private sector. Should the government be allowed to issue debt to undertake such projects, with the current account budget reflecting the amortization payments on the debt so issued? Despite the evident logic of such a budget split, the public choice case for the rule of overall budget balance is overwhelming. Otherwise, excessive investment spending is inevitable, with the future amortization of price-tags left to be picked up by succeeding in-period governments.

Of course, there will be those who will argue, especially from within the Keynesian school, that a balanced-budget constitution limits the instruments available to the government for demand-management of the economy. In an obvious sense, of course, this cannot be denied, although many economists would emphasize the limited apparent effectiveness of such interventions, in both the UK and the USA, over the past fifteen years. In any event, the requirement of budget balance does not rule out all relevance for fiscal policy, since the balanced-budget multiplier, if it exists at all in practice, implies that the changing scale of the budget itself may influence aggregate demand even when balance must be maintained. To the extent that tax limits combine with the balanced budget to place upper bounds on the public sector, the scope for such discretion undoubtedly *is* reduced. But, in the last analysis, liberals will always sacrifice a degree of *potential* demand-management gain for a positive increment in liberty, especially in the light of the self-seeking impulses which are known to govern actual budgetary decisions in the real-world marketplace of democratic politics.

(iii) *The public provision of commodities should be reduced.* The rent-seeking opportunities available within the public sector, as a consequence of monopolistic trading markets, monopolistic bureaucratic provisions and the willingness of unconstrained governments to deficit finance their expenditures already have been outlined in this chapter. With the relentless relative advance in the size of the public sector such a pronounced feature of most advanced economies, rent-seeking behaviour has become a major economic activity with deleterious consequences both for economic efficiency and for the maintenance of a liberal society. Without doubt, some combination of tax limits and budget balance, constitutionally enshrined, would rein in many of the rents currently available within the public sector and, to that extent, would curtail rent-seeking activities. Whether or not such constitutional constraints would survive the ravages of rent-seeking in the absence of significant institutional reform, however, must be considered uncertain, even if they were to be introduced by qualified majority voting in a national referendum. If constitutionalism is to be introduced by self-seeking citizens, either behind the veil of ignorance or in reaction to the horrors of the Hobbesian jungle, public sector reforms must be viewed as a complementary necessity.

In essence, rents can be removed by displacing monopoly power within the public sector where currently it offers management and workers the opportunity to exploit. An essential, relatively straightforward first step on the path to such reform is the removal of all statutory monopoly provisions from the trading and non-trading public sectors, allowing potential competition from the private sector to limit the size of public sector rents and, thereby, to curtail rent-seeking activities. This measure alone will not suffice, however, either in the case of public enterprise or of the bureaucracy of government.

The problem with public enterprise, even with statutory monopoly removed, is the willingness of in-period politicians to engage in the deficit-financing of enterprises which prove unable to cover their costs with revenues even over an extended period of time. Even the requirement of overall fiscal balance would not prevent such outcomes of the vote motive in the political marketplace. The only fail-safe solution to this problem, which inevitably would take some time, if capital markets were not to be disturbed excessively, is to adopt a long-term policy of privatization of all public enterprises, reintroducing capitalist constraints on rent-seeking possibilities. During the period of transition, deficits should be disallowed or *de minimis* should be reflected in specifically named deficit taxes imposed on the income-tax base as a means of bringing pressure to bear from taxpaying voters upon the politicians who underwrote such inefficiencies.

Bureaucracy poses less tractable problems than public enterprise from the viewpoint of rent elimination because it does not encounter even the limited market test imposed on public enterprise, and because it offers to its sponsors little insight into the true nature of the production functions which underpin its commodity provisions. A combination of reforms is necessary to make inroads into the rents which are currently exploited within this vexatious area of government.

The most radical reform, which is feasible in the case of bureaux provisions that are not characterized by public good or natural monopoly qualities, is that of bureaux elimination in favour of capitalist market provision. Education, medicare, telecommunications, waste disposal, water supply provisions etc. certainly are susceptible to such adjustments. Where relevant, financial support via voucher or insurance provisions might be introduced to prevent any potential under-consumption of such facilities by individual citizens.

During the inevitable transition phase to privatization, charges should be introduced save where publicness characteristics are pronounced and the bureaux simultaneously should be decentralized to the local level. Thus, competition between local government organizations would constrain the rents that any local bureau could extract, whilst citizens who so wished could vote to some extent with their feet, migrating from the more to the less profligate authorities. For the rest, the fiscal constitution together with the tax limits that might be imposed would have to take the strain in reforming this least amenable area of the public domain. Rent-seeking is a pervasive feature of the public sector. No single group acting alone can be expected to relinquish its rents or rent prospects as a piecemeal contribution to economic efficiency. Yet, if faced in aggregate with the prospect of constitutional reform, applicable to all groups, a sufficient majority might endorse rent destruction policies. If the minority then obstructed such a constitution, the issue of democracy itself would move centre stage, with dictatorship and anarchy waiting in the wings as potential substitutes should it fail this crucial constitutional test.

REFERENCES

1. Arrow, K., *Social Choice and Individual Values* (New Haven, Conn., Yale University Press, 2nd ed., 1970).
2. Berlin, I., *Four Essays on Liberty* (Oxford, Oxford University Press, 1969).
3. Black, D., *The Theory of Committees and Elections* (Cambridge, Cambridge University Press, 1958).
4. Breton, A., *The Economic Theory of Representative Government* (London, Macmillan, 1974).
5. Bradford, D. A. and Rosin, H. S., 'The optimal taxation of commodities and incomes', *American Economic Review*, 66 (1976), 94–101.
6. Brennan, G. and Buchanan, J. M., *The Power to Tax* (Cambridge, Cambridge University Press, 1980).
7. Breton, A. and Scott, A., *The Economic Constitution of Federal States* (Toronto, University of Toronto Press, 1978).
8. Buchanan, J. M., *The Limits of Liberty* (Chicago, Chicago University Press, 1975).
9. Buchanan, J. M. and Wagner, R., *Democracy in Deficit: The Political Legacy of Lord Keynes* (New York, Academic Press, 1977).
10. Buchanan, J. M., Tollison, R. and Tullock, G., eds, *Towards a Theory of Rent-Seeking Security* (Texas, A & M University Press, 1980).
11. Downs, A., *An Economic Theory of Democracy* (New York, Harper & Row, 1957).
12. Frey, B., *Modern Political Economy* (London, Martin Robertson, 1978).
13. Friedman, M., 'Lerner on the Economics of Control', *Journal of Political Economy*, 55 (1947), 405–16.

14. Hahn, F., 'Reflections on the invisible hand', *Lloyds Bank Review*, No. 144 (April 1982), 1-21.
15. Hayek, F. A., *The Constitution of Liberty* (London, Routledge & Kegan Paul, 1960).
16. Hayek, F. A., *Law, Legislation and Liberty: Vol. 3, The Political Order of a Free People* (London, Routledge & Kegan Paul, 1979).
17. Hemming, R. and Morris, N., 'Taxation policy' in C. D. Cohen, ed., *Agenda for Britain: 1, Micro Policy* (Oxford, Philip Allan, 1982).
18. Hobbes, T., *Leviathan* (London, J. M. Dent, 1943).
19. Hume, D., 'Of the independency of Parliament' in *Essays, Moral, Political and Literary* edited by T. H. Green and T. H. Grose (Oxford, Oxford University Press, 1963).
20. Jones, P. and Sugden, R., 'Evaluating choice', *International Review of Law and Economics*, 2 (1982), 47-66.
21. Keynes, J. M., *The General Theory of Employment, Interest and Money* (London, Macmillan, 1936).
22. Locke, J., *Two Treatises of Government* (London, Everyman, 1924, originally published in 1698).
23. Lucas, R. E., 'Expectations and the neutrality of money', *Journal of Economic Theory*, 4 (1972), 103-24.
24. Mirrlees, J., 'An exploration in the theory of optimal income taxation', *Review of Economic Studies*, 38 (1971), 175-208.
25. Mirrlees, J., *Arguments for Public Expenditure* (Association of University Teachers of Economics, 1979).
26. Mill, J. S., *On Liberty* (Harmondsworth, Penguin, 1974, originally published in 1859).
27. Nozick, R., *Anarchy, State and Utopia* (New York, Basic Books, 1974).
28. Peacock, A. T. and Shaw, G. K., *The Public Sector Borrowing Requirement* (Buckingham, University College, 1981).
29. Price, R. W. R., 'Public expenditure' in C. D. Cohen, ed., *Agenda for Britain: 2, Macro Policy* (Oxford, Philip Allan, 1982).
30. Rowley, C. K. and Peacock, A. T., *Welfare Economics: A Liberal Restatement* (London, Martin Robertson, 1975).
31. Rowley, C. K., 'Liberalism and collective choice: a return to reality', *Manchester School*, 4 (1978), 224-51.
32. Rowley, C. K. and Wiseman, J., 'Inflation versus unemployment: is the government impotent?' *Journal of Economic Affairs* (forthcoming, 1982).
33. Seldon, A., *Charge* (London, Maurice Temple Smith, 1977).
34. Sen, A. K., 'The impossibility of a Paretian liberal', *Journal of Political Economy*, 78 (1970), 152-7.
35. Sen, A. K., 'Personal utilities and public judgements: or what's wrong with welfare economics?' *Economic Journal*, 89 (1979), 537-58.

36. Solow, R., *Price Expectation and the Behaviour of the Price Level* (Manchester, Manchester University Press, 1970).
37. Sugden, R., 'Social choice and individual liberty', in M. J. Artis and A. R. Nobay, eds, *Contemporary Economic Analysis* (London, Croom Helm, 1978).
38. Sugden, R., *The Political Economy of Public Choice* (London, Martin Robertson, 1981).
39. Tobin, J., *Asset Accumulation and Economic Activity* (Oxford, Basil Blackwell, 1980).
40. Wagner, R. E. and Tollison, R. D., *Balanced Budgets, Fiscal Responsibility and the Constitution* (San Francisco, Cato Institute, 1980).

3 Critical Political Economy

ANDREW GAMBLE

THE MEANING OF POLITICAL ECONOMY

Political economy in recent years has acquired a bewildering variety of meanings. It has been taken to mean both the principles and problems of economic policy and the relationship of the state to the economy. There is accordingly considerable confusion as to what the term currently embraces. Is political economy a branch of policy analysis or a more ambitious science of social formations; an extension of economic theory to the analysis of political behaviour and the public sector, or a series of reflections on the principles underlying the conduct of policy?

In orthodox economics several writers have sought to distinguish between political economy and economic analysis. According to Lionel Robbins, political economy is concerned with principles of public policy in the economic field and therefore with prescription rather than description. The political economist searches for solutions to problems of policy, whereas the concern of the economist is not with policy at all but with creating and testing 'value free generalizations about how the economy works'.[1] Robbins' approach was shared by Joseph Schumpeter, who at the start of his *History of Economic Analysis* contrasted political economy with economic analysis. Political economy was defined as 'an exposition of a comprehensive set of economic policies that its author advocates on the strength of certain unifying normative principles, such as the principles of economic Liberalism, Socialism.'[2]

This notion of political economy as a discourse concerned with ends and with policy in contrast to value-free economic science has been implicitly challenged by the rise of the 'new political economy' which believes that economic analysis can yield value-free generalizations about how the political system works and how government behaves.[3] The older type of discourse becomes unnecessary or at least drastically reduced in its scope. The explanation of why governments behave as they do is sought not in their ideological principles but in the constraints which determine the range of choices before them and in the actual logic of rational choice. A similar desire for technical knowledge is found in Marxist writing that sharply distinguishes between science and ideology and offers Marxism as an objective science of social formations.[4] Faced by this challenge two responses are possible. The term 'political economy' might be confined to a discourse on the principles and ends of policy. The new political economy would then be designated public choice theory and recognized as a branch of applied economics rather than as a legitimate usurper of the traditional ground of political economy. The alternative would be to recognize that the traditional distinction between a value-laden discourse on ends and a value-free examination of processes was never soundly based and if adhered to strictly would impoverish both political economy and economics. It always represented a major departure from the concerns and approach of classical political economy. From this second perspective all modern variants of political economy, including public choice theory, have arisen from two systems of political economy which combined in their analysis the discussion of ends as well as means, policy as well as processes. These two systems are liberal political economy and Marxism. Other schools of political economy exist but none approach the systematic character of these two. This chapter will be primarily concerned with Marxism and with the debates that have been carried on within and over its theoretical framework. Marxism is a form of critical political economy in the sense that it criticizes the assumptions, the methods, and the conclusions of liberal political economy. It arises in opposition to liberal political economy but is inconceivable without it, and does not simply reject it but incorporates in its own theory what it regards as valid. Before turning to examine it directly it is first necessary to review briefly the basic assumptions of liberal political economy in order to understand the Marxist critique and how it differs from other critical approaches.

LIBERAL POLITICAL ECONOMY

The origins of liberal political economy lie in the classical political economy of the English and French schools which flourished from the end of the seventeenth to the middle of the nineteenth century. In Adam Smith's hands political economy was at once an inquiry into the nature and causes of the wealth of nations and a discussion of the principles on which economic policy should be conducted. The one informed the other. The very notion of political economy owed much to the Greek origins of the term. For the Greeks the economy was the household and economics was the art of balancing revenue and expenditure. Political economy therefore meant the art of managing the public finances, the revenue and expenditure of the public, i.e. royal household. This is one set of meanings that has never been lost; economy and economizing have always suggested the husbanding of scarce resources and the planning of expenditure. For Adam Smith the purpose of political economy was to provide guidance to the statesman as to how he might maximize prosperity and so revenue by freeing rather than obstructing the natural energies of the people. To do this effectively required an understanding of economic behaviour.

Adam Smith relied on observation of contemporary circumstances and historical evidence to fashion his pioneering study. But the economists that built upon his work, especially Ricardo, elaborated Smith's insights into a systematic theory of market exchange. With the increasing universalization of exchange that accompanied the establishment of a capitalist economy, a new primacy came to be accorded to the economy over the state. The 'economy' came to mean the market order, the sphere of exchanges between individuals, a sphere possessed of its own internal principles of order and its own internal momentum, governed by specific laws. The state retained only residual functions.

Liberal political economy as it emerged in the nineteenth century was organized around the concept of a market order. Whereas Adam Smith's advice to the statesman had been cautious and contingent, liberal political economy proclaimed universal laws of economic behaviour which could not be transgressed without serious consequences. The preservation of the market order itself became the main object for policy. Policy was not concerned with the aims and outcomes of market exchanges but only with the framework of rules that governed them.

Three crucial assumptions about market exchange are involved in liberal political economy: the assumptions of rationality, egoism and freedom. Individuals are assumed to be rational to the extent that they choose the most efficient means of realizing whatever aims they have. They therefore attempt to maximize their utility by calculating the costs and benefits involved in different courses of action. This leads directly to the second assumption, egoism. The unlimited egoism of market agents is derived from rational pursuit of whatever maximizes their utility. Market agents are therefore self-interested but not selfish, because the pursuit of self-interest takes place within an agreed framework of rules, which ensures that it coincides with the promotion of social welfare. There is a natural identity of individual and general interests because only those exchanges are made from which all parties benefit. In order for this to be so the third assumption, freedom, has to be made. For the market order to work individuals must be able to make choices freely. This implies a minimum of restraints upon individual behaviour, but that minimum is all-important since it specifies the conditions that have to be created in order for a market order to exist and for the individual and the general interest to coincide. This minimum cannot be provided by the process of market exchange itself, hence there remains an irreducible need for a public authority. The key functions of this authority are, firstly, to maintain legal equality between all market agents—all individuals must be free to buy and sell, competition must be open and fair; secondly, to maintain order and peace—contracts must be enforced and the security of property and persons guaranteed; thirdly, to establish a medium of exchange and maintain its stability and acceptability.

The concept of a market order carried with it a number of implications both for society and politics. It suggests that decision-making will be relatively decentralized and that the economy will be ruled by the forces of supply and demand that result from a myriad of individual decisions. This in turn implies impersonality, the undermining of relations of personal dependence and local self-sufficiency, the growth of inter-dependence as every individual, every region, and every country specializes in producing what it can produce most cheaply for the world market. In a market society everything becomes a commodity, everything has its price, everything can be ranked in terms of the resources it uses and the alternative uses to which such resources can be put. Such a society is characterized by social relations that are essentially harmonious. To the extent that the public authority guarantees the framework of rules for the market order the individual interest is reconciled with the general interest and coercion of one individual by another individual or by a group other than the state itself is an aberration. Classes are accidental not necessary features of a market order, which is distinguished by the unforced cooperation of the owners of all factors of production in economic activity.

The market order is the sphere of private interests and private activity and a great chasm separates it from the public sphere, the realm of the state and politics. Liberal political economy is ambivalent towards the state. On the one hand it acknowledges the necessity for a strong state if the market order is to exist at all; on the other hand it is suspicious of the state's powers. The state has to guarantee the conditions for fair exchange and fair competition, but ways have to be found to restrain the extension of state intervention from guaranteeing the framework of rules to influencing what exchanges are made and what the outcomes are. This is why liberal political economy has always insisted upon the notion that the state is dependent upon society. This principle finds concrete expression in the manner in which the state is financed—through exactions on individual incomes.

This suggests that the state should adopt a neutral policy stance, confining itself to interventions that guarantee the framework of rules for the market order and removing the obstacles to competition and the free play of market forces.[5] The removal of market rigidities becomes the dominant element of its policy. The famous trinity, free trade, economy, and *laissez-faire*, perfectly expressed, and still expresses, the conclusions for policy that flowed from liberal political economy.

THE ORIGINS OF CRITICAL POLITICAL ECONOMY

Liberal political economy has been the most dominant form of political economy because its analysis is based upon tracing the consequences for the state and the economy that arise from the development and universalization of individual market exchange and commodity relationships. But from the outset it did not go unchallenged, especially since what emerged as a critical form of thought so rapidly became transformed into a confident ortho-doxy. The notion of a critical theory derives in part from the Enlightenment. Criticism means criticism of established author-ity. Abstract morality and 'truth' were counterposed to the corrupt world of politics.

In this sense of critical, a political economy emerged quite early that was critical of the assumptions and conclusions of liberal political economy. Two criticisms are to the fore. Liberal political economy was condemned for its defective moral outlook and for its failure to describe reality accurately. This produced not a systematic alternative theory, but a number of diverse and specific criticisms of liberal political economy. The objections frequently centred not on the analysis which under-lay liberal political economy but on the conclusions which were derived from it. The Ricardian socialists, for example, criticized the notion of distribution, arguing that if labour was the source of all value then labour was entitled to the full share of its product. Proudhon accepted the analysis of market exchange but criticized the growth of monopoly, and presented as an ideal the competitive economy of independent self-employed artisans. List criticized the doctrine of free trade and the law of comparative advantage, arguing that free trade in practice gave disproportionate benefits to the nations whose industries enjoyed the highest productivity. Malthus, from a different perspective, criticized the doctrine of free trade because it meant the sacrifice of agriculture in the interests of industry and commerce, and the consequent loss of self-sufficiency and a 'balanced' economy.

What emerged from such diverse criticisms was a set of ideas to challenge the dominant logic of liberal political economy. They centred around a concept of national economy, of the interests of local and national communities threatened by the corrosive power of individualism, market exchange and com-modity production. Liberal political economy was criticized because while its principles proclaimed the universal interest, its policies promoted some interests and sacrificed others. Free trade meant the enrichment of the owners of capital and the subordination of the owners of labour; the concentration of economic power and the undermining of independent pro-ducers; the dominance of some nations and the dependence of the rest; the triumph of industry and commerce and the decline of agriculture and the landowners as a powerful independent interest.

To those specific early criticisms were later joined analyses which criticized the inability of liberal political economy to explain central features of capitalism as it developed on a world basis in the second half of the nineteenth century. No unified school emerged but major emphasis was placed on the historical and institutional analysis of the economy and economic policy rather than on the abstract and deductive models of the liberal economists. The German historical school was particularly influential on British writers such as Cunningham, Hobson, Ashley and the Webbs. Much of this work provided the intellectual foundation for the rise of themes in political economy which emphasized collectivism and sought to justify greater intervention by the state. The social imperialism of the Tariff Reform Movement and the new collectivism of the emerging Labour Party were founded on this kind of critical political economy.

These disparate themes of national political economy have been further developed by many different writers, among them Veblen, Keynes, Galbraith, Schonfield, Myrdal and Rostow. What has prompted much of this critical work in political economy has been dissatisfaction with the ability of the theoretical models of liberal political economy adequately to explain the character of modern capitalism—the degree to which production has been centralized and concentrated, markets eroded and individualism undermined; the rise to dominance of companies, unions and government agencies, the bureaucratization of economy, politics and society; the regular appearance of fundamental economic crises and the inability of market forces to overcome them; the growth of the range of state intervention, the unequal distribution of resources and the growth of collective provision of welfare; the existence of world poverty and persistent conflicts between national and regional communities.

Although 'national' political economy has never generated a body of theoretical principles to rival liberal political economy and often relies on the economic analysis which liberal political economy provides, nevertheless its emphasis on realism and relevance and its general focus on problems of national economies and the legitimation of industrial societies has allowed it to become influential. So much so that liberal political economy itself now sometimes appears as a form of critical political economy because of the onslaught its adherents have launched on Keynesian management of demand, collective welfare provision, and state influence over market outcomes, all of which have gradually become part of the political consensus in most advanced capitalist states.[6] Together liberal political economy and national political economy furnish alternative intellectual frameworks for thinking about problems of economic policy and responding to the pressures and specific circumstances of managing modern mixed economies.[7]

MARX'S CRITIQUE OF POLITICAL ECONOMY

The critique of political economy originates with Marx and provides the most comprehensive alternative to liberal political economy. Marx's political economy is critical in the sense already outlined, but it goes further than other varieties of political economy because Marx understands critique in the two further ways in which it was employed in the German tradition: as reflection on the conditions for possible knowledge, and as reflection on a system of constraints which are produced by human actions and which limit human activity.[8] The critique of political economy, therefore, has several aspects. In the first place Marx criticizes the premises on which liberal political economy is based. He recognizes the scientific importance of the analyses produced by classical political economy, but he identifies ideological assumptions which limit its range and restrict its further development. As a result, classical political economy is only partly successful in its aim of achieving a scientific analysis of the economy. In his writings in the 1840s Marx singles out two such assumptions—timelessness and the necessity of private property.

Marx argues that the categories of classical political economy are timeless; they treat the capitalist mode of production as though it were the culmination of historical development. For the political economists, wrote Marx, there was history, but there is no longer any. The relationship between capitalism and previous modes of production is obscured because the latter are understood simply as imperfect realizations of capitalism, and the character of capitalism as a historically specific rather than as an everlasting and universal mode of production is never grasped. The importance of this idea for Marxist political economy is to encourage a historical comparative approach to the study of capitalism. Because Marxists have a precise concept of the capitalist mode of production they have engaged in analyses of non-capitalist modes of production in different historical periods and within capitalist social formations. This is why Marxists have been in the forefront in analysing questions like the role of domestic labour and migrant labour, uneven and combined development in the world economy, and the character of state expenditure in modern capitalist economies.

The second ideological assumption Marx criticized was the idea that the modern economy must be founded upon private ownership of the means of production. The effect of this, he argued, was to treat capital as a thing, rather than as a social relation, and so obscure the nature of production and distribution of the social product in a capitalist economy. Capital instead was treated simply as a stock of money, tools, and raw materials, ownership of which was rewarded by an income (profits). For Marx capital is a social relation between the owners of the means of production and the owners of labour power. Without wage labourers there is no capital and no capitalists in Marx's sense. The importance of this conception, and the theory of surplus value which Marx develops from it, is that it directs attention to the struggles between capital and wage labour and to the importance of understanding the dynamics of the labour process.

Marx wanted his critique of political economy to remove the obstacles he saw to a fully scientific analysis of capitalist economy. But at the same time it was a critique in the second sense, a reflection on the humanly produced constraints which were obstacles to the creation of a free society. Demystifying the social world, by criticizing the categories within which it was understood and lived, was one of the conditions for the emergence of a revolutionary consciousness and a revolutionary movement. For Marx the existence of private property destroys the basis on which liberal thinkers proposed that the individual and the general interest could be reconciled: a community of independent owners of commodities who were equal both as producers and as consumers. Private ownership of the means of production rests on the alienation of their labour power by wage labourers to capitalists. This creates a social system not controlled by its individual members but controlling them, and so denying freedom, autonomy, and the realization of human potential. This critique is rooted in Marx's concept of the human species, of labour and of nature, which form the premises for his analysis of history. Out of this critique comes Marx's rejection of the claims of bourgeois society to be the first classless society, and his attempts to prove that capitalist society is a new form of class society despite the formal freedom and equality of its citizens. He always presented his critique as a critique from the standpoint of the working class, the class which potentially represented the general interest because the overthrow of the social relations that subordinated it could only be achieved by the overthrow of class society.

The enduring strength of Marx's critique lies in his ability to see capitalism as a historically specific mode of production. The manner of organizing the labour process—the interaction between human communities and the natural physical world—is for Marx what differentiates human societies. Labour is a nature-imposed necessity, but in class societies the labour process is organized to produce a surplus which is appropriated by the class owning the means of production. For Marx the crucial question in analysing capitalism was explaining how a surplus arose and how it was appropriate in an economy which claimed to have abolished exploitation and oppression and to be founded upon the principle of exchange of equivalents between independent sovereign individuals. What distinguishes Marx's critique from all other branches of critical political economy is the specific weight he gives to liberal political economy. He presents the market order in its ideal form as a society of independent commodity producers. Such a community suffers no exploitation but also lacks control over the conditions of its own existence since the labour process is coordinated and resources allocated through the operation of the forces of demand and supply. But, as Marx demonstrates, in such a society based on individual production and exchange of commodities, there is no exploitation, injustice, or fraud that is inherent in the social relations themselves. Commodities are exchanged according to their values whose measure is the socially necessary labour time required for their production and which finds concrete expression in money, the medium of exchange, the commodity that is the universal equivalent for all commodities.

Marx's purpose in *Capital* was to show how, on the basis of the exchange of value equivalents, capital and surplus value can arise. He argues that it depends on certain preconditions— the formation of money hoards in the hands of particular individuals through their participation in the circulation process, and the availability of labour power as a commodity alongside the other elements of the production process. Purchase of the one commodity whose unique use value is the creation of more value gives the owner of capital control over the labour process. Marx contrasts the freedom and equality of individuals in the market with their coercion and exploitation at work. The production process becomes a battleground between the owners of labour power and the owners of capital, for the interest of capitalists is to extract as much surplus labour from their work-force as is possible, whereas the interest of the workers is to give back to the capitalists only that amount of labour that compensates them for the wages they have paid out. From this organization of the labour process Marx derived his conception of capital as self-expanding value, possessed of an inner drive to expand constantly. There is nothing metaphysical about this. The dynamism of capitalism arises directly from the central social relationship on which it is founded— between owners of capital and owners of labour power. The constant struggles between them over the organization of the labour process—the length of the working day and the introduction and deployment of machinery—were conflicts over the extraction of surplus value and helped determine the way in which capitalism developed. Of the two, the raising of labour productivity proved more important than extending the working day because the limits to it as a mode of extracting surplus value were less immediate. They would only be reached when the production process had been automated and living labour expelled from it, and the capitalist mode of production had come to dominate the whole world. Marx argued that in the long run the limit to increasing the productivity of labour was the tendency for the rate of profit to fall. To avoid this tendency becoming actual capitalists were compelled to manage their affairs in ways which greatly increased the productivity of labour and brought nearer a fully automated production process. Competition compelled them to concentrate production in larger plants and centralize it in fewer hands, to introduce new technological innovations to cut costs, and to create a world market by searching for areas of the world economy where the structure of costs was significantly lower. The tendency of the rate of profit to fall is a concept which refers to the problem of maintaining profitable accumulation by means which, while they alleviate the crisis of profitability in the short run, in the long run exacerbate it. The process of capital accumulation is highly unstable and uneven. It creates poverty and a surplus population. It creates and destroys skills in the work force, it reduces almost everyone in capitalist society to the status of a wage labourer.

Marx's critique of liberal political economy has proved so long lasting because he provided a genuinely alternative standpoint for judging public policy and analysing the historical development of modern societies. On the basis of his analysis he saw a political economy of the working class challenging the political economy of the bourgeoisie. The former was concerned with the emancipation of labour which meant a political programme that pointed to an eventual abolition of wage labour and individual market exchange. The latter was concerned with maintaining the conditions under which the market order could be preserved and extended. Marx saw the struggles to limit the working day to secure trade union rights and to win universal suffrage as essential moments in the creation of a socialist movement capable of overthrowing the rule of capital and transforming industrial society.

RECENT DEVELOPMENTS IN MARXIST THEORY

The success of Marxism as a theory is much disputed. There are naturally many aspects of it which do root it very firmly in the nineteenth century. But there are others which give it undeniable relevance to the second half of the twentieth century. Marx's ideas continue to stimulate and to inform a wide range of work in the social sciences. This is partly because Marx was so successful in foreseeing so many of the long-run developments of capitalism as a world system. Considering how little developed capitalism actually was at the time he was writing (even in England) the accuracy with which Marx charted its progress is remarkable.[9]

This must be set alongside Marx's major failure, his prediction and his hope that the inability of capitalism to resolve its internal contradictions, except by violence and wars, would generate a revolutionary consciousness and a revolutionary movement centred on the industrial proletariat. Marx was right to see the relationship between labour and capital as a key political relation but he obviously failed to foresee how the achievements of the political economy of the working class, having tightened the limit within which capital could operate at least within national economies, would become one of the major obstacles to the emergence of a revolutionary socialist consciousness.

The tension between the continuing insights offered by the theory of capital accumulation, in the long-run development of capitalism, and the evident passivity and in some cases marginality of the Western proletariat, became acute in the 1950s. Western capitalism had not only survived the slump and depression of the 1930s and the tremendous economic and political upheaval of World War II, but had also emerged stronger and more united, and was launched on the fastest period of expansion in its history. The association of Marxism with Stalinism and the new fears about totalitarianism, coupled with the newfound resilience of the economy and the democratic institutions of Western capitalism, raised fundamental questions about the Marxist analysis. Was the economy still subject to crises or had state intervention succeeded in permanently moderating them? Was the working class in any sense revolutionary? Was it gradually disappearing and being transformed into a quite different social formation? Was the state still a class state or did the achievements of social democracy mean that it had been transformed into a neutral instrument which would advance reform and maintain prosperity? Together these questions contributed to one central doubt— was the economy still capitalist? Did it make sense to analyse it any longer in class terms or as a process of capital accumulation, founded on the antagonism between wage labour and capital?[10]

The return of major economic crises in the 1970s gave new relevance to traditional Marxist ideas but at the same time it brought a major revival of Marxist studies which initiated fundamental debates on how Marxist political economy should be utilized in analysing modern capitalism. Two debates have been of major importance—one on value theory, the other on state theory.

The first of the great controversies concerns the status of Marx's concept of value.[11] This is a debate that has never been entirely quelled, partly because the concept is so central to the whole of Marx's theory of capitalism, partly because it so obviously distinguishes Marxist 'economics' from mainstream economics. The rejection of the labour theory of value of classical political economy and its replacement by the marginal utility theory became one of the cornerstones of modern economic analysis. Economists ever since have tended to treat the labour theory of value as a rejected theory and Marxist economics as a survival from a pre-scientific era. This is why Samuelson once felt able to refer to Marx as a minor post-Ricardian.

One strand in the debate on value has attempted to reconcile Marx's concepts with neo-classical concepts. Models of considerable mathematical complexity have been erected to demonstrate how under certain assumptions labour time measures of value can be transformed into prices. But even if Marx's theory could be rescued in this way its utility as a method of analysis of how prices were formed would be highly questionable, because it would be so cumbersome.

A very different approach stems from the work of Sraffa and others influenced by him at Cambridge. They have been labelled by their opponents as neo-Ricardians[12] and although the label is not entirely accurate it does indicate that their concern is to return to the formulations of the labour theory of value of Ricardo and classical political economy and find solutions to the problems Ricardo could not resolve, which are different to the solutions Marx proposed. The ideas that emerge are neither Ricardian nor Marxian but they are closer to both than they are to neo-classical economics, whose theoretical foundations they entirely reject.

What several of the neo-Ricardians wish to do is to find an alternative way of theorizing a surplus producing economy which does not have what they regard as the theoretical shortcomings of Marx's work. They reject the concept of the economy

that is to be found in neo-classical economics which sees production as the result of mutual cooperation between the owners
of the various factors of production. Instead they share with
classical political economy the notion of an economy that
produces a surplus which is appropriated as profit, interest and
rent, and they put forward a class analysis of the way in which
production is organized and the product distributed. But they
argue very strongly that the whole framework of value analysis
is redundant for this purpose. Labour time values are irrelevant
for explaining prices. They favour instead a cost of production
theory derived from Sraffa, which sees prices determined by
the socially necessary conditions of production, i.e. the actual
physical quantities of machines and raw materials employed,
combined with the wages paid to the work-force. Prices emerge
as a mark-up on these costs.

The neo-Ricardians are anxious to point out that their theory
does not exclude the possibility of coercion or exploitation in
the labour process. They see no reason to alter Marx's analyses
of the working day and machinery in *Capital*. Rather they argue
that for the first time a genuinely scientific account of capitalism
can be developed which does not rest upon 'metaphysical'
foundations. Obsession with value, they argue, has been one
reason why Marxism has made such little progress. As Ian
Steedman says: 'The project of providing a materialist account
of capitalist societies is dependent on Marx's value magnitude
analysis only in the negative sense that continued adherence
to the latter is a major fetter on the development of the
former.'[13]

The neo-Ricardians regard themselves as developing Marx's
theory in the most fruitful manner, discarding only what is
theoretically suspect, but retaining many important features,
including class analysis and the analysis of the labour process.
But what is discarded is the analysis, derived from value theory,
of the tendency of the rate of profit to fall and the long run
tendencies of development of the capitalist mode of production.

The argument against the neo-Ricardians has concentrated
on two themes. The first position, expressed most clearly by
Erik Olin Wright,[14] is that there is a basic complementarity
between the two approaches. He argues that value analysis is
concerned with establishing the structural limits within which
the accumulation of capital develops, while the Sraffian analysis

shows how specific outcomes are selected. The range of possible outcomes is not infinite but limited by the forms in which value is expressed, such as the commodity, money and capital. The second argument is more uncompromising. It rejects the neo-Ricardian analysis on the grounds that it misunderstands the methodology that is involved in the value analysis. On this reading most of the arguments that it is impossible to derive a coherent theory of prices from Marx's theory of value are mistaken because value and price are not, for Marx, separate variables. Values cannot be calculated or observed independently of prices—prices are the necessary form through which values are expressed; but it is impossible to measure both separately and then theorize about the relationship between the two. This approach puts great emphasis on Marx's theory as an integrated set of concepts which defines its field in a way that makes it accessible to knowledge.[15]

This position has several variants but one of the more influential has been the attempt to study the forms which social relations take under capitalism, both their logical connection and their historical origins and development. This can lead to a fatalistic and at times reductionist emphasis on the invariant succession of forms in the circuits of capital, but it can also lead to a focus on the manner in which there are continual conflicts over the imposition of capitalist forms—particularly the production of commodities, and wage labour. This is considered further, below.

The debate on value has often been conducted at a fairly high level of abstraction but it has implications for most other areas of substantive research within Marxist political economy, particularly the debates on the labour process, and the debates over the state. There is a lot at stake in the controversy. Rival conceptions of the capitalist economy, disputes over the correct method of analysis, and the problem of a normative basis of socialist political economy are all involved. None of these are trivial questions, but that means they are most unlikely to be settled by intellectual debate. The strength of the neo-Ricardians is that they wish to develop concrete analyses of the contemporary capitalist economy and they find much of the conceptual apparatus of the major alternative to liberal political economy an encumbrance. They particularly dislike the way in which value analysis is used to portray an inevitable sequence of development and promote political fatalism. The neo-Ricardian future is a much more open future because they reject the idea of necessary trends. Each situation has to be analysed afresh. But there remains a basic doubt as to whether neo-Ricardianism succeeds in creating an alternative theoretical basis for a socialist political economy. Marx gave central importance to the labour process and pinpointed the structural conflict between labour and capital as the centre of his analysis. Neo-Ricardians deny that their main interest is in the circulation of capital. They too assert the primacy of the labour process. But it is difficult to see why they should insist on this while rejecting the theoretical analysis which first established this primacy. They wish to remain in the terrain Marxism has established while disowning the means by which it was constructed.

The divide over method is not trivial since it runs right through the substantive debates on the nature of contemporary capitalism. This is particularly evident in the debates over the nature of capitalist crisis and the analysis of inflation, recession, and the activities of the modern state. One central issue is how far an analysis of the long-run tendencies of capital accumulation, as presented for example in classical form by Ernest Mandel,[16] can deal adequately with the novel elements of the crisis of the 1970s, particularly the combination of rising unemployment and rising prices, the growth of state activities, and the increasing domination of the world economy by multinational capital. The neo-Ricardian position, in sharp contrast to this, emphasizes in its analyses specific institutional features of modern capitalism, in particular the oligopolistic structure of markets. In this way it tends to converge with radical formulations in national political economy.[17] At the heart of its explanation of inflation, for example, is the idea of continual bargaining between different groups over the basic costs of the production process, the outcome of which is determined by the degree of monopoly each side can exercise. The liberal theory of the market order is entirely rejected. Inflation is a result of a power struggle between organized labour, organized capital, and government. Indeed the characteristic feature of this whole branch of critical political economy is to abandon the individualist foundations of economic analysis and pose all questions of economics as matters involving relations of power as well as relations of exchange.[18] Liberal political economy by contrast has to treat instances of coercion as aberrant not integral elements of markets and economic relations. The opposition between Marxist and neo-Ricardian (or Sraffian) perspectives is fairly plain. But among those Marxist who continue to accept value analysis there has also been considerable dispute about the classical Marxist theory of crisis. Some of the criticisms are technical. Has the organic composition of capital actually risen during the 1960s and 1970s?[19] Is the crisis in the 1970s a classic crisis of overproduction, an expression of the tendency of the rate of profit to fall, or does it have more immediate and transient causes?[20] The more general criticisms are directed at reductionist and functionalist presentations of the Marxist theory of crisis. In such accounts the laws of capital accumulation are conceived as the reproduction of an economic system. A crisis is an interruption in this process of reproduction, caused by the appearance of barriers to further accumulation. Social and political crises are conceived as symptoms and effects of economic crisis. Classical Marxism never supposed there was any inevitability about the outcome of such social and political crises. An economic crisis—the breakdown of capitalism as a functioning economic system—was not a sufficient condition to produce revolutionary consciousness (a determination to overthrow the system of wage labour) but it was certainly thought of as a necessary condition.

This approach has been fundamentally challenged within Marxism by much of the recent work on the theory of the state. Crisis theory and state theory have become inextricably connected. Until recently the analysis of the state and of politics has always remained relatively undeveloped within Marxism. *Capital* has long been treated as a book about economics rather than politics, and within the Marxist tradition, and still more among the critics of Marxism there has been a deep-rooted tendency to interpret Marxism as a form of economic determinism and to approach the study of ideology and politics from the side of economics. In this way the traditional division between politics and economics, promulgated by liberal political economy and fundamental to its understanding of the relation of economists and politics, was restated within Marxism. The liberal idea of the self-correcting and self-sufficient market was echoed by the Marxist notion of capitalism as a self-contained economic system, governed by its own inexorable laws of motion. In both conceptions the state hovered uneasily outside as an external and largely passive guarantor of the conditions needed to maintain and reproduce the social order. Much early Marxist writing on the state reflected this notion.

Yet one of the fundamental points of Marx's critique of political economy was the denial of the separation between politics and economics. The consequences of this were not worked out in Marx's own writings. He never lived to write the book on the state that he planned, and his formulations are often ambiguous and capable of many different interpretations. The questions that he posed and some of his remarkable insights have given rise to the modern Marxist debates on the state.[21] These debates have centred around the relationship between the state and the economy and have led to a fundamental re-evaluation of Marxist political economy.

Two major strands in this literature will be identified here. The first stems from those theorists, in particular Poulantzas, who have challenged explanations that treated the state as an instrument of the ruling class and have emphasized instead its relative autonomy from 'economic' class interests.[22] The state is conceived instead as an arena of conflict between diverse political and social forces. Political institutions such as legislatures, the Civil Service, and parties are not seen as direct representatives of classes, and classes themselves are recognized as being composed of many fractions. The hegemony of the ruling class has to be forged and maintained politically.

This approach owes much to Gramsci. Its main weakness is identifying precisely the limits of the autonomy which the state enjoys. One solution is to modify the idea of economic determination by defining the limits in terms of class struggle. The laws of motion of capital appear then not as some inexorable force, but the result of a continual contest between the forces of labour and capital, and the state becomes not just an arena for conflict but a set of policies and agencies which are not orchestrated by a single will and are not subordinated to a single class interest. Another solution is to get rid of the idea of economic determination altogether.[23] One influential perspective draws a sharp divide between competitive and monopoly capitalism. Under competitive capitalism, it is argued, the economy did operate according to the laws of capital accumulation, but as a result of several major transformations this is no longer the case. State and economy have become closely interlinked—the boundaries are increasingly hard to determine, the state moreover has assumed responsibility for crisis management, steering the economy so as to minimize the social and economic impact of disturbances in the accumulation process. States have assumed this role partly in response to the needs of the giant corporations, which increasingly dominate markets and industries and whose operations span the world, and partly because of the industrial and political strength of subordinate classes, particularly labour movements.

It is often argued that changes such as these mean that a qualitatively new stage in capitalist development has arrived— one in which the former laws of motion of capital accumulation no longer function as they once did. This requires a major redirection of analysis. For if political intervention is sufficient to displace crisis tendencies, then politics has become dominant over economics, and Marxist political economy becomes transformed into political analysis. Economic factors become just one aspect of any political situation, but they are not necessarily central to it.[24]

This perspective, which ultimately leads away from political economy, has been challenged by the state derivation school. The starting point of this approach was stated very clearly by the Russian legal theorist, Evgeny Pashukanis, when he wrote: 'Why does the state take the form of an impersonal mechanism of public authority isolated from society?'[25] Pashukanis and those who have followed him have attempted to derive logically the forms of the state from the categories of Marxian political economy. The weakness of this approach is that it can easily lapse into an uncritical functionalism, identifying functions which the state must fulfil if the system is to survive, but not analysing the actual history and the circumstances which determine whether or not they were fulfilled. Its great strength is that although its starting point is the way in which the economic and the political are divorced, it works towards demonstrating their underlying unity. This unity is not something that has only recently been achieved, because the theory does not suppose that there was ever a time when the economy was independent and self-sufficient, powered by its own internal laws of motion. Instead the form the state assumes is *derived* from the functions that must be performed if the economic system is to be maintained and reproduced and which cannot be performed by market agents themselves. Security of contract, the enforcement of competition, the rights of property, and acceptability of money, are all shown to be necessary conditions for the existence and reproduction of a commodity producing economy, the subject of analysis in Marx's opening six chapters in *Capital*. Appropriate institutions and agencies are organized to maintain them. But the sale of labour power as a commodity and the coming into being of the relations between capital and wage labour further requires that the state extends its activities to secure the profitability of the process of accumulation. This means confronting the obstacles that periodically arise to continued profitable accumulation, chief among which is the organized working class.

The state derivation approach removes the need to see state policy as the expression of identifiable class interests or as an ideal collective capitalist which can intervene omnisciently to prevent crisis, or as a power suspended above society. It forms the basis on which political analysis of the state can be integrated with the value analysis of capital accumulation. All the pitfalls remain of mistaking levels of abstraction and substituting the logical categories for detailed historical research, or mistaking functional explanations for causal ones. But it does open the way for a critical political economy that neither reduces politics to economics, nor substitutes political analysis for economics, but instead treats both economics and politics within the framework of value analysis.[26]

This was Marx's own procedure in *Capital*. He developed the logical structure of his argument out of his empirical researches, but he did not mistake this logical structure for the actual pattern of reality. In *Capital*, for example, having already discussed the specific form the labour process takes under capitalism, he shows logically how the capitalist mode of production depends on the extraction of surplus value. The actual extraction of surplus value, however, is by no means a smooth functional process, as he shows so clearly in his discussion of the tremendous struggles over the length of the working day. For Marx nothing was ever automatic about the reproduction or continuation of capitalism. He never viewed it primarily as a system of economic reproduction, but as a system of social and political domination.

CONCLUSION

Marx's critique of political economy remains powerful because of its ability to inspire new insights into the way capitalist economies are organized and are developing, and to provide a political project for human emancipation. Although there have been attempts to develop a self-contained Marxist tradition, it has always been strongest when it has renewed itself as a critique of liberal political economy, identifying what is scientific and what is ideological in the dominant theories and analyses of capitalism, criticizing the assumptions which both limit understanding of the forces that shape the capitalist mode of production and which provide the basis for the justification of capitalist social relations. Marxism is always first and foremost a critique of ideology, including its own, rather than an independent science of society. But a critique of ideology does not entail a complete rejection of ideology. One of the main strengths of Marx's critical political economy was the scientific status he was willing to accord to many of the conclusions of classical political economy. He was able to go beyond classical political economy through his concept of value, which allowed him to grasp and set out the basic forms—commodity, money, capital—of the capitalist mode of production, tracing their inner connections with one another. On this basis he claimed to have established the central tools for analysing the specific conditions and circumstances under which capital and capitalist social relations arise in a market economy which shape the space within which the accumulation of capital develops and determines the limits within which it moves.

Marxism has made little contribution to price theory but it has given a major impetus to studies in many areas, such as those exploring the nature of the capitalist mode of production as a world system and its interrelationship with other non-capitalist modes of production; to studies of the labour process and the labour force; the nature of political and economic crisis; and, increasingly, to the theory of the state.

Many unresolved questions remain and new doubts and

uncertainties have been created. But there can be little doubt that in the past twenty years Marxist political economy has renewed itself as a critical and open study. The controversies over value and the state have by no means resolved the difficulties but they have sharpened Marxist concepts. Marx's theory of the state has been firmly grounded in his critique of political economy and the indispensability of value theory has been successfully reasserted. Its adherents have been able to maintain against the neo-Ricardian critics that certain problems can only be posed within the framework of value analysis. It has become clear that two very different methodologies, two very different kinds of critical political economy are involved in the debate on value.[27]

So much actual work in political economy, however, concentrates on relatively straightforward historical and institutional analyses of policy. The marrying of these to the major theoretical frameworks is not always easy. But the frameworks are still important in the way in which they define facts, identify problems, and provide criteria for evaluation. In Marxist political economy a number of major areas for future research have changed. Firstly, the analysis of crises—the role of debt and credit, the role of the public sector, and the role of technological revolutions.[28] Secondly, the analysis of the state—the political and policy responses to the slump; the programmes and strategies of different political groupings; and the nature and limits of state involvement in the economy.[29] Thirdly, the analysis of the world market and the changing world division of labour, particularly the unevenness of industrialization, the character of modern imperialism, the nature of the Soviet economy, and the possibility of new centres of accumulation in the Third World.[30] Fourthly, the analysis of the labour process—the impact of the new technology, the implications of mass unemployment, the changing character and composition of the labour force and the industrial reserve army.[31]

The recovery of the positive features of the Marxist critique of political economy means that all these questions are being fruitfully pursued and new knowledge is being produced.

NOTES AND REFERENCES

1. Lionel Robbins, *Political Economy Past and Present* (London, Macmillan, 1976), pp. 2-3.
2. J. A. Schumpeter, *History of Economic Analysis* (London, Allen & Unwin, 1954).
3. A good survey of this literature is D. C. Mueller, *Public Choice* (Cambridge, Cambridge University Press, 1979).
4. In the 1960s and 1970s this was most pronounced in work influenced by Louis Althusser.
5. The most authoritative restatement of this idea and the other ideas of liberal political economy can be found in F. A. Hayek, *The Constitution of Liberty* (London, Routledge & Kegan Paul, 1961).
6. See, for example, Milton Friedman, *Inflation and Unemployment* (London, Institute of Economic Affairs, 1977) and F. A. Hayek, *A Tiger by the Tail* (London, Institute of Economic Affairs, 1972).
7. This is not to argue that policy can ever be treated as a simple implementation of ideas. For a forceful reminder of this see Jim Tomlinson, *Problems of British Economic Policy 1870-1945* (London, Methuen, 1981).
8. I have drawn here on the discussion by Paul Connerton in his *Introduction to 'Critical Sociology'* (Harmondsworth, Penguin, 1976).
9. See, for example, J. A. Schumpeter, *Capitalism, Socialism, and Democracy* (London, Allen & Unwin, 1950) and the more recent assessment by Krishan Kumar, *Prophecy and Progress* (Harmondsworth, Penguin, 1978).
10. The most important work of Marxist political economy produced in these years was P. Baran and P. Sweezy, *Monopoly Capital* (New York, Monthly Review Press, 1964). See also John Strachey, *Contemporary Capitalism* (London, Gollancz, 1956).
11. There are two recent valuable collections of articles on value theory: Diane Elson (ed.), *Value* (London, CSE Books, 1969) and Ian Steedman *et al.*, *The Value Controversy* (London, New Left Books, 1981).
12. See the important essay by Bob Rowthern, 'Neo-Classicism, Neo-Ricardianism and Marxism', in *Capitalism, Conflict and Inflation* (London, Lawrence & Wishart, 1980).
13. Ian Steedman, 'Ricardo, Marx, Sraffa', in Steedman *et al.*, op. cit. Steedman provides the best statement of the neo-Ricardian position in *Marx after Sraffa* (London, New Left Books, 1977). See also the contribution of Hodgson in Steedman *et al.*, op. cit.
14. Erik Olin Wright, 'The value controversy and social research', in Steedman *et al.*, op. cit., pp. 36-74. His positions are set out more fully in *Class, Crisis, and the State* (London, New Left Books, 1979).
15. Three different approach are M. Itoh, *Value and Crisis* (London, Pluto, 1980); Ben Fine and Laurence Harris, *Re-Reading Capital*

(London, Macmillan, 1979); and Geoffrey Kay, *The Economic Theory of the Working Class* (London, Macmillan, 1979).

16. Ernest Mandel, *Late Capitalism* (London, New Left Books, 1975) and *The Second Slump* (London, New Left Books, 1978). See also Itoh, op. cit.; Paul Mattick, *Marx and Keynes* (London, Merlin, 1970); and the important articles by David Yaffe, 'The Marxian theory of crisis, capital and the state', *Conference of Socialist Economists Bulletin*, Vol. 1 (1972); and 'Value and price in Marx's Capital', *Revolutionary Communist*, Vol. 1 (January, 1975).

17. See, for example, the writings of the Cambridge Economic Policy Group and the work of some socialist economists, notably Stuart Holland, in *The Socialist Challenge* (London, Quartet, 1975).

18. A textbook introduction to this approach is Joan Robinson and John Eatwell, *An Introduction to Economics* (Cambridge, Cambridge University Press, 1973).

19. See, for instance, the very astute criticisms of Mandel by Rowthorn, reprinted in Rowthorn, op. cit., pp. 95-128.

20. See the transcript of the Australian radio debate between Ernest Mandel and Bill Warren, 'Recession and its consequences', *New Left Review*, 87-8 (September-December, 1974), pp. 114-24.

21. Only a few brief comments are possible here. For a valuable survey see R. D. Jessop, 'Recent theories of the capitalist state', *Cambridge Journal of Economics*, 4 (1977), pp. 353-74.

22. Nicos Poulantzas, *Political Power and Social Classes* (London, New Left Books, 1973); *State, Power, Socialism* (London, New Left Books, 1978).

23. This approach has been particularly evident in writing of the Frankfurt school and those influenced by them. See, for example, Jurgen Habermas, *Legitimation Crisis* (London, HEB, 1976). It is also prominent in much American Marxist writings. See Baran and Sweezy, op. cit.; and J. O'Connor, *The Fiscal Crisis of the State* (New York, St Martin's Press, 1973).

24. See A. Cutler *et al.*, *Marx's Capital and Capitalism Today* (London, Routledge & Kegan Paul, 1976).

25. E. Pashukanis, *Law and Marxism* (London, Ink Links, 1978), p. 139. The best introduction in English to the state derivation debate is J. Holloway and S. Picciotto (eds), *State and Capital* (London, Edward Arnold, 1978).

26. Significant recent work in this direction which attempts to give due weight to the mechanisms of economic reproduction with the mechanisms of social reproduction includes Fine and Harris, op. cit. Their work is particularly important for the emphasis they place on the circulation process as well as the production process.

27. In Britain one of the main arenas for these debates has been the Conference of Socialist Economists, at its annual conference and through

its journal, *Capital and Class*. Other important journals for these debates include *New Left Review, Marxism Today, Socialist Economic Review,* and *Economy and Society*. A useful general survey of recent debates is in Ben Fine and Laurence Harris, 'Controversial issues in Marxist economic theory', *Socialist Register 1976*, pp. 141-78. See also the rejoinder by Hodgson in *Socialist Register 1977*, and the reply by Fine and Harris.

28. Cf. J. O'Connor, *The Fiscal Crisis of the State*, op. cit.
29. Cf. Ian Gough, *The Political Economy of the Welfare State* (London, Macmillan, 1979).
30. Cf. for a survey of a vast literature, Ian Roxborough, *Theories of Underdevelopment* (London, Macmillan, 1979).
31. Cf. Jack Braverman, *Labour and Monopoly Capital* (New York, Monthly Review Press, 1974).

PART III

THE POLITICAL ECONOMY OF THE ADVANCED INDUSTRIAL STATE

4 The Political Economy of Economic Policy

DAVID McKAY

Few subjects have received more attention from the social science community over the last few years than the relationship between Britain's economic performance and her political and social structure. However, as far as the role of government in the economy is concerned, much of this effort leaves the reader unsatisfied. There is, in particular, an intellectual hiatus between those scholars (mainly political scientists) giving primacy to institutional relationships and those (drawn from several disciplines) who view social structural variables as the key to both economic performance and government policy. In addition, the economists are usually reduced to vague references to 'irrational' policies or 'political expediency' which help rather little. A fourth group, appreciating the intimate (and obvious) links between political institutions and social structure do attempt some synthesis, but their efforts frequently founder on an unnecessary deference either to Marxist or to liberal ideology.

The purpose of this chapter is twofold. First, briefly to review these various approaches with the specific purpose of testing how useful each is in improving our understanding of economic policy-making. Second, an attempt will be made to provide an alternative view of economic policy-making in Britain by synthesizing the more convincing of the institutional and social structural approaches. This will not be an exercise in economic analysis; measuring the contribution of government policy to Britain's economic malaise in any precise way is a virtually impossible task. Instead the main purpose will be to help explain why policy has taken the shape it has. Implications for economic performance will be discussed, but in a general and speculative rather than precise fashion. As a very large body of literature is involved, discussion will concentrate on the more important and influential contributions.

THE ECONOMISTS

It is apt that we should start with the economists, for they are easily the most respected and influential group of academics commenting on Britain's economic ills. This is naturally so, given the relative ease with which economic variables, including emotive and politically loaded indicators such as unemployment and inflation, can be measured. However, although economists are at their technical best when measuring productivity differences among industries or the effects of different exchange rate levels on industrial competitiveness, they almost always fail to link their analysis to the political economy of government policy or to broader social structural influences. This is so even when they accept that these are, in fact, of paramount importance. Hence we come across sometimes extraordinary findings which effectively relegate economics to the trivial or obvious. Caves and Krause, for example, in their now celebrated Brookings study of the British economy, conclude: 'The studies in this volume indicate that Britain's economic performance stems largely from its productivity problem, whose origins lie deep in the social system.'[1] What these origins are we are not told, although individual chapters hint at trade-union power, poor management and an undermotivated workforce as the probable roots. Following often very careful statistical and econometric analysis of productivity, exchange rates and taxation, such vague references leave the reader intellectually stranded. Above all, this particular volume tells us virtually nothing at all about the role of government in encouraging or inhibiting productivity and investment. The same accusation can be levelled at another influential collection of essays edited by Frank Blackaby on 'De-industrialization'.[2] Economic policy is discussed, naturally, but usually in terms of its nuisance value or in terms of what government should do now that de-industrialization has occurred.[3]

What is remarkable about these economists is the almost casual way in which the role of the state is either ignored or played down. Yet we now know enough about the economic development of other societies to appreciate that, either directly or indirectly, governments can and do play a crucial role in encouraging investment, innovation and economic growth.[4] The question remains. Why have British governments apparently failed to play this role—especially as, until very recently at least, the UK government activity was, by the simplest quantitative measure (percentage GNP in the public sector) very large?[5]

Of course another group of economists specifically identifies a high rate of government spending as the major cause of economic malaise. Hardline free marketeers see government intervention as almost always dysfunctional and especially so when major pricing and investment decisions are influenced by 'non-market' factors such as prices and incomes, regional or social and industrial policy.[6] Simply to assert that government intervention prevents the achievement of Pareto optimality is, however, of little value. Much depends on the nature of intervention and the exact role played by the state in relation to major economic actors and interests—a fact now appreciated by a number of economists and public choice theorists.[7] Rarely, however, do these commentators view governments in anything but an unfavourable light. The reasoning is usually that government intervention in 'pluralist' (or democratic?) countries such as Britain and the USA is bad because it leads to an over-provision of public goods. In Japan and France where societal forces are weaker in relation to the state, intervention is less destructive because governments are not obliged constantly to make concessions to competing and independent interests.

Finally, mention should be made of those economists who accept that governments are important both in terms of what they have done (or not done) in the past and in terms of what they should do by intervening more positively in the economy in the future. Hence the group of economists associated with the Cambridge Department of Applied Economics have long pleaded for selective import controls and the introduction of a 'Japanese style' industrial policy.[8] Predictably, these advocates do not tell us *why* past policies have taken the shape they have and their pleas in support of protection, planning agreements and a greatly strengthened National Enterprise Board take little cognizance of the likely political obstacles which would result from such policies being identified with a politically isolated Labour left.

Perhaps the most interesting recent contribution in this context comes from an economic historian. Sydney Pollard argues forcefully (and very convincingly) that chronic under-investment is at the root of the British problem and that governments have played a major part in aggravating this tendency.[9] Moreover, Pollard singles out the Treasury, Civil Service and

specific government policies as deserving of particular oppro-
brium.[10] But we are not told why the Treasury and Civil Service
are so antipathetic to taking a direct hand in investment.
Certainly some hints are given when Pollard discusses Civil
Service values and successive governments' continued loyalty
to 'imperial' policies (defence of sterling, high defence spending), but they remain hints, not analysis.

Generally, then, the economists have contributed rather little
to the puzzle of British postwar economic policy. Given their
status and influence in the Anglo-Saxon world, their record
must be considered disappointing. For all the elegance of their
theorems and econometric models they have generally failed to
solve the riddle of why governments have pursued the policies
they have and what impact these policies have had on the real
world economy.

THE INSTITUTIONALISTS

By institutionalists is meant those academics (mainly political
scientists) who have sought to explain economic policy-making
primarily in terms of how political institutions have behaved
over time. The category includes a large and varied body of
work. What holds it together is its assumption that political
institutional relationships are the independent variable in the
policy system. The broader society obviously relates to institutions but usually it reacts to them rather than moulds them.
By implication, at least, institutional reform can achieve a great
deal. Although now out of fashion, the institutionalists were
extremely influential during the 1960s and early 1970s. As
Geoffrey Fry has recently documented, the assumption during
this period that administrative reform could solve Britain's
problems was widespread.[11] The mood was predominantly
technocratic. By implication, at least, neither the party or
electoral system nor the broader society was at fault. And
the actual policies of government, underpinned as they were
by the twin pillars of Keynesian demand management and the
welfare state, were also accepted as indispensable. What apparently was lacking was the linkage between government and
the broader society. So the Civil Service and central machinery
of government was branded inefficient and unresponsive, as was
the local government system.[12]

In economic policy such sentiments led to a number of by now familiar experiments, from the creation of the National Economic Development Council to the Department of Economic Affairs. The experience of these innovations is well documented,[13] but it is well worth numbering the assumptions behind what might be called the 'technocratic critique':

(a) Government policy can and does make a difference to economic performance; the market is manipulable by political actors.

(b) Failure in the past has been one of administrative coordination and control. Improve this through central planning and industry and commerce will respond positively.

(c) More specifically, a shortsighted Treasury and an old-fashioned Civil Service have inhibited adoption of the longer view—especially as far as exchange rate policy, investment and output are concerned.

In sum, all that is required to improve performance is the political will to reform the machinery of government. Indeed, the technocrat's faith in reform measures and condemnation of politicians for lacking the political will to implement them extended into the 1970s. As late as 1976 Michael Shanks was showing a touching faith in planning:

. . . What is the strategy to be followed and, once agreed, how are we to make it happen? The evidence of this book suggests that it is precisely on this point that successive British governments have failed to provide the leadership and the coherent thought required, by refusing to make the necessary choices between mutually incompatible alternatives. To this extent the planning exercises carried out between 1961 and 1976 have been charades rather than serious exercises in national growth and revival. It remains to be seen whether the 1976 industrial strategy will have a happier outcome.[14]

Shanks is, of course, quite right to condemn the planning policies as 'charades', but he completely fails to explain not the immediate causes of their failure—Treasury opposition, deference to the value of sterling, indifference from industry— but the deeper causes which explain successive governments' continued belief that such measures *can* work. We will return to this theme later.

A second group of institutionalists identify the electoral and party system as the villain in the piece. So the two-party system in combination with the single-member district, first-past-the-post electoral arrangements have produced adversary politics[15] and consequent frequent changes in policy. Certainly a cursory glance at postwar economic policy confirms this tendency, with 1951, 1970, 1974 and 1979 being election years characterized by sharp changes in economic policy. However, on closer examination it is clear that there have been as many changes within the lives of governments—1949, 1959, 1966, 1972 and 1976 being obvious 'U turn' dates. The political/business cycle thesis represents a related argument: governments will reflate (or inflate) the economy and create employment and short-term increases in income at that point most likely to increase their chances of re-election. Following elections governments will be forced to deflate to correct the worst consequences of the earlier reflation. The more precocious of the political/business cycle advocates see the even more damaging tendency for each cycle to produce a higher rate of inflation than the last. Faced with the spectre of Phillips curves moving ever upwards and rightwards these scholars conclude that the only logical corrective course of action is to suspend democracy.[16]

But both the adversary and political/business cycle claims are built on very flimsy empirical evidence. True, exchange rate, fiscal and monetary policy have fluctuated with changes of government but there is no clear relationship between changes of government (or policy changes within the lives of governments) and what Sydney Pollard rightly identifies as the key indicator—industrial and infrastructural investment. *All* governments have underinvested or, for reasons to be examined later, have been reluctant to encourage industry to invest.[17] Similarly, the political business cycle thesis simply does not stand up to the evidence. As Brian Barry points out, the literature cannot support the claim that inflation and employment are directly related either to electoral strategy or to electoral fortune.[18]

Even if governments cannot manipulate the economy in the ways claimed by the institutionalists, we cannot dispute the very real institutional advantages which British governments appear to enjoy compared with many other countries. Britain is a unitary state with (until very recently) a simple two-party system. On coming to power, Cabinet government and party discipline in Parliament should ensure governments an unusual degree of control over policy-making—especially as the British Civil Service is loyal, incorruptible and protected by the Official Secrets Act. As we know, the reality is somewhat different— a fact which would appear to add weight to those who see Britain's problems as emanating from the broader society rather than from the political system. But as will be argued later, Britain's institutional arrangements *are* an important clue to the puzzle—even if not in the way the institutionalists would themselves accept.

THE SOCIAL STRUCTURALISTS

Again, this is a broad category embracing a number of approaches. What combines them is the belief that the problems of managing the British economy—and indeed British economic performance—have their origin in the social structure. In its crudest form this perspective is familiar and influential. Lazy workers, Luddite trade unions and incompetent management are at the heart of the 'British disease'. Sociologists have attempted to characterize changes in working-class perceptions and behaviour in more academic terms. John Goldthorpe, for example, relates heightened social conflict and in particular increased pressures from workers for more pay and better conditions to the decay of the status order (or decline of deference), the strengthening of citizenship rights and the emergence of a mature working class.[19] These very general assertions have but limited value for our purposes. As Goldthorpe himself accepts, he is concerned only to explain what economists cannot, economic policy being supposedly one of the factors they can explain. In any case, broad sociological claims about working-class behaviour seem seriously at odds with the evidence of significant productivity differences between different sectors and industries and even between firms in the same industry.[20] These differences imply (and the experience of Japanese-managed firms in Britain confirms) that worker behaviour *can* be changed in spite of putative developments in working-class perceptions and expectations.

Another academic interpretation points to the strength and independence of economic interests as the cause of economic stagnation. Hence Mancur Olson in his audacious theory of comparative economic growth rates claims that the absence of cathartic wars and social upheavals has left organized interests in Britain (and the USA) intact. Able to act collectively on behalf of their members these organizations effectively undermine market mechanisms. The resulting restrictive practices leave the economy operating at well below the optimal. Governments, unable to resist the demands of these groups—and especially trade unions—pursue high-expenditure, consumer-satisfying policies which are destructive to the common economic interest.[21] Samuel Brittan's thesis in the 'Economic contradictions of democracy' is broadly similar, only he extends the argument by incorporating claims that rising expectations lead to ever intensifying frustration as the economy fails to deliver.[22] This is, of course, part of the 'overload' thesis which has generated a flurry of (mainly Anglo/American) political science publications over the last few years.[23] In some ways it is surprising that political scientists should have pioneered the overload argument, as it does place first causes in society rather than polity. This said, overload advocates do focus on the problems which political institutions and processes (and, indeed democracy itself) face as a result of increasingly intense and strident societal pressures. In so doing they limit the explanatory power of their argument, for we are told rather little about the nature of state/societal linkages. Above all, how the polity relates to society is rarely placed in comparative and historical perspective. At its simplest the argument goes something like this:

(a) Universal suffrage and other democratic processes were established when social cleavages were comparatively simple. In Britain there followed a long stable period when politics was dominated by class divisions. In the USA the division was less acute, but at least from the New Deal onwards politics took on a loose left/right dimension. In both countries demands on government were broadly limited to those articulated by party politics.

(b) More recently party dealignment and the strengthening of special interest politics have upset this fragile equilibrium. As society and social cleavages have become more complex so governments' capacity to respond and satisfy everyone has diminished.

(c) Worse still, the trend towards a more open and accessible polity has come just at the time when economic problems have intensified. Governments have therefore been forced to accommodate competing demands in the context of a diminishing cake.[24]

Little hope is placed in institutional reform by the 'overloaders'. Bureaucratic rationalization may, indeed, confuse the situation further.[25] What governments should do instead is lower public expectations and disengage from a direct role in resource allocation.

The overload thesis has much to commend it. Who, after all, could dispute the facts of rising expectations and increasing demands on government? However, as an explanation of British economic policy in the postwar years it is less helpful. For much of the period governments were remarkably free from societal pressures. Underinvestment, stop-go policies and Treasury orthodoxy had almost nothing to do with union power or electoral expediency. And why should Britain and the USA be so prone to democratic overload compared with the 'successful' economies of Japan, France and West Germany? Some would quickly respond that because these countries have more authoritarian and *dirigiste* traditions (or because their independent economic interests were destroyed by war and occupation) their governments have been given greater leeway to pursue 'productive' policies. But the overloaders cannot have it both ways. 'Productive policy' implies a central role for the state in stimulating investment or creating the right environment for capital accumulation and profit-making. A strong state role, whether directly (nationalization and infrastructural investment as in France) or indirectly (guiding and encouraging private investment through central state agencies as in Japan) is anathema to the neo-conservative overload critics. They plead for the very opposite—disengagement of the state and a return to the market.[26]

But perhaps the Anglo-Saxon social structures are so different from those of the successful economies that they can accommodate only a limited (and not necessarily optimal) range of policy solutions. If this is so, it is not claimed explicitly by the overload analysis, which has very little to say in a comparative context.

Comparative research on state/societal linkages has, of course, been undertaken and has become increasingly influential over the last decade. Moreover, much of this work is concerned with the economy and economic policy. One of the most interesting contributions is the collection of essays edited by Peter Katzenstein, *Between Power and Plenty*,[27] on the foreign economic policies of advanced industrial states. Katzenstein and his contributors identify distinctive state/societal linkages in each country as the major explanation of contrasting economic strategies. Britain and the USA are categorized as being weak states, where the control exercised over organized interests (corporations, unions, peak associations) is limited. This sharp differentiation between state and society is contrasted with Japan's symbiotic state/society linkages where the wheels of economic policy are oiled by pervasively intrusive state bureaucracies.[28] The reluctance of the British state to intervene directly in the micro-economic or industrial policy is buttressed by liberal ideology. And when intervention is attempted it falls foul either of weak peak associations unable to control their members or of a hesitant or even obstructionist Civil Service.

Implicit in this analysis is the assumption that governments need to have a micro-economic industrial strategy to succeed in an increasingly interdependent and competitive world. Those whose institutional and ideological arrangements inhibit such a strategy are clearly at a disadvantage. But Britain and the USA have sharply contrasting institutional structures; how then can they be placed in the same weak state category? Katzenstein's answer here is not entirely satisfactory. He acknowledges that the British system places great power at the centre and that Cabinet government is aided by a pliant Parliament and loyal Civil Service. In spite of these apparent 'advantages' British governments have failed to develop a coherent industrial and economic strategy because of the formidable independent power of individual firms, the 'City', unions and shop-floor organizations, all of whom tend to act unilaterally with little respect for government or peak associations—or even other unions and firms within the same industry. As suggested, liberal ideology also plays a part in undermining economic policy, but we are not told exactly how.

Why is it, exactly, that British governments have made such feeble efforts to intervene directly in investment and pricing decisions? Surely such efforts that have been made have floundered not only because of the opposition of organized actors acting unilaterally, but also because governments have themselves been internally divided, uncertain or hesitant when implementing micro-economic policy? We will return to this point later.

In a similar, though more historically based analysis, Pierre Birnbaum goes even further in pursuing the weak state thesis:

> Just as France seemed to offer the example of a society in which the state appeared to be the ideal type of state, so Great Britain was the model of the country in which government was carried out by civil society, the state being reduced to a minimum.[29]

In arguing his case, Birnbaum invokes what is by now a rather familiar body of evidence drawing on politico/economic relations during feudal times and earlier. In contrast to France and Prussia, peripheral economic interests in England gained access to the centre (via Parliament) very early in history. Steady economic progress and the absence of an external threat enabled government to evolve as the agent of established economic interests. Moreover, with early industrialization and the startling success of capitalism, the state was required to do very little, so strengthening an emergent liberal ideology.

The development of Prussia and France (and Japan?)[30] was quite different. In feudal times, external threat and internal competition from warring barons obliged the state to differentiate itself from society and to acquire and build a statist ideology—neutral, autonomous and strong. Nothing embodied the state more clearly than the central state bureaucracy whose function was to reach down into society; to control and eliminate competition, administratively, fiscally and, if all else failed, through the exercise of police power.[31] In contrast to Britain, industrialization was led by the state (or by state bureaucracies)[32] and in spite of wars, occupations and other traumas, the state remains strong in these countries even today. Certainly the evidence that European administrative elites are more sympathetic to state intervention than is the British Civil Service is considerable.[33] Also, the lack of integration between bureaucratic, political and economic elites in Britain is quite marked. Recruitment is from a variety of sources and inter-elite social and political linkages are poorly developed.[34] All of this would seem to give credence to the weak state thesis—and also to further undermine the already largely discredited charge that Britain is becoming a corporate state.[35]

Nevertheless the weak state thesis, although in some ways helpful in explaining British economic policy, contains a number of flaws and omissions. In particular:

(i) Whatever the validity of the claim that over the last several centuries economic interests have dominated government via Parliament, such a claim looks absurd today. Of course, the weak state advocates accept this,[36] but if economic interests no longer dominate Parliament, what role do they play? Until quite recently it was popular to assert that finance capital, the most resilient of organized economic interests, was effectively in control of government via the Treasury. But the first careful study of the City shows this not to be the case. The City had, until recently, remarkably few links with government.[37] If governments deferred to the interests of the City in exchange rate and other policies, it was not because they were the slaves of finance capital; it must have been for some other reason.

Moreover we have already established that economic interests in Britain, although independent, are highly fragmented vertically and horizontally. Finance capital is organized separately from industrial capital; individual firms and unions often go their own way; peak associations have limited control over their members. Individual firms—and especially unions—may exercise considerable *negative* power over government policy but usually in response to macro- rather than micro-economic measures. And it is in micro-economic policy that the British appear so backward and unresponsive compared with the 'successful' economies.

The message, then, is clear: British economic interests may not be incorporated into a central state bureaucracy (or completely excluded from access through coercion), but at the same time they patently do not control government nor, in micro-economic policy at least, have they actively obstructed government measures. Failure in micro-economic policy would appear, then, to be partly attributable to the characteristics—institutional, cultural, ideological—of the political and administrative elites themselves.

(ii) A major implication of the weak-state position is that British government *cannot* intervene directly in the economy. They are always constrained by economic interests, a weak and reluctant central bureaucracy and the absence of long established vertical linkages between state and society. Curiously, however, there have been occasions when the British state has formulated and implemented micro policy to great effect. During the 1930s, and more especially World War II, resources were mobilized and investment and manpower directed in a manner which put the supposedly state-dominated French and German systems to shame.[38] True, much of the machinery of control was dismantled during the late 1940s and 1950s, but its very existence surely puts paid to the more reductionist of the strong society/weak state theories.

Even more significant is the record of the 1945–51 Labour Government's industrial policy. On inheriting wartime controls, an enviable world trading position, and an extraordinarily solid platform of public support, Labour probably pursued those policies most likely to alienate economic interests and least likely to aid long-term economic growth. Nationalization was the key element in industrial policy, but its effects on the economy were small. As Jacques Leruez has observed:

Labour leaders quite failed to see the possibilities of using the new public sector as a way of steering the whole economy in the direction they desired. They behaved as if, while carrying through their plans for nationalization, they had no understanding of the real meaning of what they had done. Ownership changed; power did not.[39]

Although established industries loathed nationalization and wartime controls, there is little evidence that they objected strongly to government-led investment planning, a 'picking winners' strategy or infrastructural investment. Schonfield's 1965 analysis remains valid: Labour Governments failed to develop a coherent industrial strategy not because of opposition from industry or labour, but because they and the civil servants around them were reluctant to create direct and intimate links with private firms.[40] Even those enterprises nationalized by the government were left pretty much to their own devices.

A similar pattern emerges when later micro-economic initiatives are examined. Most flounder not because of opposition from industry—indeed in some instances, such as the work of the National Economic Development Council industry was highly supportive—but because of opposition or indifference to micro-economic planning from within governments and administrations.[41] Neddy, the DEA, the NEB and planning agreements all suffered from what at best was ambivalence and at worst open hostility shown towards them even by members of Labour governments. Conventional wisdom has it that planning agreements, the latest of these measures, were indeed opposed by industry.[42] But it could be argued that by the mid 1970s the whole debate had taken on a highly ideological rather than technocratic slant. The language and style of the *1973 Labour Programme* from which the Planning Agreements system derives was combatitively socialist and anti-private capital. Nothing could better ensure opposition from industry than this.

INSTITUTIONAL AND SOCIAL STRUCTURAL EXPLANATIONS: A SYNTHESIS

From the foregoing discussion we can conclude the following:

(i) A major characteristic of postwar economic policy has been a reluctance by governments to engage in direct or indirect investment. Micro-economic policy has nearly always played second string to macro-economic policy, whether it be of the Keynesian or monetarist variety. Considerable evidence exists to suppose that this investment failure has put Britain at a serious disadvantage in relation to other industrial states.

(ii) Adversary politics and political/business cycle arguments are at best tangential to any explanation of economic policy. The 'technocratic critique' is more convincing, but puts too much emphasis on the machinery of government *per se*. Links with the broader society are generally ignored and the techocrats' explanation of why micro-economic initiatives have failed—Treasury opposition, lack of political will, external constraints—are inadequate. Most institutional explanations also fail to link the institutional *advantages* which Britain enjoys to the particular mix of economic policies pursued over the last thirty years.

(iii) As an explanation of the failure of micro-economic policy, social structural theories are quite appealing. If the state is weak in relation to society, or economic interests are autonomous and resistant to intervention, then indeed micro-economic policy must have limited potential. Moreover, if the trend has been towards the strengthening of society in relation to the state then the problems of economic management will be that much greater—especially if the external economic environment has been growing ever more hostile. But as catalogued, there is little evidence that economic interests have overtly resisted micro-economic policy. The fiercest battles over economic policy have involved resistance to *macro* measures —monetary, fiscal and non-selective prices and incomes policy. Until the changes in the ideological climate of the 1970s industry and unions either welcomed or were largely indifferent to micro-economic policy. This said, Britain does appear to have weaker state/societal linkages than some other countries. Politicians and civil servants dislike intimate involvement with the day-to-day investment decisions of private firms or even of nationalized enterprises. Inter-elite linkages are also poorly developed and almost certainly have inhibited development of the sort of symbiotic relationship between industry, government and finance which is so often identified as a key to Japanese economic success. Whatever the historical origins of this political fragmentation, there have been occasions when it has been successfully overcome, and although in its crudest form the corporatist thesis is clearly inappropriate in Britain, evidence of increased consultation between government and industry (and within government and within industry) is discernable.[43]

If British governments are not always constrained by societal pressures, then the implication is clear: the characteristics, values and ideologies of governments themselves must be a factor in explaining economic policy. Does this mean that we are obliged to seek refuge in such vague generalizations as politicians and bureaucrats lacking the 'political will' or the 'ideological inclination' to pursue a coherent industrial strategy? Not entirely, for as was implied earlier, the link between institutional arrangements and policy have yet to be fully explored. What follows are some tentative pointers to this relationship.

A unique feature of British political development was the emergence of a labour movement and social democratic party in the context of a weak state.[44] In no other major country was a new socialist party obliged to implement a programme of social and economic change without the aid of a strong state bureaucracy and an established tradition of intervention. Of course, the domestic and international pressures for change and increased intervention also affected Conservative governments and led to the hesitant steps towards corporatism recorded by Keith Middlemas and others.[45]

The great paradox of the British situation was that although by the standards of continental countries the state was weak, the political system was remarkably centralized and stable. On the face of it, the interventionist solutions to the country's social and economic ills looked simple: elect a reformist government with a clear Parliamentary majority and via a loyal and efficient Civil Service implement the party's programme. Social and political stability together with a high level of literacy and political education would add to the chances of success. With such apparent advantages relatively simply policy solutions looked attractive. And as significant was the fact that the new reforming elites had themselves few linkages with the broader society and economy. Policy-making in the Labour Party was dominated not by rank and file industrial workers and trade unionists drawn from the 'provinces' but by London-based middle-class intellectuals.[46] Above all, the party was influenced by members of the Fabian Society—an organization noted for an often over-confident and crude empiricism which coincided nicely with the simple view of society which British institutional arrangements implied. Joseph Schumpeter's observations on the Fabians are characteristically perceptive:

They were careful about their facts which some of them took no end of trouble to collect by means of extensive research, and critical of arguments and measures. But they were quite uncritical as to the fundamentals, cultural and economic, of their aims. These they took for granted. They were unable to see the difference between a slum and the House of Lords. Why both of these were obviously 'bad things', that's common sense, is it not? And greater economic equality or self government in India or trade unions and free trade were no less obviously 'good things'. Who could doubt it? All the thinking that was necessary was on how to clean up the bad things and on how to secure the good things; everything else was irritating futility.[47]

This Fabian 'technocraticism' influenced leaders from all political parties. Simple solutions imposed from above were all that were required to transform society. It was almost as though politicians and civil servants were *above* rather than *in* society. The pulling of levers in Whitehall or Westminster could guide the economy or reduce inequalities without government involving itself in the messy business of establishing, strengthening and refining relationships with real world firms, industries, unions, regions and local governments. Keynesian economics reinforced such thinking with its assumption that aggregate demand could be manipulated by government spending from above. The *quality* of expenditure—on which industries, services, regions and so on it should be spent—became largely irrelevant. Andrew Schonfield observes that the 'Keynesian revolution' did not really occur in countries with strong state-societal linkages, for in such societies economic policy automatically involved *micro*-economic intervention with the state exploiting established relationships with individual economic actors.[48]

This thesis is quite compatible with the currently fashionable 'decline of industrial spirit' argument. As far as politicians and bureaucrats are concerned the 'industrial spirit' was never really present.[49] And when forced to intervene to 'manage' an increasingly volatile and complex economy they did so in a way reconcilable with centralism and a historically weak state—from above and by adopting simple 'unitary' solutions.[50] Interestingly, these solutions were often expensive, but then a high level of public expenditure does not on its own require a strong and intrusive central state bureaucracy—especially if it consists primarily of transfer payments and subsidies for autonomous state enterprises. Even when public spending accounted for over 40 per cent of GNP the actual machinery for monitoring, controlling and evaluating expenditure remained much as it had in Victorian times.[51]

Of course some state/society linkages were forged during the first half of the twentieth century—especially during the national emergency periods of depression and war. But they were always *ad hoc* and improvised by nature. It was almost as if, once the emergency was deemed over, politicians and bureaucrats could not wait to shed themselves of the uncomfortable business of corporate management. Certainly this was the experience of the 1945–51 Labour governments.[52] Later, the micro-economic experiments of the 1960s and 1970s also lacked political support. At the first sign of failure some excuse was found for abandoning them. Moreover, by the 1970s fiscal pressures had reached such a level that the reordering of priorities towards selective industrial and infrastructural investments and away from the established priorities of defence, social spending and a universalistic regional policy became especially difficult. As a result, British industrial policy became extraordinarily muddled. As Wyn Grant has accurately observed: 'There has been and continues to be considerable disagreement in the United Kingdom about whether government should have an industrial policy at all and, if so, what form it should take.'[53]

Three final points need to be added to this analysis. First, far from dying out Fabian technocraticism is still very much with us. Macro-economic manipulation of the economy from above is the very essence of Thatcherism. The policy objectives may differ from those beloved of the Fabians but the means and the underlying attitudes towards government's role in society are the same. Government is *above* not *in* society; its role is to create the right environment for private actors to behave in the desired manner—whether it be to promote equality, accumulate capital or whatever. Government does not intervene directly—either (the Fabians) because it is not necessary or (the present Conservative Government) because it is neither necessary nor desirable.

Second, although both politicians and civil servants are imbued with these values some evidence exists to suggest that politicians must take the main responsibility for the resulting policies. As repeatedly emphasized, British institutional arrangements and political culture facilitates coherent policy formulation and implementation. When national emergency demands it, politicians have moved into society to great effect.[54] Moreover civil servants can be the creatures rather than masters of politicians. The Thatcher Government's generally successful crusade against public spending demonstrates this. Admittedly, distinguishing cause from effect is difficult in this area, but it certainly seems feasible to argue that although politicians' freedom to pursue particular policies is limited by bureaucrats and societal pressures, these are much less formidable constraints than is commonly supposed.

Third, failure to adopt a coherent micro-economic strategy has had a long term depressing effect on industrial and infrastructural investment. Sydney Pollard's comment is apt:

The whole of postwar policy has been built on the assumption that whatever else can be manipulated or changed, actual production and investment cannot be and must be left to industry, and that the most the government can do is to set the scene which therefore receives top priority—at the expense of damaging the production and the investment, for the benefit of which the scene-setting is supposed to have been undertaken in the first place.[55]

Crucially, when Pollard is referring to governments' role in 'actual production and investment' he is not pleading for a command economy or for the suspension of the market place. Few of those directly involved in the private production of goods and services would argue with his call for greatly increased infrastructure investment. Neither would many object to pleas for a coherent investment programme led by a national finance corporation, a similar scheme for technological innovation,[56] or some selective protection for industries vulnerable to foreign competition.[57]

CONCLUSIONS

'But the United States is not Japan' is an oft quoted reply to those who argue that the USA should adopt a Japanese style industrial policy.[58] These critics quite rightly point out that the American institutional arrangements and social structure simply cannot accommodate a coherent micro-economic strategy. Hence the current recourse to market solutions. Although the UK is frequently placed in the same position, the foregoing analysis would suggest that this is a mistake. Britain's institutional structures are highly favourable to effective policy formulation and implementation. And while state/societal linkages are poorly developed, the evidence on economic interests being resistant to micro-economic intervention is ambivalent, to say the least. The UK may not share with Japan, France and some other countries sophisticated and well developed vertical and intra-elite linkages, but those at the apex of the constitutional system have a greater capacity to create and nurture such contacts than is commonly supposed.

Of course British governments do indulge in micro-economic intervention—in the context of a highly complex and volatile national and international economic order, they have no choice. But policy tends to be *ad hoc*, fragmented, inconsistent and often reluctant. Rarely is it strategic, and even more rarely do politicians or civil servants heartily endorse carefully worked out investment programmes. Over the last few years direct industrial investment has tended to favour lame duck state enterprises or sometimes dubious private ventures over which little day-to-day control is exercised.

Remarkably, in view of Britain's economic performance, political leaders remain unconvinced of the need for state-led programmes of investment and innovation. Were British industrial capital strong, resilient and capable of transforming the economy without state assistance, this might be understandable. But this is patently not the case. Only the Labour left endorses an enhanced state role, but it does so in a highly ideological manner which has little political support.

It is the major contention of this paper that although a more effective economic policy is constrained by societal forces and the historically weak linkages that exist between agents of the state and major economic interests, these are not as significant obstacles to change as the values and assumptions of politicians themselves. As suggested, until the 1970s it was institutionally and politically convenient for politicians, together with their major source of ideas and programmes, the political parties, to seek recourse in simple macro-economic solutions to Britain's ills. By the 1980s the intensity of decline did precipitate some intellectual regeneration within existing and emergent political parties. So far, however, this regeneration has failed to produce anything close to a consensus on the need for a nationally directed programme of investment and innovation. Until such a consensus is built—and it may never be—British economic policy is almost certainly condemned to a continuing mixture of ineffective macro-economic management and micro-economic improvisation and *ad hocery*.

NOTES AND REFERENCES

1. Richard E. Caves and Lawrence B. Krause (eds), *Britain's Economic Performance* (Washington DC, Brookings, 1980), p. 19.
2. Frank Blackaby (ed.), *De-industrialisation*, National Institute of Economic and Social Research, Economic Policy Papers 2 (London, Heinemann, 1979).
3. Notable exceptions to this criticism are the contributions by Chris

Freeman ('Technical innovation and British trade performance'), which rightly chastises the government-led emphasis on defence and aerospace research and development in the postwar period, and by A. Singh on 'North Sea oil and the reconstruction of UK industry', which pleads for a Japanese-style industrial policy. Ibid.

4. This is a major theme of later discussion when full references will be given.

5. However the established view of the UK as a country with a large public sector is now open to some doubt. Within the EEC Britain has the smallest public sector (percentage of GNP in 1980) at 43.9 per cent compared with 46 per cent in Italy, 46.4 per cent in West Germany and 46.5 per cent in France—although the relative size of the American, and especially the Japanese, public sectors remain small. Britain also has the second lowest tax burden in the EEC. See EEC, *European Economy*, various editions, 1981/82.

6. See Milton and Rose Friedman, *Free to Choose* (London, Secker & Warburg, 1980).

7. Including many identified with the right. Bacon and Eltis, for example, make a crucial distinction between marketed and non-marketed public sector goods, the former being acceptable as 'productive'. See Robert Bacon and Walter Eltis, *Britain's Economic Problem: Too Few Producers* (London, Macmillan, 2nd ed., 1978). While often highly critical of government intervention, many public choice theorists recognize that the nature of the political and social system can decide whether intervention is benign, productive or damaging. See Mancur Olson, *The Political Economy of Comparative Growth Rates* (College Park, University of Maryland, 1979); also Alan T. Peacock and Martin Ricketts, 'The growth of the public sector and inflation', in Fred Hirsch and John H. Goldthorpe, *The Political Economy of Inflation* (London, Martin Robertson, 1979).

8. See the various editions of the Cambridge Economic Policy Group's *Economic Policy Review*.

9. Sydney Pollard, *The Wasting of the British Economy* (London and Canberra, Croom Helm, St Martin's, 1982).

10. Ibid., Chapter 7.

11. G. K. Fry, *The Administrative 'Revolution' in Whitehall* (London, Croom Helm, 1981).

12. Ibid., Chapter 2.

13. Ibid., Chapters 4 and 5. See also Alan Budd, *The Politics of Economic Planning* (London, Fontana/Collins, 1978); Jacques Leruez, *Economic Planning and Politics in Britain* (Oxford, Martin Robertson, 1976).

14. Michael Shanks, *Planning and Politics* (London, Allen & Unwin, 1977), p. 106.

15. S. E. Finer, *Adversary Politics and Electoral Reform* (London, A. Wigram, 1975).

16. For a comprehensive and brilliantly critical review of this large body of literature, see Brian Barry, 'Does democracy cause inflation?', in Leon Lindberg and Charles S. Maier (eds), *The Politics and Sociology of Global Inflation* (Washington DC, Brookings, forthcoming).

17. Should there be any doubt about the underinvestment thesis a glance at any of a dozen or so indicators from value added per employee to gross capital formation per capita to productivity levels should remove them. Indicators relating to other possible causes of economic decline —strikes, the industrial structure, international competitiveness, inflation, tax burden, government expenditure are all inconclusive in comparative perspective. See Pollard, op. cit., Chapter 2, also Caves and Krause, op. cit.

18. Barry, op. cit., pp. 44-51. It could be argued that the political/ business cycle analysis is a social structural rather than institutional explanation as governments are obliged to heed the wishes of a selfish electorate. But the electorate is made up of discrete individuals, not groups, and according to this literature is ultimately manipulable by politicians. As Barry puts it: '[it is a system] characterized by a collection of rogues competing for the favours of a larger collection of dupes', ibid., p. 41.

19. John H. Goldthorpe, 'The current inflation: towards a sociological account', in Fred Hirsch and John Goldthorpe (eds), *The Political Economy of Inflation* (London, Martin Robertson, 1978).

20. Caves and Krause, op. cit., chapter by Richard E. Caves, 'Productivity differences among industries'.

21. Mancur Olson, op. cit.

22. Samuel Brittan, 'The economic contradictions of democracy', *British Journal of Political Science*, Vol. 5 (1975), pp. 129-59.

23. One of the first and clearest expositions of the thesis was Anthony King's 'Overload: problems of governing in the 1970s', *Political Studies*, Vol. 23, Nos 2-3 (1975), pp. 162-74. A more recent comparative perspective—although still dominated by British thinking— is Richard Rose (ed.), *Challenge to Governance: Studies in Overloaded Politics* (Beverly Hills and London, Sage, 1980). For the American view see the tenth anniversary issue of the *Public Interest, The American Commonwealth 1976* (New York, Basic Books, 1976), contributions by Samuel P. Huntington and S. M. Lipset; also Samuel P. Huntingdon, *American Politics: The Promise of Disharmony* (Cambridge, Mass., Harvard University Press, 1981).

24. Lester Thurow's *Zero Sum Society* (Harmondsworth, Penguin 1981) makes precisely the same argument from an economist's perspective.

25. See the chapter by Peter Self, 'Resource and policy coordination under pressure', in Rose (ed.), op. cit.

26. This may be a little unfair on the British 'overloaders' who are much less explicitly apologist for liberal ideology, but implicit in their work is the assumption that because governments have too much to do, a possible solution is to give them much less to do—or, possibly, make them more resistant to electoral pressures through coalition politics or national governments.

27. P. J. Katzenstein, *Between Power and Plenty: Foreign Economic Policies of Advanced Industrial States* (Madison, Wisconsin, University of Wisconsin Press, 1978).

28. Ibid., Chapter 9.

29. Pierre Birnbaum, 'State, centre and bureaucracy', *Government and Opposition*, 6 (1981), 58-77 and sources cited. See also Andrew Gamble, *Britain in Decline: Economic Policy, Political Strategy and the British State* (London, Macmillan, 1981), Chapter 3.

30. Birnbaum does not include Japan, but there is evidence that its development has been similar if not identical, see Barrington Moore Jr., *The Social Origin of Dictatorship and Democracy* (Harmondsworth, Penguin, 1979), Chapter 5.

31. Birnbaum, op. cit., pp. 66-77. For some fascinating quantitative indicators of the weakness of the British state during the nineteenth century, see Clive Trebilcock, *The Industrialization of the Continental Powers 1780-1914* (London, Longman, 1981), Chapter 7.

32. Trebilcock, ibid., Chapter 1.

33. See John Armstrong, *The European Administrative Elite* (Princeton N.J., Princeton University Press, 1973).

34. See Pierre Birnbaum, 'Institutionalization of power and integration of ruling elites: a comparative analysis', *European Journal of Political Research*, 6 (1978), 105-15; W. Guttsman, 'Elite recruitment and political leadership in Britain and Germany in 1950: a comparative study of MPs and Cabinets', in P. Stedworth and A. Giddens (eds), *Elites and Power in British Society* (Cambridge, Cambridge University Press, 1974); Neville Abraham, *Big Business and Government: The New Disorder* (London, Macmillan, 1974), Chapter 16.

35. For a review of the corporatist literature, see Andrew Cox, 'Corporatism as reductionism: the analytic limits of the corporatist thesis', *Government and Opposition*, 16 (1981), 78-95.

36. Including the more interesting of the 'Marxist' scholars, who do accept some independent role for institutions, see Bob Jessop, 'The transformation of the state in post-war Britain', in Richard Scase (ed.), *The State in Western Europe* (London, Croom Helm, 1980), pp. 23-94.

37. See Michael Moran, *Banking, Power and Policy: The Case of Competition and Credit Control* (London, Macmillan, forthcoming).

38. For an account of British economic policy during this period, see Keith Middlemas, *Politics in Industrial Society* (London, Andre

Deutsch, 1979), Chapters 8-10. For a comparative perspective, see J. A. Schumpeter, *Capitalism, Socialism and Democracy* (London, Allen & Unwin, 1954), Chapters 27 and 28.

39. Jacques Leruez, *Economic Planning and Politics in Britain* (Oxford, Martin Robertson, 1976), p. 76. The same can be said of regional policy, the main purpose of which was employment creation rather than industrial growth. See David McKay and Andrew Cox, *The Politics of Urban Change* (London, Croom Helm, 1979), Chapter 6.

40. Andrew Schonfield, *Modern Capitalism* (London, Oxford University Press, 1965), Chapter 6.

41. Leruez, op. cit.; Fry, op. cit., Chapter 4; and sources cited.

42. David Coates, *Labour in Power? A Study of the Labour Government, 1974-1979* (London, Longman, 1980), Chapter 3.

43. See Wyn Grant, *The Political Economy of Industrial Policy* (London, Butterworth, 1982) for a review of recent industry/government relations and some comparisons with West Germany.

44. See Birnbaum, 'State, centre and bureaucracy', op. cit., and sources cited.

45. Middlemas, op. cit., Chapters 7-10.

46. See L. J. Sharpe, 'The Labour Party and the geography of inequality: a puzzle', in Dennis Kavanagh (ed.), *The Politics of the Labour Party* (London, Allen & Unwin, 1982).

47. Schumpeter, op. cit., p. 322.

48. Andrew Schonfield, *Modern Capitalism* (London, Oxford University Press, 1965), p. 65.

49. Martin Wiener, *English Culture and the Decline of the Industrial Spirit, 1850-1980* (Cambridge, Cambridge University Press, 1981). See also his 'Conservatism, economic growth and English culture', *Parliamentary Affairs*, 34 (1981), 409-21.

50. And not only in economic policy. In planning and land use a similar tendency prevailed. See David McKay and Andrew Cox, *The Politics of Urban Change* (London, Croom Helm, 1979), Chapter 8.

51. See Fry, op. cit., Chapter 5.

52. See Fry, ibid.; also Mikkal E. Herberg, 'Politics, planning and capitalism: national economic planning in France and Britain', *Political Studies*, 39 (1981), 497-516.

53. Wyn Grant, 'UK industrial policy: the problem and its perception', *Parliamentary Affairs*, forthcoming.

54. The Falklands emergency demonstrates this point nicely. It is difficult to imagine any other Western country requisitioning ships, allocating resources and controlling information with such formidable ease. In the light of these events to label the British state 'weak' seems absurdly inaccurate. When politicians wish to exercise strong state powers they can do so.

55. Sydney Pollard, op. cit., p. 190.

56. Interestingly, there are some very good justifications for a national innovation policy drawn from economic theory. See Norman J. Schofield, 'Innovation and the socially optimal rate of investment', *Journal of Economic Affairs*, forthcoming; and also K. Pavitt and W. Walker, 'Government policies towards industrial innovation: a review', *Research Policy*, 5 (1976), 11-97.

57. Moreover, there is increasing evidence that state-sponsored investment and innovation programmes need not be a product of hierarchical, centralized bureaucracies. Indeed, *competition* between agencies is as often a feature of industrial policy. See Wyn Grant and David McKay (eds), 'Industrial policies in OECD countries'. Special issue of the *Journal of Public Policy*, 3 (forthcoming February 1982), contributions by Hills, Holmes, Grant and McKay.

58. For a discussion, see Marc Bendick, *A Federal Entrepreneur? Industrial Policy and American Economic Revitalization*, Urban Institute Working Paper 1525-01, Washington DC, 1981.

5 The Political Economy of Industrial Policy

WYN GRANT

INTRODUCTION

In despair at the slow theoretical development of their discipline, some political scientists have turned to the apparently more advanced social science of economics for theories and terminology to explain political phenomena. Some interesting insights have resulted, but the view taken in this chapter is that 'political economy' should not be a hybrid in which the economics strain is allowed to become dominant, but rather should involve an attempt to develop the insights of political science so that they can be placed alongside those of economics in the study of problems of common interest.

A wide range of government policies may affect the industrial economy. Apart from the crucial influence of macro-economic policies such as the presence or absence of an exchange rate policy, secondary forms of economic policy such as energy policy, transport policy and employment policy clearly have an impact on the state of industry. Aspects of social policy, such as education policy, can be of considerable importance because of their influence on the skill composition of the workforce. There is, thus, a very wide range of government policies that have an impact on industry, even if they are not specifically directed towards industrial policy objectives.

Government industrial policy is an amorphous subject, but there is a solid core of industrial policy that is concerned with the various measures used by government to influence the investment decisions of individual enterprises—public and private—so as to promote such objectives as lower unemployment, a healthier balance of payments and a generally more efficient industrial economy. Investment decisions are taken to cover not only the creation, expansion and re-equipment of production capacity, but also decisions about research and development facilities and product development. In many ways, policies of this kind are a response to the failure of conventional economic policy measures, although they may simply exacerbate the problems that macro-economic measures have not solved. Indeed, as Corden points out, 'The more disturbance there is on the macro-economic side, the more industrial policy is likely to become short-term oriented, to flounder around, a tool in political and economic crisis management.'[1]

On the whole, the distinction between economic policy and industrial policy is reasonably clear. It would be generally accepted that attempts to control the money supply form part of economic policy, and that a scheme to modernize and rationalize the machine tool industry would form part of industrial policy. There are, of course, boundary problems. Aid to British Leyland concerns a particular firm and would, in an ideal world, form part of a coherent government policy for a particular industry, motor vehicles. However, the consequences of the closure of a firm like British Leyland would be so widespread that they would probably show up on an aggregate model of the economy. Perhaps the greatest difficulties arise not in distinguishing industrial policy from economic policy, but from other policies concerned with particular industries, such as energy policy. For example, would a scheme to provide selective assistance to energy-intensive industries to offset high energy prices form part of industrial policy or of energy policy? Does a programme of forward ordering for power stations represent an attempt to develop a coherent energy policy or to ensure that the power-generating equipment industry has a steady programme of work?

It is very tempting to fall back on the argument that government industrial policy is what the national industry ministry does (or does not do). However, such an approach would not be helpful in a country such as West Germany which has no industry ministry but, despite its protestations of innocence, does have an industrial policy. In Britain, the Department of Industry is only responsible for some industries; others are the responsibility of the Departments of Trade, Energy, Transport, Health and Social Security, Environment, Ministry of Agriculture, etc. In any case, one must be cautious about exaggerating the impact that government can actually have on industry. In a country like Britain, most important industrial decisions are taken by individual firms or semi-autonomous state industries, or by the providers of finance. Government can exhort, cajole, provide funds, even nationalize, but what results often looks like little more than a series of hastily erected sandcastles built in the face of the incoming tide.

THE CONTRIBUTION OF POLITICAL SCIENCE

Even if one can delineate the area of study, is there a distinctive analytical contribution that can be made by political scientists? Economists can estimate the employment and balance of payments effects of a given policy measure; industrial sociologists can tell us why the organization and norms of the workplace will prevent the policy ever being implemented; accountants can explain to us different ways of arriving at the bottom line, and so on. Political scientists tend to be a sceptical group when it comes to the merits of their own discipline, but if the discipline is to have any academic credibility, it must be capable of making a contribution to the study of problems as important as those which arise in the industrial policy arena. If nothing else, political scientists must provide an antidote to the views of those politically illiterate economists who see politics as the expression of irrational prejudices which prevent the optimal policies devised by economists from being put into effect.[2]

However, many economists are more receptive than hitherto to political explanations that can contribute to the understanding of economic phenomena, if only because the variance left unexplained by their econometric equations is too large to be written off as an error term. What can political scientists offer them? It will only be possible to offer a brief sketch of the possibilities here. Perhaps most obviously, political scientists should have something to say about the ways in which industrial policy decisions are taken. How much influence is exerted by civil servants? What part does Parliament play in the policy-making process? What are the consequences of the delegation of some tasks to 'quasis' and 'quangos'? Above all, how do the different parts of the industrial policy community interact with each other? Questions such as these are perhaps rather less fashionable today than they were in the late 1960s and early 1970s. There has been an overreaction against the former widespread enthusiasm for institutional reform so that the assumption that organizational reform is the answer to every problem has been replaced by an assumption that organizational arrangements do not matter at all. However, at the very least, it does not seem unreasonable to ask how it is decided to spend the £2,000 million or so of public money allocated to industrial policy on a regular basis every year, quite apart from the not infrequent additional provision of 'crisis money' for one of Britain's ailing industries. If the answer is that most of the spending is predetermined by decisions taken in the past, that is itself interesting.

However, simply charting the hydrography of the industrial policy community will not convince the sceptical economist who believes that 'the excellence or otherwise of administrative machinery can only be judged by its results. It is the disregard of this simple point which makes public administration such a barren subject'.[3] Above all, it is important not to confine the analysis to government, which may be busy taking decisions that have little or no impact on the industrial economy. There is a clear need to examine the principal intermediaries between government and the industrial economy, the trade associations, and the complex relationships that exist between them, their members and government's 'sponsorship divisions'. The recent neo-corporatist literature may be of some help here at least in providing a starting point for analysis.[4]

Trade associations have received some attention from political scientists because they can be analysed within the familiar framework provided by the pluralist interest group literature and the more recent rational choice literature of the Olsonian variety. Regrettably, less attention has been paid by political scientists to perhaps the key unit of industrial policy analysis, the firm. The place of the firm as a basic unit of analysis in economics is long established, and important contributions to our understanding of how firms behave have been made by economic historians, organization theorists, industrial sociologists and students of business studies. Rather more arcane contributions have been made by experts in company law and in accountancy. However, one has to look very hard to find a distinctive political science contribution to the study of the firm. Some political scientists have contributed to the literature on transnational companies, but this literature deals with only one type of firm, albeit a very important one. Much of the literature is concerned with alternatives to the conventional firm.[5] This is an important subject, but it does diminish the need for analysis of the capitalist firm. For example, how far do firms see themselves as political as well as economic actors? To what extent do they build political analysis into their investment plans and business decisions? Does the growth of specialized government relations units in very large firms represent a greater sophistication in the approach of firms to political issues? All these are important questions on which political scientists should have something to say.[6]

A caricature of a politically illiterate economist's view of how a choice is made between alternative industrial policies would run something like this: governments specify policy objectives, and arrange them in a preference order; targets are derived from these objectives, and policy measures devised; these are then implemented. If the policy fails, it may be because inadequate techniques were used, or correct techniques wrongly used, in which case economists may have to be called in to advise on (or argue among themselves about) less imperfect techniques. A caricature of the 'man in the street's' view of how industrial policy is made would run something like this: the collapse of a major firm, or a crisis in a particular industry, leads to political pressures on government to act; after a period of cliff-hanging talks, accompanied by varying amounts of agonizing and handwringing depending on the personality of the particular minister, an aid package is put together; everyone then breathes a sigh of relief, and hopes that a crisis will not recur in the same firm or industry too quickly. The reality appears to be somewhat different from both of these caricatures. Government policy objectives are rarely explicitly stated and, when they are, often appear to be contradictory, and industrial policy, given the imperfect information available from the industrial economy, often looks like a series of crisis response measures. On the other hand, considerable progress has been made by government, both in developing criteria against which particular aid packages can be judged, and in devising schemes which attempt to tackle some of the basic problems of the industrial economy on a systematic basis (such as the Product and Process Development Scheme). Nevertheless, it is clear that the debate on industrial policy is conditioned by certain basic assumptions and by an almost mystical preference for some types of policy measure over others.

It is here that the political scientist can be of some assistance. Using his or her skills of conceptual analysis, the political scientist can analyse the ways in which the British debate on industrial policy is underpinned by a belief in something called the 'mixed economy', which is rarely defined, but often referred to; swamped by pleas for a 'consistent' industrial policy; and preoccupied with the notion of 'deindustrialization'. Do frequently used concepts such as these detract from, or contribute to, the quality of the debate? The political scientist can use his or her knowledge of political parties to try and explain why in Britain, particularly as far as the Labour Party is concerned, industrial policy has been preoccupied with *manufacturing* industry and has relegated labour-intensive industries, such as tourism, to a candy floss economy? The political scientist can use a range of knowledge and skills to attempt to explain why both Britain and West Germany, with their different political systems, have preferred location specific aids such as regional policy over aids to particular industries or for particular purposes. It is certainly not because such policies are efficacious. The areas that are economically disadvantaged in Britain are much the same as they were fifty years ago when regional policy was started, with the addition of the West Midlands, which may well have suffered from the diversion of new types of industry elsewhere. Indeed, there is evidence that regional policies have destroyed jobs by enabling industry to become more capital intensive.[7] The political preference for regional policy cannot be simply explained in terms of economic necessity or policy efficacy; a political explanation is required as well.[8]

There is clearly considerable scope for the comparative study of industrial policy. There is, of course, the usual danger of making superficial comparisons which take institutions and policies out of the context of a particular economy, society and polity and attempt to apply them to the United Kingdom. For example, it would be foolish to understand Japanese industrial policy without first learning something about Japanese economic history and the resultant structure of the Japanese economy, not to mention the particular character of Japanese society.

Such comparative studies as have appeared in Britain tend to be concerned with the other major West European economies. Thus, Peacock has produced an excellent comparison of British and West German industrial policy for the Anglo–German Foundation.[9] Diana Green has produced a study of recent French industrial policy and is working on a comparative study of British and French industrial policy.[10] In what is now a rather dated study, Holland reported on a visit to Italy and the state holding companies to be found there.[11]

Although population size is one important variable when considering the selection of countries for comparative study, it is not the only relevant one and can mask other important differences. For example, the British economy is much more dependent on foreign trade than those of France and West Germany. Just as there is much to be said for the study of the political institutions and processes of the smaller western democracies, so much can be learnt from an analysis of their industrial policies. Garner has produced an interesting analysis of the Austrian approach to industrial policy[12] and there have been a number of studies of the Republic of Ireland's industrial policy, which are discussed in more detail later. However, if early industrialization and an excessive reliance on traditional heavy industries are regarded as one set of causes of Britain's industrial problems, a comparison with Belgium—also an early industrializer—might be fruitful.

Experts on international relations are also in a position to make an important contribution to the study of industrial policy. The failure of the European Community to evolve anything resembling an adequate industrial policy has already been exhaustively analysed.[13] Indeed, it could be argued that the various studies of industrial policy by the OECD have had more impact on the conduct of industrial policy at the national level than any measures taken by the European Community. However, perhaps the most important area in which international relations experts can make a contribution is to the study of international trading relations. Industrial policies are sometimes criticized for being little more than a surrogate form of tariff barrier, and certainly one of the reasons for the development of industrial policies in a number of countries has been the need to cope with problems arising from the liberalization of international trade in the postwar period. The world now seems to be moving into a more protectionist phase and among the issues which require analysis are whether or not the new industrializing countries are to be viewed as a 'problem'; the increasing impatience expressed by some European Community countries about Japanese conduct in trade matters; and the future of GATT.[14]

THE INDUSTRIAL POLICY LITERATURE: AN OVERVIEW

In the preceding pages, a number of references have been made to the existing literature on industrial policy. It will not be possible to offer, in the space of this chapter, a comprehensive survey of what is already a very large literature. Instead an attempt will be made to survey the contours of the landscape. Three general statements can be made with some confidence about the industrial policy literature: it is largely written by people with no experience of either government or industry; it is uneven in its coverage; and it is prone to fashions.

It is perhaps unavoidable that most of the literature on industrial policy is written by academics with no experience of either government or industry. After all, they have the time to write the books, and career structures are such that they have few opportunities to gain direct experience in their fields of interest. However, there are three good books by practitioners on British industrial policy. Sir Arthur Knight writes from the perspective of an industrialist with extensive experience of government.[15] Edmund Dell has drawn on his experience as a minister to write a book on industrial policy which, although characterized by a certain world-weary pragmatic scepticism, at least tells us a great deal about how industrial policy has been made, rather than how it might be made.[16] Last but not least, Gerald Kaufman offers a rather rare blend of awareness of the limits imposed by established institutions, and practices, and controlled optimism about the possibilities of change.[17] What is, of course, missing is a book by a civil servant about the amorphous industrial policy community that may only exist as a community of regular meeting attenders. What would be better still is a book by a civil servant who has moved 'round the table' to a firm, a trade association or a nationalized industry. Unfortunately, people who know a great deal can sometimes explain very little.

The uneven coverage of books and articles on industrial policy to some extent reflects the uneven coverage of industrial policy itself. Thus, the preponderance of books or articles on regional policy reflects government's long standing interest in that form of industrial policy. Three good studies of policies towards particular industrial sectors have been produced by political scientists: Hogwood on shipbuilding; Jenkin on the offshore supplies industry; and Ovenden on steel.[18] There is a tendency for the literature on sectoral policies, considered as a whole, to concentrate either on 'glamour' sectors, such as microelectronics, which are rapidly expanding or sectors, such as steel or motor vehicles which are rapidly declining. Again, this partially reflects the emphasis of the policies pursued by government, although government policies towards the engineering industry have been relatively little studied, leaving aside motor vehicles.[19] Industries which are not dealt with by the Department of Industry, such as food processing, construction and medical supplies, are particularly neglected. For example, the food processing industry is the fourth largest employer in the country, and accounts for about a tenth of the gross output of all manufacturing industries, but has received little attention from academics, particularly political scientists.[20] This is in spite of a number of important technological developments such as the potential for the application of microelectronics to production process control; progress towards article numbering; and the important implications of biotechnology.

Intellectual fashions are not always undesirable as they can lead to new attention being given to an unjustifiably neglected area, or to a new theoretical perspective being applied to an established area of enquiry. For example, the recent preoccupation with industrial innovation in the British industrial policy literature resulted from a perception that too much attention had been concentrated on pure research and development and not enough on 'the whole process of analysing and developing a new idea, designing a product and a production route, setting up for production, and making the product a commercial success in the market place'.[21] The risk is that one may end up with a catchphrase that has little real policy content, particularly when, as in the case of innovation, the word carries with it 'a presumption of virtue'.[22] It is a sobering thought that a recent conference on industrial policy and innovation led to the conclusion that 'very little is being said now whch was not familiar a quarter of a century or more ago. Nor has anyone much in the way of new ideas about what is to be done about it.'[23] The political debate on industrial policy is very good at producing catchphrases or words which are popular if only because they have unpalatable opposites: consistency (rather than inconsistency); constructive intervention (rather than destructive intervention); positive adjustment (rather than negative adjustment). One task for the political scientist is to stand aside from these fashions and to expose what are often very shallow ideologies.

INDUSTRIAL POLICY IN PRACTICE

The need for industrial policy

Much of the debate about industrial policy, in Britain at any rate, is concerned less with the choice between alternative industrial policies, than with whether government should have an industrial policy at all. Apart from the intellectual case for not interfering with the workings of the market, the lessons of experience suggest that industrial policies often end up giving additional protection to already sheltered industrial interests; giving money to firms to carry out projects that would have proceeded without government help; and that when governments try to pick winners, they end up picking losers. This has led to an increasing interest in industrial policies which work with the market by responding to its signals, although it is never quite clear where these signals come from or how they are to be interpreted.

A negative justification for industrial policy is that other countries do it, therefore Britain has to do it as well if its industries are not to be disadvantaged. Of course, if other countries do it badly, then Britain would gain by doing nothing. However, it is by no means certain that other countries do it badly. At the very least, they seem able to improve the international competitive position of particular industries; and, at best, they are able to have a positive impact on the entire industrial economy.

Even market-oriented countries have had to take some industrial policy measures. Switzerland has taken steps to offset the regional consequences of the decline of its watch industry and to facilitate the diffusion of microelectronics technology. In West Germany industrial policies that were originally conceived of as complementary to the market mechanism 'have become more interventionistic and distorting'[24] since the early 1970s. Indeed, in troubled industries such as shipbuilding support measures have been introduced 'which stretch the philosophy of the non-interventionist social market economy to the limit'.[25]

Because Britain is a relatively centralized country with some attempt at the functional coordination of industrial policy, the gap in terms of the provision of industrial aid between it and a more functionally and geographically decentralized country like the United States may seem greater than it really is. A great deal of industrial aid is provided at the state and local government level and only attracts public notice when two or more states battle for a major development, as when Ohio and Pennsylvania both tried to obtain the first Volkswagen plant in the United States, with Pennsylvania eventually winning with a $200 million package that Ohio could not match. Twenty-seven states were offering finance for plant expansions and tax exemptions on new equipment by 1975.[26] In addition, a great deal of federal aid has been provided for high technology through research and development contracts, principally with the defence and space industries. For example, Lockheed's own R & D budget was $81 million in 1978, but another $120 million was contract R & D, very largely for government agencies.[27] A further source of state aid is that provided for small businesses through the Small Business Administration (SBA) set up in 1953. It is important to remember that 'small business' has been defined rather differently in the United States from other Western countries—in 1979 businesses with a turnover of up to $7.5 million and employing up to 1,500 people were eligible for aid from the SBA.

The United States has also resorted to the more traditional forms of regional, sectoral and 'bailing out' aid used by other western countries. The Economic Development Administration (EDA) was established in 1965 to provide grants to economically depressed areas to help attract business investment or revive falling industries. In 1979 funds available to the EDA totalled $558 million, although $229 million of this was used for infrastructure assistance.[28] As far as sectoral policies are concerned, the $56 million Footwear Industry Revitalisation Programme launched in 1977 looked very much like the Section 8 schemes used by the last Labour Government in Britain as part of its industrial strategy, the only difference being that the American scheme was linked with complementary voluntary restrictions on imports in a way which did not happen in

Britain. Although the scheme was experimental, it was hoped that it might be a forerunner for schemes in other industries, such as men's clothing and stainless steel utensils, but this kind of detailed intervention is unlikely to find favour under the Reagan administration.

Last but not least, the United States has not refrained from engaging in the most controversial form of industrial assistance, rescue packages for failed companies. In 1970 Congress provided $125 million in guarantees to allow the failed Penn Central Railroad to continue operation. In 1971 Lockheed, a major Defense Department supplier, applied for aid after Rolls Royce went bankrupt. Congress narrowly voted to guarantee $250 million in bank loans. The 1974 Rail Reorganization Act authorized $558.5 million for design and operation costs plus $1.5 billion in loan guarantees to consolidate seven bankrupt railroads in the Northeast and Midwest. In 1980 the Chrysler Loan Guarantees Board authorized the rescue of the Chrysler motor company with $1.5 billion in loan guarantees, the largest amount ever provided for a single company. Given the difficulty of avoiding some state aid to industry in even the most market-oriented countries, it might seem sensible to try and devise a set of industrial policy measures that attempt to cope with problems in the industrial economy before they become too serious, and to argue about how that could be done rather than whether it should be done at all.

A successful selective intervention policy?
The case of the Irish Republic

The Irish Republic's industrial policies have attracted considerable international interest because it appears to be one of the few countries that has managed to develop a successful industrial policy based on a strategy of selective intervention. Virtually all industrial aid is provided through a single public agency, the Industrial Development Authority, which is made up of five businessmen, two members from government departments, an independent chairman and the managing director. The Authority formulates and reviews IDA policy, which is executed by a board with two government members which meets weekly to take decisions on new industry grant applications.

Between 1972 and 1978 IDA grants totalling nearly £500

million supported a total investment of approximately £1.5 billion with an employment potential on completion of about 100,000 jobs—equivalent to half the current labour force in manufacturing in the Republic. The OECD has identified three beneficial consequences of this programme as far as capital stock in manufacturing is concerned: the aggregate stock of manufacturing capital has greatly increased; the average age of the stock has declined; and a larger proportion of Irish manufacturing industry now embodies best-practice technology.[29]

One consequence seems to have been that the Irish response to the 1973 oil crisis was different from that of other western countries. A European Community study of adjustment to the crisis found that 'Ireland is in a somewhat special position . . . It is the only country which has experienced both a decrease in the share of private consumption . . . and an increase in the share of investment, despite a very marked crisis in 1973–76. Public consumption has had a powerful spillover effect and foreign trade has grown at a rate which is two to three times as fast as in other countries'.[30] In 1979 investment volume in the Republic in manufacturing industry increased by 19.5 per cent compared with an EC average of 5 per cent, and jobs in manufacturing industry showed a net increase of 3.7 per cent compared with an EC average decline of 1.1 per cent.[31] Although the Republic's economy has recently encountered increasing difficulties, this is for reasons unconnected with its industrial policy, such as the relative lack of indigenous energy supplies.

The Republic has been particularly successful in attracting foreign investment, especially Japanese investment in high technology industries, a trend symbolized by the decision of Fujitsu, Japan's leading computer company, to establish a £42 million plant to manufacture integrated circuits at a site near Dublin (although the main source of overseas investment in the Republic remains the United States). In the period after 1960 the Republic was able to attract 250 foreign firms— 'a number *equal* to the number of foreign firms establishing in the United Kingdom and nine times the number establishing in Northern Ireland'.[32] Perhaps the most attractive aspect of the package to investors has been a 'tax holiday' on profits on exports up to 1990. Pressure from the European Community has now ended that particular concession, although it still applied to all new industries entering into an agreement with the IDA before the end of 1980. In future, firms will pay tax at a maximum rate of 10 per cent on all profits, still an attractive proposition. Although manufacturing firms in the UK rarely pay the full 52 per cent rate, they can still expect to pay more under the UK's complicated tax regime than they would in the Republic.

In addition, the IDA offers a range of discretionary cash grants to investors to cover land, site development, buildings and new plant and machinery. Other incentives include training grants, covering up to 100 per cent of training costs and research and development grants, normally 50 per cent. Although the IDA operates a highly flexible approach to potential investors, its exercise of discretion is related to the general objectives of its industrial plan. The central industrial strategy in the 1978–82 IDA plan is based on shifting the Republic's industry 'into products with higher added value based on good quality and design, aimed at specialist market niches using well planned professional marketing. The strategy will aim to capitalize on the strengths of the country, such as the high level of education, where we have an advantage over Third World countries.'[33] In assessing the suitability of projects, the IDA takes into account such considerations as the proportion of the plant's products that will be exported; whether there will be substantial requirements of local raw materials; how much effect it will have on national income; and whether the products which are to be made have a high value-added content, a high market growth rate and a minimal risk of obsolescence in the short term. The IDA operates its incentives in favour of labour intensive industries giving a higher percentage capital grant on average to such industries. However, the IDA recognizes that 'the capital intensity of industry is largely a function of the type of industry which we wish to develop . . . if Irish based industries wish to produce competitively, not only in price but in quality, they have little choice but to adopt competitive production processes'.[34] The IDA is prepared to bid high for plants it particularly wants, for example in the electronics field. It has approached firms in a number of growth sub-sectors which it has identified in the electronics industry and attracted Mostek, a leader in the production of memory chips, with incentives worth £19,000 per job created.

The only real failure to date was when a subsidiary of a Dutch concern closed its factory in Limerick making steel cord for tyres in 1977 with the loss of 1,400 jobs. The IDA's Rescue Unit provides assistance to firms which are experiencing short-term difficulties. During 1979 IDA grants totalling £893,000 were approved in 'rescue packages' for twenty-three firms. Where a satisfactory 'rescue' is not possible and a closure is likely, a promoter is sought to take over some or all of the company's assets, twenty-four such projects being negotiated in 1979. The 1977 Industrial Development Act gave new powers to the IDA to encourage the rationalization of sensitive sectors of Irish industry, but the 'response from Irish industry was disappointing'.[35] However, £12 million had been committed up to the end of 1979 to a re-equipment and modernization programme with job preservation objectives.

In a sense, the IDA's programme has been a victim of its own success. The creation of a larger number and, perhaps more important, wider range of more attractive jobs in the Republic has led to the disappearance of the traditional pattern of migration from the Republic. Hence, the industrial investment programme has not had the impact on unemployment in the Republic that had been hoped for. Moreover, the Republic's industrial policy has been criticized on the grounds that the new industries attracted to the Republic have relatively low linkages with the rest of the economy; that too much emphasis has been placed on export enterprises relative to import competing firms; and that the policy has led to increasing foreign dominance of the economy.[36] Although the policy was relatively successful in the 1970s, at least in terms of attracting new investment, it is likely to encounter growing difficulties in the 1980s as the Republic encounters increasingly fierce competition from other countries for what is likely to be a shrinking pool of internationally mobile jobs. The very stiff international competition encountered by the IDA in attracting the electronics and mechanical engineering industries was reflected in an increase in the average grant cost in real terms per job approved in new overseas industries from £4,998 in 1978 to £7,063 in 1979 (1979 prices).

The Irish Republic is Britain's main competitor for inward industrial investment and the policies pursued by the Irish government had been watched with interest and some concern in the United Kingdom. Mr Gavin McCrone, an academic expert on regional policy who became a senior Scottish Office official, has bluntly stated, 'If we are trying to land investment in competition with Ireland we cannot fight them on financial incentives'.[37] The Republic also benefits from having 'one door' for inward investors to come through in contrast with the bewildering number of agencies and government departments concerned with inward investment in Scotland, Wales and Northern Ireland, although the Northern Ireland Department of Commerce believes that it is the nature of the Republic's incentives, rather than its organizational arrangements, which have been the main factor in promoting new investment. In particular, the Department believes that the Republic's fiscal incentives are 'particularly attractive to those projects where there is a rapid profit build-up. Such projects tend to be attractive high technology sectors like electronics and pharmaceuticals.'[38] In other words, in so far as the Republic's incentives package attracts some industries rather than others, it discriminates in favour of those which are likely to be profitable and to expand in the future. British industrial policy often seems to result, whatever the intended objectives may be, in the propping up of those industries which have a glorious past rather than a promising future.

Nevertheless, doubts have been expressed about the usefulness of comparisons between the industrial policies of the Irish Republic and the United Kingdom. The House of Commons Committee on Scottish Affairs concluded that 'there is no question of simply importing the Irish model to Scotland, partly for constitutional reasons and partly because of the differing relative importance of inward investment to the two countries'.[39] Certainly, the Republic's industrial economy is at an earlier stage of development than that of the United Kingdom, as is reflected in the higher proportion of the population employed in agriculture, and the poor condition of important parts of the industrial infrastructure such as roads and telecommunications, although steps are being taken to remedy these deficiencies. Thus, 'The Republic *needs* overseas investment more than Scotland, and might therefore be expected to pay more.'[40] Indeed, a cynical interpretation would be that the additional level of grant and lower rates of tax in the Republic just about compensates for infrastructure deficiencies and the Republic's proneness to long industrial disputes in key sectors such as banking.

In addition, the Republic is entitled to provide higher levels of grant under European Community rules. It is allowed to give very high levels of regional grant assistance throughout its territory, a special status it shares with the six counties forming Northern Ireland, the south of Italy, the French overseas territories and West Berlin. Moreover, Protocol 30 of the Treaty of Accession explicitly takes account of the Irish government's programme of industrialization and economic development. In this Protocol, the high contracting parties recognize that it is in their common interest that the objectives of the policy be attained and, in particular, that 'in the application of Articles 92 and 93 of the EEC Treaty, it will be necessary to take into account the objectives of economic expansion and the raising of the standard of living of the population.'[41] In fact, the Republic does not provide grants up to the EC limit of 75 per cent of initial investment, and the maximum effective value of the Republic's package has been costed at 34.5 per cent, compared with a 20.9 per cent figure for Britain (presumably in special development areas).[42]

Comparison is also made difficult by the discrepancy in population size between the Republic and the UK. The Republic is able to enjoy 'complete independence of policy-making, in an economy sufficiently small not to provoke retaliation if its policies broke international trading rules and conventions'.[43] Nevertheless, considerations such as these should not be allowed to detract from the considerable achievements of an industrial policy which has managed to increase the Republic's share of jobs promoted in the British Isles from 5 to 6 per cent in the late 1960s to about 30 per cent in the late 1970s.[44]

The Republic's approach could not be applied to the UK as a whole and is clearly most attractive to Nationalists and radical devolutionists. Nevertheless, there are some lessons to be learnt which could be applied within the framework of a UK industrial policy. First, the entire Irish grant is discretionary, whereas much of British assistance is tied up in the 'automatic' regional development grant which is often provided for highly capital-intensive projects which would probably have located in the same place without government assistance. Second, the Irish approach recognizes that jobs and exports can be provided by services just as much as by 'making things'. In addition, 'Service industries, by their nature, can get into operation very quickly.'[45] Under the Service Industries Programme initiated in 1974, the IDA had by the end of 1979 approved 116 projects which now employ 3,000 persons, mostly graduates and their equivalent. Third, the IDA places considerable emphasis on identifying potential projects, as distinct from reacting to enquiries from interested businessmen. The IDA's Project Identification Unit provides market information on new product opportunities and twenty-five new enterprises were set up as a result of its activities in 1979. The Unit has recently established a product research facility which collates information on, for example, technology transfer opportunities and successful products in other countries. This facility is open to entrepreneurs and is used by about twenty persons per month. The Republic's approach to the development of a selective intervention strategy is clearly one of the most thorough and innovative in the Western world.

CONCLUSIONS

It is not possible to offer a comprehensive treatment of either the academic analysis, or the substantive issues, of industrial policy in the space of one chapter. The account offered here has had four main purposes: to establish that there is scope for a political science contribution to the study of industrial policy; to point to some of the deficiencies of the existing literature; to argue that all Western countries are obliged to resort to some form of industrial intervention; and that this intervention can sometimes have moderately beneficial consequences. This does not amount to a political economy of industrial policy, but it does illustrate some of the ways in which such a political economy could be constructed.

NOTES AND REFERENCES

1. W. M. Corden, 'Relationships between macro-economic and industrial policies', *World Economy*, 3 (1980), 167–84, p. 183.
2. This position held by some economists is effectively exposed and demolished in B. Hogwood, 'Analysing industrial policy: a multi-perspective approach', *Public Administration Bulletin*, 29 (1979), 18–42.

3. R. Pryke, *Public Enterprise in Practice* (London, MacGibbon & Kee, 1971), p. 457.
4. It is used as the basic theoretical perspective in the nine-country comparative project on business interest associations organized from the International Institute of Management by Wolfgang Streeck and Philippe Schmitter.
5. See, for example, L. Tivey, *The Politics of the Firm* (Oxford, Martin Robertson, 1978) where the longest chapter is about alternatives to the conventional firm.
6. A preliminary attempt to tackle them is made in the writer's *The Development of the Government Relations Function in UK First* (International Institute of Management, Berlin, 1981).
7. See, for example, J. F. F. Robinson and D. J. Storey, *Employment Change in Manufacturing Industry in Cleveland 1965–76*, County of Cleveland Planning Department, Report No. 176, typescript.
8. For an attempt at such an explanation see the writer's *The Political Economy of Industrial Policy* (London, Butterworth, 1982), Chapter 3.
9. A. Peacock, *et al., Structural Economic Policies in West Germany and the United Kingdom* (London, Anglo-Germany Foundation, 1980).
10. D. Green, *Managing Industrial Change* (London, HMSO, 1981) examines recent French industrial policy.
11. S. Holland, ed., *The State as Entrepreneur* (London, Weidenfeld & Nicolson, 1972).
12. In National Economic Development Office, *A Study of the UK Nationalized Industries* (London, 1976), Background Paper 2, pp. 35–51.
13. An analysis of enduring value is to be found in M. Hodges, 'Industrial policy: a directorate-general in search of a role', in H. Wallace, W. Wallace and C. Webb, eds, *Policy-Making in the European Communities* (London, John Wiley, 1977), pp. 113–35. See also W. Wallace, ed., *Britain in Europe* (London, Heinemann, 1980), especially Chapters 1 and 6.
14. Some of these questions are dealt with in W. Diebold Jr., *Industrial Policy as an International Issue* (New York, McGraw-Hill, 1980).
15. A. Knight, *Private Enterprise and Public Intervention* (London, Allen & Unwin, 1974).
16. E. Dell, *Political Responsibility and Industry* (London, Allen & Unwin, 1973).
17. G. Kaufman, *How to be a Minister* (London, Sidgwick & Jackson, 1980).
18. B. Hogwood, *Government and Shipbuilding* (Farnborough, Saxon House, 1979); M. Jenkin, *British Industry and the North Sea* (London, Macmillan, 1981); K. Ovenden, *The Politics of Steel* (London, Macmillan, 1978).

19. An exception in A. Daly, 'Government support for innovation in the British machine tool industry: a case study', in C. Carter, ed., *Industrial Policy and Innovation* (London, Heinemann, 1980), pp. 52-67.
20. See, however, P. Maunder, 'Food Manufacturing' in P. Johnson, ed., *The Structure of British Industry* (London, Granada, 1980), pp. 80-105; and W. Grant, 'The politics of the UK food processing industries', *Critical Rural Sociology*, forthcoming.
21. Cabinet Office/Advisory Council for Applied Research and Development, *Industrial Innovation* (London, HMSO, 1978), p. 13.
22. C. Carter, 'Reasons for not innovating', in Carter, *Industrial Policy and Innovation*, op. cit., pp. 21-31, p. 21.
23. C. Carter, 'Report of the discussion', in Carter, ibid., pp. 225-33, p. 233.
24. J. B. Donges, 'Industrial policies in West Germany's not so market-oriented economy', *World Economy*, 3 (1980), 185-204, p. 189.
25. Peacock, *et al.*, op. cit., p. 90.
26. R. Goodman, *The Last Entrepreneurs: America's Regional Wars for Jobs and Dollars* (New York, Simon & Schuster, 1979), p. 12.
27. M. Marks, 'State and private enterprise', *Business Economist*, 11 (1980), 5-15, pp. 10-11.
28. Organization for Economic Co-operation and Development, *Regional Policies in the United States* (Paris, OECD, 1980), p. 30.
29. OECD Annual Economic Survey on the Republic of Ireland, 1979.
30. Commission of the European Communities, *Changes in Industrial Structure in the European Economies since the Oil Crisis*, special issue of *European Economy*, p. 15.
31. Industrial Development Authority, *Annual Report 1979*, p. 1.
32. B. Moore, R. Rhodes and I. Tarling, 'Industrial Policy and Economy of Ireland', *Cambridge Journal of Economics*, 2 (1978), 99-114, p. 108.
33. *IDA Industrial Plan 1978-82*, p. 5.
34. Ibid., p. 17.
35. IDA *Annual Report 1978*, p. 14.
36. For a summary of these criticisms see D. C. McDonald, 'Issues in industrial development policy', in J. W. O'Hogan, ed., *The Economy of Ireland: Policy and Performance* (Dublin, Irish Management Institute, 2nd ed., 1978), pp. 264-71.
37. Evidence to the Select Committee on Scottish Affairs, Second Report, 1979-80, p. 15.
38. Ibid., p. 242.
39. Second Report from the Committee on Scottish Affairs, 1979-80, *Inward Investment*, p. 11.
40. Ibid., p. 19.
41. Commission of the European Community, *Report on Irish Economic Law* (Competition—Approximation of Legislation Series, 1977), p. 22.

42. Ibid.
43. Moore, Rhodes and Tarling, op. cit., p. 100.
44. Evidence to the Select Committee on Scottish Affairs, op. cit., p. 242.
45. IDA *Annual Report 1978*, p. 17.

6 Corporative Industrial Relations and the Welfare State*

COLIN CROUCH

INTRODUCTION

The Functions of the State in Capitalist Society

Recent work on the theory of the state in capitalist society has heavily challenged the old social democratic formula that state intervention in a democracy usually represents action in the workers' interests against the operation of unbridled *laissez faire*.[1] Instead, state intervention has been seen as necessary to protect capitalist interests from working-class pressures (e.g. arbitration of labour disputes to limit and institutionalize industrial conflict) or to provide for certain general interests of capital which the competitive nature of the system prevents individual capitalists doing for themselves (e.g. subsidized transport and housing to accommodate workers in the urban agglomerations which capitalist production generates; or incomes policies to prevent employers competing for labour and bidding up its price under conditions of full employment).

These developments in state theory have been extremely important in drawing attention to previously ignored social processes, but they do need to be approached critically. Because of the Marxist assumption of a necessary and complete contradiction between the interests of capital and labour, these theories often ignore or distort points of congruence and compromise.[2] For example, the capitalist interest in a healthy work-force, at least when labour is relatively scarce, does coincide at certain points with workers' own interest in being healthy. Of course, there are limits to this congruity; the capitalist's interest in the health of his work-force is limited to aspects of health relevant to their performance as workers and to public health measures necessary to the control of infectious diseases, though some Marxist theories would also claim a capitalist interest in the health of workers' dependents.[3] But

*An earlier version of this chapter was first published as 'Korporatistische arbeidsverhoudingen en de interventiestaat', in P. van der Kley, *et al.*, eds, *Interventiestaat en ongelijkheid* (Nijmegen, 1981).

all this misses some of the dynamics of state intervention in welfare fields. The professions and bureaucracies which are brought into existence by any major step of state intervention quickly develop their own occupational and career interest in extending and safeguarding their field of work. Given the relative autonomy in their task areas enjoyed by professions and bureaucracies, even within the state apparatus, this drive for progress in the service concerned irrespective of the interests which first willed it into existence often liberates the areas of state intervention from any close dependence on the class interests which are effective at the policy-making stage.

For example, it is hardly in the interests of capital that large sums are devoted to expensive heart surgery for a tiny number of working-class patients within a public health service. However, if the career interests of medical scientists seem closely bound up with such developments, and if the medical profession has successfully acquired a powerful voice in the determination of health policy as a result of the indispensable specialized knowledge of its science, then it is quite likely that such expensive surgery will be developed. (By the same token, of course, there will be a similiar interference with the intentions of policy in the case of those developments which at least some Marxists are prepared to concede are the result of successful working-class struggle; this is an issue to which we shall return at the end of this chapter.)

These examples of professional and bureaucratic interests interfering with the simple logic of capitalist interests in the interventionist state are found most easily in the field of welfare policy, but there are some important instances in the sphere of industrial relations. Arbitrators and incomes policy agencies, trying to gain space for exercising discretion and to make it worth while for unions and employers to gain their good will, will always try to secure some autonomy, freeing themselves from close government dictation of their practice. Somewhat differently, the practice of Keynesian economic policy gained a certain entrenched place among Treasury officials and economic advisors in several countries. Keynes provided a set of devices which enabled policy administrators to avoid the nightmare of the interwar Depression, and Keynes's own sympathies with the problems of the administrator (as opposed to the capitalist) make his characteristic policy instruments attractive to them. It is partly as a result of this that government economic policies did not everywhere immediately jettison Keynesianism once capital came to feel its interests would be better served by the unimpeded pursuit of monetarist policy.

These points of caution are needed, as are those Marxist theories which treat at least some aspects of state intervention as the result of successful working-class struggle, if state theory is not to find itself badly caught out by recent developments. Theories of the welfare state as a capitalist interest seemed most plausible during the period of apparent compromise between social democracy and a 'reformed' capitalism: that combination of an elaborate welfare state alongside a labour movement virtually devoid of all radicalism of which the Netherlands have probably been the most striking example. In the past few years this pattern has begun to change. Under pressure from the growing tensions of capitalist economic development, the government interventions attendant on the maintenance of full employment have in many countries been withdrawn; public spending has been reduced; and right-wing political parties have advocated an end to the various measures of state intervention in the economy which had grown up in the previous period—this particular pattern being seen most strikingly in the United Kingdom following the election of a Conservative Government in May 1979. If the introduction of all these measures in the first place simply constituted a response by governments to capitalist needs, then presumably the labour movement should regard with complete indifference the end of the full-employment era, of the welfare state and of government intervention to aid industries in difficulty. The fact that this has *not* been the case is itself an indication of the inadequacy of simple theories of the capitalist state.

While many Marxists may be willing to concede the force of this point where welfare policy as such is concerned, they may consider that state intervention in industrial relations, especially in the field of income determination, is a far more clear-cut case. Surely the opposition here is between a state that is acting on behalf of capital in order to prevent workers achieving pay rises and changes in working conditions that threaten profit shares? In fact, I believe that the case of state

intervention in this area is just as complex in its class implications as, say, health or education policy; that it is best treated
as an aspect of the same set of issues; and that the two areas of
policy have important implications for each other.

State intervention and centralized industrial relations

First, however, it is necessary to establish what is being meant
here by state intervention. There is of course a good deal of
intervention within the simple administrative state: laws which
establish and limit union rights, provision for arbitration and
mediation, etc. All this remains within the province of a capitalist state which is required merely to provide conditions of
stability and order for capital. It is the state which is called
upon to do more—to participate in organizing detailed relations between the productive forces, including pay determination—which is our primary interest here. There are, however,
problems in taking as the object of study the extent to which
the state intervenes formally and directly in incomes questions.
In some cases, it is true, this appears, misleadingly, to be the
crucial factor. In the Netherlands a high degree of statutory
determination of incomes has for long been set against incipient
shop-floor movements for a more decentralized wage determination process. In the UK the government has often tried to
intervene with a range of incomes policies in order to stem the
advance of extensive and often very militant shop-floor bargaining. Direct state intervention, often backed with compulsory
powers, would seem to be the crucial variable. But from the
perspective of other countries this is a less useful criterion.
For example, for the bulk of the postwar period there has
been very little direct government intervention in incomes
questions in Germany, Sweden or Norway; or in France or
Italy. Classification of countries on the dimension of formal
government incomes policy would therefore rank the Netherlands (and Austria) with the UK, but separate them from
Germany and the Scandinavian countries, which would in
turn be ranked alongside France and Italy!

Setting the cases of the Netherlands and Austria aside, there
is some evidence that governments try to intervene directly
in incomes issues when there is crisis, when normal collective
bargaining is producing what the government regards as un-
satisfactory results.[4] The UK is the clearest case, but there

have been similar developments in Finland, Denmark, in part in the USA, Canada, Belgium, France, Sweden in the early 1970s and Germany during the early years of *Konzertierte Aktion* in the late 1960s. The Netherlands and Austria seem exceptional in that detailed government intervention has been a norm, an expression of the consensus within those societies, rather than the stopgap for lack of consensus, which it seems to be elsewhere. It is significant that in both these countries there have been, since the war, lengthy periods of 'consociational' government, or very broad coalitions between parties which, while constituting the main established political rivalries in the country, have nevertheless felt sufficiently close to one another to govern together—a strong sign of elite consensus. The actions of a consensual state being, presumably, less contentious than those of a state whose policy decisions are essentially contested by whichever parties are in opposition, one can assume that in these countries there was, at least originally, less opposition to an active state role in incomes policy.

If this exception is allowed, one may venture the generalization that the state will intervene directly in incomes issues if it is not satisfied that the bargaining partners, left to themselves, will produce satisfactory results—that is, accepting the theory of the capitalist state, results compatible with the logic of the capitalist economy. 'Satisfactory' bargaining in this sense will occur either (i) when trade unions are weak or (ii) when collective bargaining is centralized. The first condition is simple and need not detain us here; the second is more interesting. A centralized labour movement engaged in centralized bargaining will necessarily have regard for the macroeconomic consequences of its actions. For example, if a single union confederation bargains for all workers in the country, it knows that a wage demand going far beyond the rate of productivity must lead to very high inflation, wiping out nearly all the apparent gain in wages, or to widespread unemployment, or to some combination of both. These consequences being hostile to labour's immediate interests, it is unlikely that such a confederation would make such a demand. The limiting case would be a genuinely revolutionary union movement, which would make such a demand in the conscious knowledge that the demand could not be met, hoping thereby to promote a breakdown of social order from which it believed would emerge a regime more suited to the workers' long-term interests. It is always possible that such a movement might one day exist. However, for it to exist conditions must be such that a union movement which had acquired sufficient strength to engage in totally centralized bargaining would nevertheless believe that it stood to gain more by destroying completely the conditions under which it had achieved this pre-eminent position. It is therefore reasonable to assume that, in the majority of cases, a centralized movement will act in the way anticipated here. In other words, it will act in a manner broadly compatible with the logic of the capitalist economy, preserving a certain relationship between the returns to capital and labour.

The situation of a decentralized movement is very different. Again to take an extreme case, in a system in which all bargaining took place at the level of the work group, no one group would have any concern for the macro-economic implications of its actions, because the impact of its actions on the economy as a whole would have only infinitesimally small repercussions on its own position. The consequence for a capitalist economy of a large number of uncoordinated demands by individual groups are therefore likely to be far more threatening than anything attempted by a tightly centralized movement. This will be the case irrespective of whether the workers concerned are militant revolutionaries or conservative craft workers determined to maintain their differential over unskilled labour.

The crucial variable is therefore the centralization of the system. If it is centralized the capitalist state is likely to have far less *need* to intervene than if it is fragmented, because restraints of the kind which it is likely to impose are built into the system itself. Further, the state has easier access to the participants in a centralized system—the actors are few in number, and can be subjected to informal, face-to-face pressures. In a decentralized system the state can operate only by addressing the mass of actors through public appeals (likely to be highly ineffective unless there is an extraordinary degree of social consensus) or through laws and administrative controls. In the limiting case of a centralized movement which became revolutionary one would of course expect state action though of a very different kind! Certainly, if there are centralized industrial relations without massive state intervention it must be assumed that the results of the centralized system are broadly satisfactory to the state; no government could stand aside while a centralized system of industrial relations paid no attention to economic stability. The relevant unit of study is therefore not state intervention as such but the centralization of industrial relations.

CENTRALIZED INDUSTRIAL RELATIONS AND INEQUALITY

Have centralized collective bargaining systems, or government incomes policies, reduced or increased income inequality? And how do decentralized systems with powerful shopfloor movements compare on this question? This complex task is a question of econometrics rather than sociology. It would involve examining the effects on earnings of the operation of centralized pay bargaining or of government incomes policy, and comparing them with the results in cases where non-coordinated bargaining at industry, company or plant level had taken place. So far there have been no attempts at such a complicated task on a cross-national basis.[5] Were it to be attempted my own expectation would be that it would show no clear conclusions. It is *possible* that countries with centralized incomes policies alongside strong labour movements would have more egalitarian results than centralized systems with relatively weak labour movements, on the grounds that in the former case the terms of the policy would be more heavily determined by labour. But how these would compare with decentralized systems is difficult to assess, since so much depends on where the weight of the decentralized system lies. If it is with skilled workers, as has often been the case historically, then one would expect decentralization to increase their differentials over the low paid, and possibly also to improve their position against white-collar groups and managerial staffs. But this will not always be so. In cases of imperfect centralization, with incomes policy being primarily enforced through government intervention, that policy is usually most effective in the public sector, where the government has most control. Since manual workers in the public services tend to be among the lowest paid, the breaking of incomes policy by decentralized action among these workers may well have a redistributive effect.

Such evidence as one has on this complexity of factors in Britain serves only to show the lack of clarity. Britain is an interesting if untypical case to take since policy there has varied so much in recent years. In the latter 1960s (1965–9) there was a government incomes policy, initially voluntary but with increasing statutory elements. Even when statutory it is difficult to relate what happened in collective bargaining to the policy, because it was vulnerable to so many breaches. However, research on the *attempts* of the policy already shows considerable ambiguity;[6] on the one hand the National Board for Prices and Incomes was expected to have regard for problems of the low paid, but on the other hand in much of its work it was concerned to increase differentials. When that incomes policy was finally broken, low-paid public-service workers were important in restoring free collective bargaining.

The next phases of incomes policy, 1972–3 and 1975–8, were far more egalitarian in their intentions. Both the statutory Conservative policy (1972–3) and the voluntary Labour one (1975–8) expressed pay norms in either flat rates or combinations of flat rates and percentages, in the latter case also temporarily incorporating a provision where those on very high salaries would receive no increase at all. When this policy collapsed it was from a combination of pressures from higher-paid workers wanting to restore their eroded differentials and again low-paid public-service workers who had been exceptionally held down during the period of restraint. Evidence on the movement of pay during the period of 1970s incomes policy shows a considerable though probably temporary redistribution from those on the highest incomes, but not much change within the mass of wage and salary workers.[7] However, these patterns are confused by such developments as a considerable erosion of the male/female differential and various contradictory movements among the pay of public-sector employees. While manual workers were perhaps being held back in the public services, several public-service professional groups (such as teachers and nurses) experienced particularly large settlements in the mid-1970s, partly as a catching-up exercise after the preceding periods of restraint. Effects of different forms of pay determination on the distribution between capital and labour are particularly hard to disentangle, since one has to take account of the response made by capital to any gains on the labour side. The first question concerns the extent to which increases in labour's share will lead to inflation as capital acts to preserve its share. There is then the secondary problem of allocating the effects of inflation on different income groups, which is itself a difficult task.

The available evidence suggests that during the past few years of economic crisis the share of profits in national income in the advanced capitalist societies has dropped.[8] While there are several causes of this, one has probably been increased labour militancy, especially at the shopfloor level. If this is the case, then in the first instance the collapse of coordinated bargaining which ensures a relative balance between the position of labour and capital has been associated with a decline in class inequality. However, it is not possible for a full assessment to end there. If the decline of profits leads to a flight of capital from the countries concerned, there will almost certainly be increased unemployment and a reduction of working-class incomes. There is increasing evidence that such a process has been taking place. There is also evidence of a 'counter-attack' by capital against the economic policies which seemed in the long run to generate this increased labour strength: the move away from Keynesian full-employment policy towards monetarism. The effects of this are almost certain to be increased unemployment, a decline in working-class industrial and political power and a reduction in that public spending which primarily benefits workers.

But does this end the causal chain? Will monetarism lead, as its advocates hope, to a strengthened economy? If so, organized labour may then again become powerful. Or will it lead to prolonged recession, with a long-term weakening of organized labour? This latter possibility needs to be set alongside two further developments: the recent flight of capital to newly industrializing Third-World dictatorships and the threat to employment in the industrialized countries from the micro-processor and other highly automated industrial processes. The possibility of a long-term decline in the power of organized labour within capitalist society has to be seriously considered. While the causes of this development are varied, among them is the increasing instability of industrial relations and income developments which has taken place since the late 1960s. Certainly the flight of capital has been greatest in those countries where labour's decentralized power developed furthest, such as Italy and the United Kingdom.

In discussing these possibilities one is already moving into the world of speculation; to go beyond them to consider whether a new emiseration of the working class and a collapse of capitalism would have revolutionary potentiality is to go further beyond the scope of scientific discussion, but it is obviously an important aspect of the whole question.

The new instability of labour–capital relations disturbs what is often regarded as the social-democratic compromise in capitalist society, which in several countries characterized the 1950s and much of the 1960s. The appellation is not really accurate: the pursuit of policies associated with social-democratic parties was only one constituent of a balance of forces which also included a conservatism which was willing to make compromises in order to integrate and incorporate labour, and the partly coincidental occurrence of sustained high levels of economic growth which made possible more class compromises than had hitherto been thought attainable in capitalist societies. For social democrats and progressive conservatives the optimal class balance in late capitalist societies included the following elements: full employment; a high level of social-welfare spending; but disciplined industrial relations to ensure that full employment did not lead to inflationary pressure. Within that consensus there was considerable scope for political conflict, but it provided an agreed frame of reference, which preserved both the existence of private capital and a strongly organized, secure and fully employed working class.

The cessation of economic progress (so important to the maintenance of that balance) has clarified the positions of two major sources of opposition to the social democratic compromise. First, and more powerfully, capitalist interests are breaking with the stance adopted by progressive conservatives. The guarantee of full employment, they argue, has produced an intolerable rise in labour's strength which is not being kept in check by the apparent compromises on labour's side. In particular, wage restraint cannot be relied upon because it is undermined from the base. On the other side Marxists argue that social democracy, by accepting a compromise with capital and restraint on shopfloor wages pressure, is holding back the collapse of capitalism which must bring in its train a socialist society. The counterarguments of social democracy are, against capital, that dismantling the compromise will lead to prolonged economic recession, extensive civil strife and possibly a suppression of liberties; and against Marxists that only reactionary interests are likely to gain from social chaos and collapse.

CENTRALIZED INDUSTRIAL RELATIONS AND SOCIAL WELFARE

The foregoing arguments assume a certain connection between social democracy and centralized, or corporatist,[9] collective bargaining systems. How might that assumption be tested?

That the interventionist state also tends to be the social democratic state can be demonstrated with some precision. While intervention in terms of substantive interventionist *policies* is difficult to measure, intervention can also be seen in terms of the share of the society's economic product which is taken by government, either for its own consumption or for transfers. This is of course quantifiable as the percentage of Gross Domestic Product taken in government revenue. Available statistics collected on a comparable basis enable computation of these data for twelve OECD countries for the decade 1968–77 (see Table 6.1, col. (*b*)).[10] For eleven of these it is also possible to assess the share of GDP expended by the state on broadly defined 'welfare' goals (Table 6.1, col. (*c*)).[11] Finally, for the somewhat less satisfactory datum of government *taxation* revenue as a percentage of GDP, figures are available for all eighteen major advanced capitalist liberal democracies (Table 6.1, col. (*d*)).[12]

Subject to some reservations, the strength of social democracy in a state can be regarded as a function of the presence in office of labour-movement political parties, which can be calculated as the proportion of cabinet seats held by a particular party over a certain period. The problems of such an approach include the following. In some countries major parties are either in office, alone or dominating coalitions, or in opposition; in others they are permanent majority partners in coalitions; in others permanent minority partners. These differences, as Shalev has pointed out,[13] have different implications for the ability of the party to dominate policy. However, we are here not arguing just that labour-movement parties can, by their presence in office, force through policy changes, but that they represent a compromise of class forces. Their presence as long-term minority coalition partners may therefore sometimes represent their ability to secure policy compromises with bourgeois parties. We shall proceed here on the assumption that participation in governments by labour-movement parties provides some kind of index of political strength of social democracy.[14] Participation is calculated in terms of proportion of cabinet seats held by labour-movement party representatives over successive periods of time.

There remains the problem of which parties to count as labour-movement parties. How does one cope with the American Democratic Party, which has been closely linked with the union movement but which is also responsive to several other separate and important constituencies? Or the Dutch parties, other than the Labour Party, which have strong labour-movement links while being primarily confessional, bourgeois parties? Or Christian Democratic parties claiming a link with the labour movement? Or Italy, where a Socialist Party which is only a minority tendency within the union movement has held office, but *not* the dominant Communist Party; while the Social Democrats, who have only a marginal footing with the unions, have frequently held Cabinet seats? A simple approach has been adopted to these questions here. Where a political party developed historically alongside an autonomous union movement, it is counted; others are not counted. To summarize the difficult cases, the American Democrats are not counted; only the Labour Party in the Netherlands; none of the Christian Democrats; the Socialists but not the Social Democrats in Italy; and the Communists as well as the Socialists in Finland.

Calculations have been based on the parties' record of office-holding throughout the postwar period, and not just during the decade under consideration; countries' public spending patterns do not vary dramatically with changes of party composition of government, and it is therefore reasonable to assume that the effects of party on this variable are gradual, cumulative and slow to change (Table 6.1, col. (*e*)).

Figure 6.1 shows the results of plotting this relationship. The

Table 6.1: State intervention and social democracy

(a) Country	(b) Govt. revenue 1968-77 (% of GDP)†	(c) 'Welfare' spending 1968-77 (% of GDP)‡	(d) Tax revenue 1968-77 (% of GDP)§	(e) Labour- movement party govt. particip. 1945-7 (% of Cabinet seats)¶
Australia	29.57	19.22	27.34	21
Austria	41.09	31.88	37.37	53
Belgium	37.51	29.44	37.81	28
Canada	35.84	–	31.96	0
Denmark	–	–	40.93	62
Finland	39.15	28.28	36.09	38
France	–	–	36.62	10
Germany	40.00	30.94	34.99	26
Ireland	–	–	32.15	8
Italy*	34.21	31.12	31.79	11
Japan	–	–	20.63	3
Netherlands	48.39	37.50	42.80	23
New Zealand	–	–	29.52	30
Norway	47.24	33.79	43.20	80
Sweden	51.53	35.90	44.39	90
Switzerland	–	–	26.35	19
UK	39.72	27.30	35.86	48
USA	31.15	21.88	29.60	0

*Estimates have had to be made of Italian economic data for 1968, 1969.
†*National Accounts of OECD Countries*.
‡Ibid.; see reference 11 for the limitations of these statistics.
§*Revenue Statistics*, OECD.
¶Korpi and Shalev, 'Strikes, industrial relations and class conflict in capitalist societies', *British Journal of Sociology* (1979).

number of cases involved is too small, and the data too rough, for much confidence to placed in statistical calculation, though equations have been calculated and their lines are indicated. For the record, significance tests on the three equations indicated the following: for government revenue, $r = 0.9098$, $F = 48.0504$ (significant at the 0.001 level); for welfare spending,

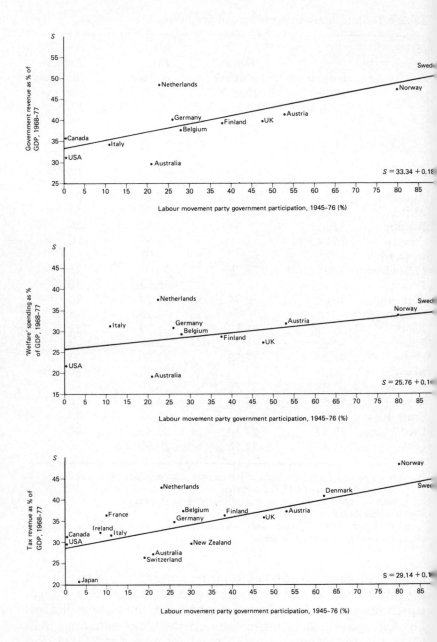

Fig. 6.1   State intervention (*S*) and social democracy (*L*).

Table 6.2: Standardized residuals for equations shown in Figure 6.1*

Country	*Govt. revenue*	*'Welfare' spending*	*Tax revenue*
Australia	*−1.62*†	*−1.73*	−1.16
Austria	−0.38	0.16	−0.17
Belgium	−0.19	0.18	0.85
Canada	0.54	n.a.	0.61
Denmark	n.a.	n.a.	0.27
Finland	−0.22	−0.26	0.11
France	n.a.	n.a.	*1.25*
Germany	0.42	0.52	0.31
Ireland	n.a.	n.a.	0.36
Italy	−0.24	0.85	0.17
Japan	n.a.	n.a.	*−1.95*
Netherlands	*2.34*	*1.89*	*2.11*
New Zealand	n.a.	n.a.	−1.02
Norway	−0.11	0.01	0.10
Sweden	0.43	0.23	−0.01
Switzerland	n.a.	n.a.	*−1.30*
UK	−0.48	−0.65	−0.31
USA	−0.47	−0.78	0.10

*Standardized residual = residual/standard error.

†Italicized numbers indicate cases in which prediction error, or residual, of the equation in a particular case was at least 1.25 times the standard error of the equation.

$r = 0.5298$, $F = 3.5120$ (not significant); for taxation revenue, $r = 0.7218$, $F = 17.4056$ (significant at the 0.001 level).

It is perhaps most instructive to examine the spread of individual countries around the equation line rather than to be impressed by aggregate statistics. For convenience we take as outliners those countries whose actual revenue/spending levels either exceed or fall short of predicted levels by more than 1.25 times the standard error of the equation concerned. The relevant data are given in Table 6.2.

On this basis, the Netherlands has far 'too high' a level of state intervention. This really shows up the inadequacy of our measuring instruments rather than the theory. It has long been recognized that, as a result of the *verzuiling* or 'pillarization' of Dutch society, the religious parties, while being primarily bourgeois parties, do try to represent the interests of the labour movements with which they are associated. In that sense the input of labour demands in the political economy of the Netherlands is considerably greater than is registered by the presence in office of Labour Party ministers.

The other country with an 'excessive' level of state activity is France. This marks a genuine exception to our hypothesis. France has long been recognized as having an unusually high level of state activity despite being a polity highly resistance to labour influence—at least until the change of government in 1981—the answer to which lies in the long history of the strong state in French society, rendering it an exception among bourgeois states. It may well be relevant that comparative research on the redistributive effect of taxation in the early 1970s showed France to be the only case among eleven Western industrial countries studied where the effect of taxation was to leave the poorest 20 per cent of households relatively *worse* off—that is, French taxation redistributed income to the more wealthy![15]

The remaining exceptions are all cases of 'inadequate' state intervention: Australia, Japan and Switzerland. Japan may be understood in terms of the unique pattern of *private* corporatism whereby employers provide social services for employees in the protected sector of the economy, services which in Western countries have typically been provided by the state as a result of labour pressure. For different historical reasons, Switzerland too has a welfare system based on private effort. These two cases therefore constitute real exceptions to generalizations about the relationship between state intervention, social democracy and openness—though it may be noted that neither are countries which one would have expected, on the basis of the independent variables, to have particularly strong levels of state intervention. The Australian case is more difficult to explain. It may be noted that New Zealand too has a rather low level of intervention, and certain regional or demographic factors may explain the Antipodian exception.

By and large, therefore, there is a clear association between the variables being related here. Can it also be shown that the social democratic, interventionist state is also associated with centralized industrial relations? There are no convenient figures that can be used as an index of this, but I have attempted a simple threefold division based on qualitative assessments.

Austria, Denmark, Germany, the Netherlands, Norway and Sweden have been classified as centralized. In the case of all except Germany this is on the grounds of the strong role played by union confederations in collective bargaining. The German case is slightly more complex, but counts as centralized on the grounds that the internal structure of individual unions is highly centralized, while the unique pattern of industrial unions makes coordination of national policy particularly easy.[16] At the other extreme come countries in which a range of individual unions carry on bargaining with little reference to each other and with at best spasmodic attempts at coordination by national confederations: Australia, Canada, France, Italy, Japan and the USA. In between comes a more ambiguous group in which periods of attempted coordination have alternated with those in which coordination has broken down: Belgium, Finland, Ireland, New Zealand, the UK; and one case, Switzerland, in which considerable national activity by confederations co-exists with a good deal of bargaining by individual unions. Table 6.3 sets out the data for the four indicators of the social-democratic/interventionist state being used here. That there is a reasonably strong relationship with centralization is clear. The numbers involved are really too small to attempt statistical difference-of-means tests, but this has been done for the two which involve eighteen countries. For the tax revenue data, the difference between the centralized and intermediate and the centralized and decentralized groups are significant at the 1 per cent level, but that between the intermediate and decentralized groups failed to achieve a recognized significance level. For the labour-movement government participation variable the difference of means between the centralized group and the decentralized group, and between the intermediate group and the decentralized group were significant at the 1 per cent level, but that between the centralized and the intermediate group at the 10 per cent level only.

In general, therefore, and using these fairly rough indicators, one is justified in claiming a relationship of some strength between the political strength of organized labour, the level of state intervention in distribution of the national product, and the degree of centralization of industrial relations.

Table 6.3: Centralized industrial relations and the interventionist state

High centralization	*Intermediate*	*Low centralization*
(a) Centralization and total state revenue		
Sweden (51.53)		
Netherlands (48.39)		
Norway (47.24)		
Austria (41.09)		
Germany (40.00)		
	UK (39.72)	
45.65*	Finland (39.15)	
	Belgium (37.51)	
		Canada (35.84)
	38.79	USA (31.15)
		Australia (29.57)
		32.19
(b) Centralization and 'welfare' spending		
Netherlands (37.50)		
Sweden (35.90)		
Norway (33.79)		
Austria (31.88)		
Germany (30.94)		
	Belgium (29.44)	
34.00	Finland (28.28)	
	UK (27.30)	
		USA (21.88)
	28.34	Australia (19.22)
		20.55
(c) Centralization and tax revenue		
Sweden (44.39)		
Norway (43.20)		
Netherlands (42.80)		
Denmark (40.93)		
	Belgium (37.81)	
Austria (37.37)		
		France (36.62)
	Finland (36.09)	
	UK (35.86)	

High centralization	Intermediate	Low centralization
Germany (34.99)		
	Ireland (32.15)	
40.61		Canada (31.96)
		Italy (31.79)
		USA (29.60)
	New Zealand (29.52)	
		Australia (27.34)
	Switzerland (26.35)	
		Japan (20.63)
	32.96	
		29.66

(d) Centralization and labour party government participation

Sweden (90)		
Norway (80)		
Denmark (62)		
Austria (53)		
	UK (48)	
	Finland (38)	
	New Zealand (30)	
	Belgium (28)	
Germany (26)		
Netherlands (23)		
		Australia (21)
55.67	Switzerland (19)	
		Italy (11)
		France (10)
	Ireland (8)	
		Japan (3)
	23.55	Canada, USA (0)
		7.5

*Figures beneath groups of countries indicate mean scores for the group.

STRENGTHS AND WEAKNESSES OF SOCIAL-DEMOCRATIC CORPORATISM

What links the variables whose association has been discussed here? Historically, one suprisingly important variable has been the openness of the economy (defined in terms of a country's exports and imports as a proportion of Gross National Product).

Openness being associated with vulnerability to international competition, the governments of such economies are more likely to intervene to protect and assist their industries in international markets. At the same time, small, open economies tend to exhibit a high degree of industrial concentration, again an aspect of international competitiveness.[17] Concentration is associated with both strong organization of employers and strong centralized labour movements. These will in turn be associated with greater government involvement in the economy than in more market-based systems.

Cameron[18] and (dealing in particular with the Swedish case) Stephens[19] have argued broadly as follows: openness leads to high industrial concentration; which leads to strong unionization and widespread collective bargaining; which in turn lead to a politically strong labour movement that exerts pressure for high public spending. This is an impressive argument, though it possibly slightly oversimplifies by ignoring the direct connection between openness and a large public sector (irrespective of the strength of labour), and by leaving out certain feed-back effects among the variables. Cameron, who is concerned with the recent *expansion* in public spending rather than continuing patterns, also leaves out of his account enduring structural phenomena of which corporatist arrangements are major examples. Openness, by encouraging cooperation between a highly concentrated industry and government, facilitates corporatist developments and, through government involvement, state intervention in the distribution of the social product.

The historical association between social democracy and corporatism needs to be explored in greater detail. Cameron and Stephens may well have identified an important source in the link between industrial concentration and labour strength, but attention needs to be paid to those cases of strong union movements existing in non-corporatist economies—e.g. the UK and Australia. It is possibly the case that social democratic policies of state intervention can only become thoroughly institutionalized in a political economy with an existing predisposition to state intervention, such as corporatism provides. It is interesting that Australia (in the early years of the century) and the UK (after World War II) were pioneers of welfare-state development, establishing a lead in state intervention *which they have not sustained.* But without detailed research this remains speculation.

Figure 6.2 attempts an overall summary of possible causal interrelations in social-democratic corporatism. As the above account has already suggested, an important originating factor has been the strength of corporatist traditions. Unfortunately the search for the causes of differences in that strength between countries lies outside the scope of this chapter. In addition to helping promote the centralization of industrial relations, these traditions may also have assisted high levels of public spending by facilitating state intervention in social and economic life, and possibly also either social-democratic party strength or consociationalism by facilitating compromise. *In turn*, labour political strength will have helped reinforce centralization, because labour leaders could both trust the state and be willing to help it by being economically 'responsible'. Several authors have also argued that public spending contributes to peaceful industrial relations by reducing workers' dependence on their wages for the maintenance of their standard of living.[20] That labour political strength will increase social spending is particularly clear.

There are also strong grounds for assuming a strong feedback from a high level of centralization to high levels of public spending. The leaders of a centralized social-democratic labour movement are likely to accept the importance of public spending and will therefore be less likely than the actors in a decentralized movement to try to claw back in pay rises what has

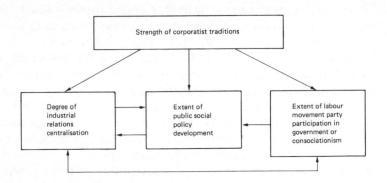

Fig. 6.2 Relations within the model of social democratic corporatism.

been lost in taxation to finance social spending. Governments trying to embark on large public-spending programmes without the confidence that a centralized union leadership will be able to restrain compensatory pay claims may well have to finance expenditure by heavy borrowing, which cannot be indefinitely sustained. Whether high centralization and high public spending then act together to favour the election of social-democratic governments or maintain the strength of consociationism is less easy to discern.

The reinforcing tendencies of the model suggest a persistent strength for social-democratic corporatism in the countries in which it has developed. However, there are also weaknesses. The welfare state, like centralized industrial relations, tends to concentrate decision making in the hands of bureaucracies and to reduce the possibilities of widespread participation. Earlier in the chapter attention was drawn to the ways in which professional and bureaucratic interests can wrest control of welfare policies away from capitalist interests. The elimination of participation is the equivalent toll levied by those forces on working-class interests. The point is of great importance because historically labour has often been a centralizing, bureaucratizing force in capitalist politics. As Weber observed, it is through the power of 'party', or as we might better express it, organization, that underprivileged groups in class society press their claims; and organization, as Weber's disciple Michels was to argue,[21] means centralization. Labour movements centralized because 'unity means strength' for weak groups, and because they wanted to pit the power of the democratically responsive state (a centralized force) against market forces, which are inherently decentralized. There have always been important decentralizing traditions within labour movements—e.g., syndicalism in France, or G.D.H. Cole's Guild Socialism in Britain, but in virtually every case it was the centralizing forces that won the day during the formative periods, partly because in this way labour was able to ally itself to changes taking place within capitalism itself, especially when these consisted of corporatist forms of centralization or relations between the state and powerfully organized interest groups.[22]

But for several years now that situation has been changing. There are growing signs, in several countries, of dissatisfaction with centralized forces. These signs are heterogeneous and associated with very varied class interests; some may object to their being linked, but it is important to grasp the extent of the discontent with centralization. Within industrial relations this has been evident in the growth of shop-steward movements and unofficial strikes.[23] There have also been radical campaigns for decentralization, participation and the revival of the community as a decision-making level in urban political struggles in several countries, often over issues of collective consumption (i.e., the welfare state).[24] Closely related to these have been (especially in Germany) ecological movements which, while not necessarily anti-centralist, tend to be such in their orientation, stressing community resistance to damage perpetrated by governments or international capital. In several countries there have been revivals of long-dormant regional loyalties and demands for devolution away from the nation state (e.g. in all the Scandinavian countries, the UK, Italy, Canada and, rather differently, Belgium). Finally, there has been a reaction against the centralized welfare state in the form of right-wing backlash movements against high taxation and state welfare—the most dramatic examples being the formation of new political parties organized on this basis in Denmark and Norway and the shift in the position of the British Conservative Party.[25]

Disparate though these movements are, they are all united, not only in their opposition to centralization, but in the fact that most social democratic parties have been 'caught on the wrong foot' by all of them. Shopfloor militancy challenges the dependence of social democracy on centralized industrial relations, which we have discussed here. The ecology movements have embarrassed labour-movement parties committed to large-scale technology in Sweden and West Germany. Regional loyalties have had a similar effect. And the very different pressures for community control and for low taxes and less welfare both challenge the social-democratic heartland of the welfare bureaucracy.

There is a more direct link between the ostensibly 'left-wing' development of shopfloor militancy and 'tax-payers' revolts' against the welfare state. There is evidence from Britain that increases in taxation may generate wages pressure,[26] and consistent with this it is notable that governments in several countries (including Britain, Germany, Sweden, Norway and Denmark) traded income tax reductions for wage restraint in the mid-1970s. If, as has been argued here, centralized wage bargaining enables governments to raise the taxation needed to finance welfare spending, the disintegration of centralized control in the 1970s has led governments to *reduce* taxation in order to regain centralization.

An important determinant of this has been the deteriorating economic situation. As increases in real income have become more difficult to achieve, so workers have both become dissatisfied with the restraint exercised by central negotiators *and* resisted the increasing encroachment of taxation on what income they do earn. In turn, taxation has risen during the recession, partly because several aspects of public spending are directly related to economic hardship, such as unemployment benefit, and partly because, for a variety of reasons, it is difficult to reduce the scale of social-services provision even if the ability of the economy to finance it at constant rates of taxation is declining. But it is doubtful whether the widespread dissatisfaction with centralized control is a result entirely of these economic factors. For example, ecological and community participation movements cannot easily be interpreted in this way; if anything, the 'green' parties contradict the logic of policies for economic recovery. Similarly, regionalism can be only partly interpreted as disillusion with the economic achievements of the nation state.

In his analysis of the crisis of the interventionist state, Offe shows how logically, increased popular participation in running state institutions could resolve some of the dilemmas, but also argues that the capitalist nature of the state renders such participation impossible.[27] The history of social-democratic politics has been the history of attempts at making possible developments and compromises which others have deemed impossible. Some of these attempts have been successful; others less so. What are the chances of successful moves in decentralization in the management of the welfare state? Or of combining coordination with grass-roots participation in industrial relations? Several countries already have examples of participation in welfare state administration. A combination of centralizing and decentralized forces in industrial relations is more difficult, unless the German model of centralized bargaining alongside *Mitbestimmung* and active *Betriebsräte* is accepted as an example. It certainly seems now to be the case that little further progress can be made along the lines of bureaucratized centralism on which labour movements have for so long relied. In addition to the crises presented by the collapse of the Keynesian world economy, the long-term viability of social democracy now depends on its ability to respond to the challenge of participation.

I am aware that in this chapter I have dealt speculatively and inconclusively with several questions, each of which merits far more substantial concentration. This is because my main aim is to show the links between a series of questions which are not always related in public debate. In doing so I hope I have mapped out an agenda for future concentration of study, and also suggested an approach to the interventionist state which differs somewhat from the preoccupations of most recent Marxist observers.

REFERENCES

1. For example, the works of Nicos Poulantzas; of the German school represented in J. Holloway and S. Piociotto, eds, *State and Capital* (London, Arnold, 1978); also J. O'Connor, *The Fiscal Crisis of the State* (New York, St. Martin's, 1973).
2. But see the far more balanced position adopted in I. Gough, *The Political Economy of the Welfare State* (London, Macmillan, 1979).
3. Ibid., ch. 6.
4. For surveys of post-war incomes policies, see A. Romanis, 'Cost inflation and incomes policy in industrial countries', *IMF Staff Papers*, by the same author, March 1967; and A. Braun, 'The role of incomes policy in industrial countries since World War II', ibid., March 1975; and J. L. Fallick and R. F. Elliott, *Incomes Policies, Inflation and Relative Pay* (London, Allen & Unwin, 1981).
5. Works on the general economic effects of incomes policy suggest that its impact may well be slight. See, for example, L. Ulman and R. J. Flanagan, *Wage Restraint: a Study of Incomes Policies in Western Europe* (Berkeley, University of California Press, 1971).
6. C. J. Crouch, 'The drive for equality: experience of incomes policy in Britain', in L. Lindberg *et al.*, eds, *Stress and Contradiction in Modern Capitalism* (Lexington, Mass., D. C. Heath, 1975), pp. 215–41; C. J. Crouch, *Class Conflict and the Industrial Relations Crisis* (London, Heinemann, 1977); J. Hughes, 'The low paid', in P. Townsend and N. Bosanquet, eds, *Labour and Inequality* (London, Fabian Society, 1972), pp. 162–73.
7. W. Brown, 'Incomes policy and pay differentials', *Oxford Bulletin of*

Economics and Statistics, 38 (1976), 27-50; A. J. H. Dean, 'Incomes policies and differentials', *National Institute Economic Review*, No. 85 (August 1978), 40-8. There is also interesting recent evidence of the extent to which union membership is associated with increased wages in R. Layard, D. Metcalf and S. Nickell, 'The effect of collective bargaining on relative and absolute wages', *British Journal of Industrial Relations*, 17 (1979), 287-302. This shows that the effect of collective bargaining in Britain seems to be to narrow differentials between skilled and unskilled workers.

8. A. Glyn and B. Sutcliffe, *British Capitalism, Workers and the Profits Squeeze* (Harmondsworth, Penguin, 1972).

9. In this chapter I am using corporatism in the sense of pluralistic corporatism, in which governments try to have autonomous labour movements do the job of regulating their own members in exchange for a range of positive and negative sanctions, including participation in various kinds of decision making. Similar strategies will probably also be pursued by the state towards other class interest groups, such as capital and agriculture. This usage has become common in recent literature (see, for a survey, P. C. Schmitter, 'Modes of interest intermediation and models of societal change in western Europe', in P. C. Schmitter and G. Lehmbruch, eds, *Trends Toward Corporatist Intermediation* (Beverly Hills, Sage, 1979), pp. 63-94, and is to be distinguished from both nineteenth-century corporatist ideology and the corporatism of twentieth-century fascism.

10. OECD, *National Accounts of OECD Countries*, annually.

11. Unfortunately published statistics do not make possible a really accurate estimate of welfare spending, especially since several countries do not even disaggregate their spending returns to the limited degree which OECD attempts to standardize. All I have been able to do is to deduct from government final consumption figures expenditure on defence, and to add to this sum the following transfer payments: subsidies, social security benefits, social assistance grants, current transfers to private non-profit institutions serving households and unfunded employee welfare benefits. In addition to 'welfare', *stricto sensu*, these figures will include several subsidies of economic activities (though I should be prepared to defend much of that as being of a welfare nature), and general public administration (which is very small). More serious however is the total inability to include tax expenditures. Since various economic and welfare transfers may take the form of tax exemptions, and since countries vary in their preference for measures of this kind rather than straightforward expenditure, these data may give a rather poor estimate of overall welfare activity. This may explain why, in the following account, the welfare spending statistics are often less well explained by the independent variables than are revenue statistics.

12. OECD, *Revenue Statistics*, annually.
13. M. Shalev, 'Strikers and the state: a comment', *British Journal of Political Science*, 8 (1978), 479-92.
14. Data based on those used by W. Korpi and M. Shalev, 'Strikes, industrial relations and class conflict in capitalist societies', *British Journal of Sociology*, 30 (1979), 164-87.
15. M. Sawyer, 'Income Distribution in OECD Countries', *OECD Economic Outlook, Occasional Studies*, 1976.
16. W. Streeck, 'Organizational consequences of corporatist co-operation in West German labour unions: a case study' (Berlin, Institut für Management und Verwaltung, mimeo, 1978).
17. G. K. Ingham, *Strikes and Industrial Conflict* (Cambridge, Cambridge University Press, 1974); P. Jackson and K. Sisson, 'Employers confederations in Sweden and the United Kingdom and the significance of industrial infrastructure', *British Journal of Industrial Relations*, 14 (1976). It should also be noted that openness is very closely related to sheer smallness of an economy, in terms of persons employed in economic activity; and organizational centralization is far more easily achieved in a smaller than a larger group.
18. D. R. Cameron, 'The expansion of the public economy: a comparative analysis', *American Political Science Review*, 72 (1978), 1243-61.
19. J. Stephens, *The Transition from Capitalism to Socialism* (London, Macmillan, 1979).
20. This has been argued by D. Hibbs, 'The political economy of long-run trends in strike activity', *British Journal of Political Science*, 8 (1978), 153-75; see also Korpi and Shalev, op. cit.; and E. Shorter and C. Tilly, *Strikes in France, 1830-1968* (Cambridge, Cambridge University Press, 1974). The argument, especially that of Hibbs, is that where social spending is high, workers are not so dependent on what they achieve in the market place for their standard of living, and therefore have less need to strike to try to improve their position. However, this ignores the fact that for the individual group of workers industrial action is a far more direct way to try to improve their standards than waiting for improved welfare. It is therefore probable that only a centralized union leadership, which may feel it has some capacity to affect the level of social spending, will accept this argument as some kind of grounds for not pressing wage claims. Prior centralization would seem to be a condition of the Hibbs hypothesis. However, once centralization exists, a high level of social spending may reinforce the centralization in turn, since peaceful industrial relations tend to stabilize relationships within them. On the other hand, if shop floor groups begin to feel restless that little is being done to take advantage of labour-market opportunities while the union leadership relies on welfare-state progress, there may be a growth of unofficial action. This opens the possibility of 'revolts' against the

pattern of centralization and high social spending discusssed below—developments of which Hibbs himself is well aware.

21. R. Michels, *Political Parties* (English edn: Glencoe, Ill., The Free Press, 1905).
22. See also H. Wilensky, *'The New Corporatism', Centralization and the Welfare State* (Beverly Hills, Sage, 1976).
23. S. Barkin, ed., *Worker Militancy and its Consequences* (New York, Praeger, 1975); C. J. Crouch and A. Pizzorno, eds, *The Resurgence of Class Conflict in Western Europe*, 2 vols (London, Macmillan, 1978).
24. E. Cherki *et al.*, 'Urban protest in western Europe', in Crouch and Pizzorno, op. cit., pp. 247–75.
25. Also relevant are changes which have taken place in the Swedish Centre Party, which changed itself from being an Agrarian Party with a declining social base to become an anti-centralist, anti-nuclear, 'green' party attracting support from a wide political spectrum.
26. F. Wilkinson and H. A. Turner, 'The wage-tax spiral and labour militancy', in D. Jackson *et al.*, *Do Trade Unions Cause Inflation?* (Cambridge, Cambridge University Press, 1972).
27. C. Offe, 'The theory of the capitalist state and the problem of policy formation', in Lindberg *et al.*, op. cit., pp. 125–44.

PART IV

THE POLITICAL ECONOMY OF INTERNATIONAL RELATIONS

7 Perspectives on International Political Economy

R. J. BARRY JONES

INTRODUCTION

Developments in both the politico-diplomatic and the economic spheres have prompted the noticeable revival of academic interest in international political economy since the early 1970s. While the virulence of the 'cold war', in particular, and the salience of purely 'political' sources of international conflict, generally, appeared to be on the wane[1] the world was suddenly confronted by new concerns over the possible shortage of vital resources, the dramatic 'oil-diplomacy' of the mid-1970s, a pernicious combination of widespread inflation and economic stagnation, and, most latterly, general recession.

The clear salience of international political economy has not, however, secured the resolution of a number of pressing and persisting issues of both theory and methodology. The very definition and demarcation of the subject remains in dispute, while controversy continues to rage over the most fruitful and valid intellectual approach to a complex and dynamic arena of human affairs.

Prior to the empirical and intellectual developments of the early 1970s political economy, both domestic and international, assumed one of two manifestations. The first, and the most well-entrenched, was that of the specifically policy-orientated work of those who remained within the mainstream of conventional macro-economic theory and analysis. Such policy-orientated economists enjoyed virtual intellectual hegemony, despite their frequent lack of critical awareness, as they faced no serious opposition. For many years the Marxist alternative to mainstream economics remained a minority taste which could, in days of seemingly endless economic well-being, be deemed the fantasy of a lunatic fringe.

Mainstream economics was also under no serious threat from the second emergent form of political economy for this could, if anything, be viewed as complementing and complimenting it. Analysts were now seeking to deploy the methodological premises and analytical tools of the mainstream economists in the study of various facets of political and international life.[2] In mimicking conventional economics this new 'formal' or 'economistic' study of politics thus offered it the greatest form of flattery.

Both mainstream political economy and the more recent formal/economistic political analysis have clearly contributed much to our understanding of facets of national and international life. They are not, however, the main focus of the present discussion, the attention of which is drawn, rather, to the dramatic clash between a number of competing approaches to the international political economy that re-emerged during the mid and later 1970s. It is through this clash that many of the major issues confronting the contemporary global political economy have been, and may best be, highlighted and avenues to their understanding (if not speedy resolution) charted.

At the heart of the current debate are alternative views of the central relationships between economics and politics: alternative views of both the actual and the desirable relationships. *Liberals*, while asserting the analytical separability of economics and politics, maintain an empirical association between modest, democratic government, on the one hand, and a *laissez-faire* economic system, on the other. The *classical mercantilists* of yore recognized the distinction between politics and economics but asserted, prescriptively, the need for the latter to be totally subordinated to the requirements of the former: for all aspects of a nation's economic life to serve the political interests of the state or its 'prince'. Contemporary *neo-mercantilists* have extended such an approach to incorporate a wide range of social and economic purposes within the list of considerations that should direct the state in its control of economic life. *Classical Marxists*, in marked contrast, asserted the primacy of economic developments in the empirical world with, in some extreme formulations, political developments being viewed as little more than opaque reflections of the economic dimension.

The diversity of viewpoint, both analytical and prescriptive, presented by the contending perspectives upon the international political economy is thus considerable and provides the student with a potentially rich source of insight and understanding.

CRITERIA

Insights will be provided and understanding promoted only if clear criteria are established for identifying that which is genuinely helpful and valid within the plethora of contending ideas and approaches. The introductory chapter to this volume indicates some of the shortcomings of naïve empiricism and, in contrast, the advantages of hypothesizing non-observable forces and factors. These considerations, however, create considerable difficulties for the establishment of clear and generally acceptable criteria for the evaluation of theories about, and approaches to, aspects of human activity. Such a situation, in turn, should encourage modesty in proclaiming the virtues of any approach and, perhaps, a greater willingness to deploy perspectives in a flexible and non-exclusive manner.

Empirical analysis may be advanced by a flexible and catholic use of perspectives but there may yet be grounds for preferring one approach to any other. The theoretical power of a perspective may here constitute the soundest criterion: power to acknowledge that which is inevitably problematical about its own epistemological foundations, power to accommodate other approaches or, at least, their more useful features; and, finally but by no means least, power to embrace the widest slice of empirical reality.

ESTABLISHED PERSPECTIVES UPON THE INTERNATIONAL POLITICAL ECONOMY

The literature reveals many approaches to the study of the international political economy and schemes for classifying such approaches. Each classificatory scheme illustrates *something* of the purposes of, and differences between, the established writers and analysts; not all, however, are equally sound of illuminating.

Robert Gilpin's threefold classification of perspectives upon the global political economy[3] remains the most effective and persuasive as a means of categorizing the range of approaches. Many of the established studies can be reduced to one of the three categories—'Sovereignty at Bay' or *liberal*; 'Dependencia' or *Marxist*; and 'mercantilist' or *neo-mercantilist*—with little or no violation to their superficial, though often rather visible, differences. Given their general significance, and the brevity of the outlines usually provided in works on international political economy, it might be valuable to sketch out the main features of each of these three major perspectives.

The liberal or neo-classical approach

While of lesser antiquity than mercantilism the liberal perspective remains dominant within the West and thus warrants initial consideration. Enshrined in such global arrangements as the General Agreement on Tariffs and Trade (GATT) and espoused by the governments of a number of advanced industrial countries (AICs), and a few newly industrializing countries (NICs), the liberal perspective proffers a thoroughgoing justification of private enterprise, *laissez-faire* and international free trade.[4]

Stripped of the considerable subtlety, sophistication, and not a little sophistry, that now surround the bare bones of the liberal perspective it asserts, in essence, that in a free, competitive market rational consumers will seek to maximize their satisfactions through their purchasing decisions. The desires of purchasers will be signalled to producers through movements in the prices of various goods and services or through the formation of queues or surplus stockpiles for other goods. Rational producers will seek to maximize their profits through producing more of those goods and services which experience price increases or the formation of queues and reducing production of those with falling prices or growing stockpiles. This response by rational producers will eventually ensure that a society's productive resources are used in the most efficient way: efficient in terms of the consumers' preferences as expressed through the free market. The further effect of such an optimal allocation of productive resources will be the elimination of both queues and surpluses and those price fluctuations that reflect an imbalance between supply and demand for given goods or services.

If free trade also exists among societies, the liberal perspective envisages both the most efficient use of productive resources and the greatest possible satisfaction of consumer wants on a global scale. Free trade throughout a world market should encourage each society to specialize in those goods and services that they can produce most efficently.

Liberal economists argue that the pattern of global specialization that will result from free trade will not be limited to any absolute advantages that certain societies may have: oil, for instance, being produceable only by countries that have oil deposits beneath their soil. Trade will, moreover, not necessarily reflect the patterns of overall efficiency in production that may have developed between societies. Rather, liberal theory rests upon the principle of comparative advantage which envisages a situation which initially appears to be quite strange but then becomes sensible on closer consideration.

The liberal principle of comparative advantage indicates the way in which it may benefit two or more societies, which initially produce the same range of goods and services, to specialize in production and thence trade, even though one society is more efficient at producing all the goods and services than the other(s).

Employing a grossly simplified, but yet illuminating, example of two societies—A and B—which produce two marketable goods—radios and wheat—the overall efficiencies of production can be compared by relating output to the efforts of one man working for one day (one man-day). In the current example, one man working for one day in society A might produce six radios *or* two kilograms of flour. In society B one man working for one day might produce only one radio *or* one kilogram of flour. In terms of output for each man-day worked society A is thus more efficient at producing *both* radios and flour than society B.

Despite society A's greater overall efficiency than society B it will still benefit both if society A switches workers from producing flour to producing more radios while society B switches workers from radio production to flour production and the two societies then trade part of their increased production with one another: society A now sending radios to B while B sends flour to A. The reason for this rests upon the fact that while society A is more efficient at producing flour than B—being able to produce 2 kilograms per man-day to B's 1 kilogram per man-day (a 2:1 advantage)—she is even more efficient at producing radios than B—being able to produce 6 radios per man-day against B's production of a mere 1 radio per man-day (a 6:1 advantage).

Given such a disparity between the relative efficiency of

producing radios and flour *within* society A and *within* society B, specialization of production and mutually beneficial trade is favoured. Society A has to give up producing only two kilograms of flour to produce an extra radio (by switching one man for one day of work). If it can obtain more than two kilograms of flour in trade (or obtain those two kilograms of flour for less than six radios) a clear benefit will have been achieved: more obtained back through trade than that given up in domestic production. Society B, in its turn, has had to forgo the domestic production of only one radio in order to produce each additional one kilogram of flour. It will therefore gain if it can trade one kilogram of flour for more than one radio (or obtain one radio for less than one kilogram of flour). Happily there exists a range of exchange ratios of radios for flour that will produce just such benefits for both society A and society B: the range of exchange ratios *between* three radios for one kilogram of flour and one radio for one kilogram of flour.

To illuminate this, if existing food levels were satisfactory in both society A and society B, both could take their 'gains from trade' in the form of increased consumption of radios. A trade exchange ratio of two radios to one kilogram of flour would allow such a possibility. Society A has here switched labour from flour production to radio production. Each man thus moved now produces an additional six radios while reducing domestic flour production by two kilograms. The two kilograms of lost flour production can be made good through imports from B, but only four radios have to be sent to B for each two kilograms of such imported flour (the exchange ratio of two radios for one kilogram of flour). Society A has clearly benefited from this arrangement to the tune of a two-radio profit. Society B, however, has also 'profited' by two radios because it had to give up only two radios worth of domestic production to produce the two kilograms of flour which were then exchanged for four radios from society A.[5]

Such is the principle that liberals suppose to lie behind the contemporary patterns of international trade. The real world is, of course, a multi-society world with trade in an enormous range of goods and services. In such a world simple exchange ratios are largely replaced by payments in money: the currencies of those nation states that engage in international trade.

Overall levels of 'efficiency' are then adjusted through the evaluation of one nation's national currency against the currencies of other nations (or, at least, a 'basket' of those currencies most frequently used in international commerce). The liberal formulation offers an elegant and often appealing view of the economic domain: elegant by virtue of both the simplicity of its basic assumptions and the logical rigour of its system of argument; appealing in the certainties that it seems to offer to those confronted by an uncomfortably complex and turbulent world. It is, however, these very features that are the subject of such trenchant criticism by those who adopt alternative views or by those who are less dazzled by theoretical prettiness and more impressed by the intractability of empirical reality.

Criticisms of the liberal perspective often turn upon the methodology and core assumptions upon which it is based. Here it is seen that the corpus of liberal theory rests not upon sound simplifying propositions about reality but upon simplifications which require evasions, or even distortions, of reality if they are to be useable, or *a priori* assumptions which are quite simply unwarranted.[6]

The assumption of rationality exemplifies the evasive and distorting failing. Unless an indiscriminate (and ultimately tautological) notion of rational action, as that action which maximizes the satisfaction of an unspecified and unconstrained set of possible needs, wants and desires, is to be adopted then a much more limited conception has to be introduced. Undifferentiated 'rationality' thus has to give way to 'economic rationality'; a notion which soon confines rational choice to the maximization of only those objectives which can be satisfied through market exchanges and which therefore ignores (and ultimately illegitimizes) all those other needs, wants and desires which an individual may well seek to satisfy through his actions and choices. Reality has thus been distorted by the evasion that is necessary in any approach to rationality that can provide a workable basis for the grand edifice of liberal economic theory.

The introduction of unjustifiable assumptions into the core of liberal economic theory may be illustrated by a number of assumptions which can be seen, on reflection, to be necessary to the operation, and predicted consequences, of the *laissez-faire* system but which are clearly absurd.

Prominent amongst such absurd assumptions are those of perfect information, for consumer and producer alike, and the general absence of barriers to entry, of any type, to potential producers of any good or service. Without perfect information consumers can clearly not make those purchasing decisions that will actually maximize their satisfactions, while producers cannot direct their efforts in the most profitable directions. However, in all but the most exceptional of circumstances, such perfect information is quite impossible. Barriers to entry, while reducing the possibilities of optimal quantities of the most desired products at the lowest practical prices, are also only too much in evidence in the real world, whether they be financial, technical, legal or organizational.

The liberal formulation also requires additional unrealistic assumptions about the conditions of consumer behaviour. Humanity must be more or less homogeneous in its wants and needs or expressed demand will be too diverse to facilitate a coherent market system or any kind of modern, large-scale system of production. There must also be a broad measure of equality of income and wealth otherwise the use of productive resources will be distorted in the direction of satisfying the desires of the wealthy at the expense of the needs of the poorer (which may be greater in real terms). Such a situation will reduce the aggregate level of satisfaction within the community by satisfying lesser wants while denying greater needs (unless the 'interesting' additional assumption is made that the wants of the wealthy are, in some way, of sufficient qualitative superiority to compensate for the failure to satisfy some of the more basic, but qualitatively 'inferior' needs of the poor).

A further, and related, condition for the proper functioning of the liberal order is the meeting of the general injunction that the satisfaction of one individual's desires has no adverse effect upon the possibility of satisfying the wishes of others. If one's possession of something denies possibilities to some other then a negative, satisfaction-reducing effect has been created, as it is in the case of the private ownership of sea-shores, woods and other natural facilities.

The assumptions of human homogeneity, equal income distribution, and no negative effects on others are, in Charles Kindleberger's words in his pioneering *Power and Money* 'heroic and unrealistic',[7] while Fred Hirsch, in his seminal

Social Limits to Growth[8] has demolished any hope that it is possible to avoid serious adverse consequences for the satisfaction of the majority in a capitalist, or free-enterprise, economy.

If global productive resources are to be employed optimally, and satisfactions to be fulfilled at the highest possible level, then the conditions of production also have to conform to a number of unwarranted assumptions. There must be no oligopolies or monopolies that can, and indeed will, limit supply, increase prices, constrain innovations or obstruct competition. Again, there must be no serious 'externalities': costs imposed upon some today, or possibly upon everyone tomorrow, such as to balance out the benefits that some are obtaining from the production being currently undertaken. There must lastly, but far from leastly, be no paradoxes inherent in the basic concept of rational action, upon which the entire edifice of liberal economic theory is based. In short, there must be no temptation to withold costly contributions to the provision of those collective goods—from litter-free streets through to national defence forces—that is, in fact, all too evident in reality and that has been the subject of some recent study (under the headings of 'free-riding', 'collective goods', and general 'paradoxes of rationality').[9]

Liberal theory has yet to grapple adequately with this problem of paradoxes of rationality and free-riding. The difficulty here is that 'liberal' theory enshrines cost-minimization and benefit-maximization as *the* criteria of economic rationality. These behavioural injunctions, however, impel the 'rational' individual to attempt to withhold his voluntary contribution to the costs of providing those collective goods that actually benefit both him and the community. Unfortunately a community composed of such 'rational' individuals will be a community in which everyone attempts to withhold voluntary contributions and for which desired, indeed desirable and often necessary, collective goods will not, therefore, be provided. Despite some confused and confusing attempts to wish this fundamental problem away,[10] it remains a basic weakness in the liberal perspective.

The general critic of the liberal perspective would also point to its static and ahistorical character.[11] Its implicit account of the historical development of the contemporary global division of labour is, at best, simplistic and, at worst, a gruesome distortion. Unable to apprehend history, the liberal approach is both static and denied the ability to offer cogent recommendations for the future. The principle of comparative advantage reduces, in practice, to a tautology for such comparative advantage is empirically knowable only through the existence of a competitive position in the production and sales of some good or service: a position which, in turn, reflects the acquisition of whatever 'factors of production' are necessary to achieve competitiveness. Thus comparative advantage may be achieved only with the acquisition of those production capabilities that make you competitive and the achievement of such comparative advantage is identifiable only when you prove to be competitive in practice.

Beyond such a tautology, the greatest difficulty facing the liberal perspective is the fact that most of the more salient factors of production are created by man rather than given by nature. A modern liberal transported back to mid-nineteenth century Japan would thus have faced a considerable intellectual difficulty when invited to advise on economic and development policy. Given Japan's factor endowments in the mid-nineteenth century our liberal would probably have advised the further development of fishing, rice production, the making of paper fans, and the painting of exotic, and often erotic, works of art.

The Marxist view

Marxist critics go beyond the view that the liberal perspective is merely misconceived in its assumptions to argue that it actually presents a view of reality that is systematically distorted. Indeed, the contrast between the liberal and the Marxist approaches could hardly be greater. Where the liberal sees a benign and stable system of private enterprise and market competition the Marxist sees exploitation, class struggle and ultimate breakdown.

Basic to the Marxist perspective[12] is the contention that history has been characterized by patterns of economic exploitation, and attendant class struggle, of which capitalism is but the most advanced and dynamic form. Industrial capitalism is characterized by the ownership of considerable quantities of capital equipment by one economic class—the capitalists or bourgeoisie, which hires members of another class—the workers or proletariat—to work with that equipment to create valuable goods and services. Marxists argue that all the value of any good or service is actually created by those who work to produce it. Capitalists, however, are able to pay their workers wages that are less than the exchange value of the goods and services that they have produced (surplus value) and thereby obtain exploitative profits.

One of the dynamic elements of capitalism is the continuous competition which forces capitalists to reduce prices, cut costs where they can, and invest in more productive capital equipment to save labour and wages. Many competitive advantages can also be secured through expansion of the scale of activity and the level of production of a firm. Competition and expansionist pressure thus remain at the heart of the capitalist system.

Unfortunately, the related pressures of competition and expansion bring their own difficulties. Holding down wages, as a means of lowering production costs, limits the size of the market for what is being produced (wage earners being ultimately the consumers for many goods and services). Overproduction may thus result and bring a fall in profitability, a reduction in the level of economic activity (a recession) and a crisis, of variable intensity, in the capitalist economy.

In addition to cyclical crises, there will be a general increase in the ratio of capital equipment to labour employed in production. On conventional analysis, such a process could well create problems for continued profitability. In Marxian analysis, however, a declining proportion of labour in any productive process *necessarily* creates a falling rate of profit.[13] The competitive pressures that encourage investment in more productive machinery thus underlines a general tendency for the rate of profit to fall throughout the capitalist world: a tendency which exacerbates the periodic crises of overproduction, and subsequent recession, and which leads towards the ultimate collapse of the capitalist system and its replacement by socialism.

By the late nineteenth century it became apparent to many Marxists that capitalism was actually more durable and malleable than had originally been believed. Imperialism, it seemed, had provided a significant escape valve.[14] More profitable investment opportunities existed in underdeveloped areas overseas and such investments could best be protected by the extension of political control to such territories.[15] Moreover, many such investment opportunities led, eventually, to an easing of domestic conditions within the capitalist metropoles for they provided new sources of cheap foodstuffs and raw materials. Domestic wages could thus be held down, the workers being able to maintain their real standards of living through the consumption of cheaper imported foodstuffs, while production costs were also eased by the availability of plentiful supplies of cheap raw materials. Finally, new colonies offered new and controlled markets for the manufactured produce of the imperial nations and hence helped ease the crisis of overproduction.

Such were the perceived advantages of 'capitalist imperialism' that many of the major European powers were attracted into overseas ventures. All remained well for the imperial metropoles until opportunities for new acquisitions were exhausted. The 'positive sum game' of imperialism now became the 'zero sum game' of imperial rivalry. And with the emergence of imperial conflicts came the reintensification of the internal economic difficulties of the major capitalist societies.

War between the imperial powers appeared to many who shared Lenin's outlook to be the inevitable consequence of the ultimate failure of capitalism's imperial safety-valve.[16]

Marxism–Leninism remained the orthodox Marxist view of developments within the capitalist world from the outbreak of World War I until some time after World War II. The Depression and diverse turmoils of the interwar era did nothing to dim the confidence of the 'faithful', while World War II itself could be seen, from the Marxist–Leninist perspective, to be a further spasm in the disintegration of the capitalist order.

The extensive and rapid decolonization of the post-1945 decades called forth the greatest modification in the Marxist approach, and the ascription of a central role to one of its more subtle, and powerful, concepts—that of *neo-colonialism*.[17] The argument, now, was that a change of political forms, from imperial control to political 'independence', in no way changed the underlying economic relationships between former colony and metropole. Colonies that had attained their political 'freedom' remain in thrall to their former masters through a pattern of general economic dependence and subordination, usually sustained by the operations of metropole-based multinational corporations (MNCs).

The subtlety of such a notion of neo-colonialism is that it can be applied retrospectively to accommodate some of the apparent anomalies of the nineteenth-century experience. It underpins a notion of 'informal empire'[18] extending beyond, but paralleling in economic respects, the formal empires of the imperial powers. Thus can be accommodated the self-declared 'exception' of the United States of America by indicating how similar effects can be created under differing formal political conditions—the USA being able to create a structure of neo-colonial relationships, particularly within Latin America, without resorting to the establishment of a large area of direct political control (under whatever title).

The concept of neo-colonialism is also closely allied with that of a 'world system of capitalism'[19] in which various classes of nation states are faced with quite different sets of opportunities and constraints, which reflect the basic functioning of a global capitalist system and the relationships in which such societies find themselves with it. Leading capitalist—or *core*—societies have benefited, and continue to benefit, from such a system, with high living standards domestically and relatively low prices for their imported primary commodities, irrespective of their direct participation in imperialism in the past, or in the basing of transnational corporations (TNCs) in the present. In contrast, less developed countries (LDCs)—or *periphery* countries—continue to face enormous structural obstacles, both internal and external, to their effective development and enhanced well-being. Such obstacles flow from the basic character of a capitalist world system, and the LDCs' peculiar historical experience of it, and include Western-orientated domestic elites through to TNC dominated markets for their primary exports. So strong are the effects of this world capitalist system that little can be done to alter its functioning or impact even by the existing group of avowedly socialist societies.

Many and varied have been the reactions to the Marxist formulation: from blind faith, through tactical neglect, to virulent criticism and opposition. The complexities, and inherently ideological character, of all social studies/sciences are sharply crystallized once Marxism is injected into the debate.

Criticisms of the Marxist perspective are pitched at one, or more, of three possible levels: epistemological/methodological foundations; basic assumptions made within the governing methodology; and, derivative propositions or 'predictions'.

At the most profound level are those arguments directed against the epistemological and methodological premises of the Marxist approach. Here the central issue is that between the simple empiricism of many critics and the more complex 'realism'[20] of the Marxists, in which 'non-observable' factors and forces are deemed to be legitimate and highly salient analytical elements: 'non-observables' such as structures (particularly that of the global core-periphery structure), 'labour power', 'social reproduction', and other concepts which relate to, but are not identical with, directly observable factors, developments or processes. Such 'non-observables' are ascribed a central role in many modern Marxist analyses and are held to underlie many of those events and developments that are directly accessible to the primary human senses.

The ultimate reliance of the Marxist perspective on references to such non-observables creates a number of difficulties that have considerable ramifications. Initially, this dependence upon non-observables exposes the perspective to the charge that it is no more than pure metaphysics: a belief system warranting no more claim to acceptability than a religion and, hence, not the stuff of which serious analytical perspectives are made. If not justifying the dismissal as metaphysics, then this characteristic of the Marxist perspective might encourage the claim that it is no more than a normative and politically motivated ideology that offers only a woolly pretence to 'scientific' veracity.

By the admission of most proponents, the Marxist perspective must be viewed as a metatheory: a theory, albeit replete in valuable insights, which is not amenable to testing by strict empirical scientific procedures.[21] This characteristic, however, is not one for which the more sophisticated of modern Marxists would feel the need to apologize arguing, as they would, that all perspectives upon human affairs are similarly 'untestable', regardless of their claims to the contrary.

In many ways the most serious consequence of the epistemological foundations and methodology of the Marxist perspective, however, is its inevitable lack of specificity. Great historical forces tend to take rather a long time to work themselves through and thus render it difficult to specify the precise stage currently reached. Non-observable factors are also definitionally obscured to the empirical observer and the materialization of their ultimate implications impossible to time with precision. Substantively, such a lack of qualitative and temporal specificity may amount to serious uncertainty about the present and immediate future. It may be impossible to say whether a current 'crisis of capitalism' will evoke a reformist or a revolutionary response, or whether the 'inevitable' socialist transformation is a day or a hundred years hence.

The Marxist perspective's lack of specificity, and its lack of temporal specificity in particular, is reassuring to many true-believers, but somewhat troubling to the more sceptical. It remains, however, an inherent and central characteristic which flows from the perspective's epistemological and methodological foundations. It is a feature which nullifies some of the more simpleminded criticisms of Marxism, but it does introduce considerable intellectual difficulties and indeterminacies.

Many of the basic assumptions, introduced *within* the methodological framework of the Marxist perspective, have also been subject to extensive criticism. Each basic Marxist concept constitutes an assumption about reality which may, or may not, be accepted. Such concepts include the primacy of the economic infrastructure, the ubiquity of class division and conflict; the creation of all value by labour; the nature and extent of economic exploitation, and the general tendency for the rate of profit to fall (this latter 'assumption' being, at once, both an assumption and a conclusion of the Marxian analysis). Such assumptions about the 'realities' of human affairs may be subject to two kinds of criticism: factual or interpretative. Most of the criticisms of the factual veracity of the Marxist perspective have been addressed to its derivative propositions about empirical developments ('predictions' which are held to have been proved unfounded). Such criticisms, however, usually founder upon the elusiveness that the Marxist perspective gains from its basic lack of temporal specificity. More force, and considerably more disputation, however, attaches to those criticisms that have been addressed to the interpretative features of many of the perspective's basic assumptions.

Some Marxist assumptions, for example, the primacy of the economic infrastructure, the ubiquity of class struggle or the labour theory of value, have been criticized as unduly one-sided.

Prior conceptions, it is argued, are here resulting in the exaggeration of a limited number of features of, or influences within reality to the total exclusion of a number of other highly significant features or influences. Critics of the view that the economic infrastructure is *the* determinant of historical developments thus point to the alternative influences of belief systems, religions, political institutions and traditions, and to the impact of prominent individuals.

Other basic Marxist assumptions have been challenged as ideologically governed misinterpretations of phenomena that have a morally neutral, or less misanthropic, role. Terms such as 'exploitation' exemplify such arguments. Defenders of the *laissez-faire* system point to the positive role that profits play in generating new resources for investment and encouraging those who acquire such resources to actually invest them in new or expanded business, thereby increasing the employment and consumption opportunities for society.

Widespread attention has, as suggested earlier, been drawn to the numerous supposed failures of the Marxist perspective's derivate propositions and 'predictions'. Critics during the first two or three postwar decades were keen to denounce the proposition regarding the cyclical crises of capitalism and of the general tendency for the rate of profit to fall. Such arguments have, however, become somewhat muted during more recent years!

Marxist doctrines about imperialism and neo-colonialism have also been criticized as inaccurate. Imperialism, it has been argued, was neither profitable nor, as decolonization 'proved', essential to the continued viability of capitalism.[22] A noticeable portion of today's less developed countries were, it is pointed out, never incorporated into formal European empires. Their domestic economic developments, and relations with the rich nations, cannot, therefore, be attributed to capitalist imperialism.[23]

In the contemporary era, the basic idea of neo-colonialism has been challenged by reference to the success of the newly industrialized countries, such as South Korea and Taiwan, cases which are held to demonstrate that contemporary capitalism in no way inhibits the development of LDCs or condemns them to indefinite economic subordination to the capitalist metropoles. Moreover, the multinational corporations are, in particular, held to benefit the host countries in which they operate in numerous ways, rather than to damage them.[24]

Finally, most critics of the Marxist viewpoint hold that there are no signs of any inevitable, ultimate global movement towards socialism. Indeed, in marked contrast, it is often argued that the instability and fragility of those societies that have embarked upon experiments with socialism evidence, if anything, a contrary tendency over the long term.

Some of the criticisms of the Marxist perspective clearly derive from misunderstanding, or a failure to appreciate some of its subtler points. Others, however, undoubtedly reflect central characteristics of the perspective itself, particularly its lack of specificity and the related problem of the subjective determinants of short-term behaviour and, hence, of short-term developments. This difficulty, which is suggested by the Marxist concept of 'false consciousness' (behaviour directed by an ideologically governed misconception of some central aspect of reality) poses a major, and largely unresolved, issue for Marxian analysis.

Some of the issues arising from the Marxist perspective, which have been seized upon by critics, have also become the focus of intense and, at times, impassioned controversy amongst its adherents. Two such issues[25] have riven Marxist circles in recent years: the question of whether the Marxist approach can survive the abandonment of the labour theory of value,[26] and the extent to which such superstructural elements as the state can be ascribed any independent influence over central developments.[27]

A further issue has also begun to rumble beneath the surface of Marxian analysis and threatens to emerge as a matter of major importance in the near future. Many see the multinational corporations as primarily a mechanism of exploitation of the poor South by the capitalist metropoles of the rich North. There are, however, some suggestions that the MNC should now properly be considered to be an exploiter of all the societies in which it operates, irrespective of the type of society —North or South, home or host. The sole beneficiaries of this exploitation are seen to be the managers of, and shareholders in, these corporations wherever located.[28] In Marxian terms, the transnational mode of organization and operation of the MNC introduces the vision of a new mode of production—

transnational capitalism (a 'mode of production' being the compound of the instrumentalities of economic production *and* the organization of producers and productive relations). A new form of capitalism can thus be identified which has its own characteristics and dynamic.

Neo-mercantilism

The liberals and the Marxists do not, however, hold a monopoly on interpretations of the contemporary global political economy or on influence over policy-makers. Neo-mercantilism represents a cast of mind that is finding increasing expression in the reflections of analysts and in the policy-making of governments as the global economy weathers general recession and engenders intensifying conflicts of interest.

Neo-mercantilism constitutes the modern development of an approach towards the management of states' international economic relations that has a long pedigree. Variants of mercantilism[29] have held sway over policy and analysis during many phases of European and, latterly, world history. Mercantilism, in all its forms, shares with the political 'realism' of analysts like Hans Morgenthau the basic assertion that the world is fundamentally a self-help system.[30] It is a world that lacks an uncontested and capable world authority which is able to make and enforce regulations and decisions. Societies therefore have to look to themselves for their own well-being, physical and economic. Irrespective of the means chosen—individual action or collaboration with others—self-help remains that ultimate reality and the imperative at the heart of a society's thinking.

Some writers have argued that mercantilism never actually existed as a coherent system of policy. Rather, it is contended, the idea of mercantilism was the creation of polemicists like Adam Smith, in *The Wealth of Nations*[31] who sought a 'straw man' to demolish by arguments that supported preferred economic doctrines or conditions.[32]

The squabbles of historians aside, the self-help reality of international relations remains. Equally clear is a disposition towards policy that has exerted a continuing, if variable, influence across time and circumstance.

Those analysts who do accept the historical reality of classical mercantilism discern two phases in its development. In the earliest—bullionist—phase the accumulation of precious metals was deemed to be the continuing priority for governors of societies. Holdings of such resources allowed troops to be hired and paid, armaments to be purchased and armies to be provisioned. In extreme cases entire mercenary armies could be hired and fielded in the promotion of the cause of those who could pay.

The implications of 'bullionist mercantilism' were clear and relatively simple. Exports were to be maximized to secure the greatest possible receipts of bullion, while imports were to be commensurately minimized. New sources of precious metals were to be pursued with rigour and, in the extreme case, the bullion of others might be misappropriated, particularly by maritime privateers.

Significant of such mercantilism was the clear and absolute subordination of economics to politics. The military and political purposes of princes and governments dictated the imperative of bullion accumulation to which all aspects of economic life must conform. In this there can be no clearer contrast between mercantilism and both Marxism, which subordinates politics to economics analytically, and liberalism, which prescribes the subordination of much of politics to economics (the former *ought* to be operated so as to serve the needs of the *laissez-faire* economy and should in no way impede its free functioning).

The later, and more comprehensive, form of mercantilism shared the basic subordination of economics to politics that had characterized the earlier form. The political and military needs of society, and its rulers, remained paramount but the range of economic conditions deemed to be pertinent to such purposes was now considerably extended.[33] The accumulation of bullion, while by no means disdained, was no longer viewed as the sole, or even the primary, aim of economic policy. The strength of a society was now seen to lie in a variety of economic conditions.

Domestically, later mercantilism pursued the greatest possible economic stability, vigour and general capability. Agricultural self-sufficiency coupled with productive potential were now seen to underpin military capability and political influence. To such ends, the fertility of the land had to be maintained, transportation facilitated, skills nurtured and manufacturing facilities created and sustained. The regulations designed to achieve such ends were extensive in their embrace of social and economic life and often intensive in their degree of intervention in everyday matters.

Internationally, later mercantilism deemed that all aspects of trade and commerce be subordinated to the political and military interests of the state. A positive balance of trade (the value of exports exceeding the value of imports) would secure the accumulation of financial resources. More significantly, however, the careful management of international trade might make an invaluable contribution to the balance of advantage in future conflict with any other society.

Considerable advantages might be gained if other states could be rendered dependent upon exports of vital supplies from one's own society. The resultant vulnerability to embargo might underpin an effective threat or be decisive in any confrontation, armed or otherwise.

As a corollary of maximizing the dependence of others upon one's self, mercantilists also cautioned against developing dependencies upon others. Domestic self-sufficiency was thus the ultimate ideal.

To secure the maximum dependence of others, and the maximum of self-sufficiency of one's self, called for the continuous and deep involvement of the authorities in all aspects of trade. Severe limits had to be imposed upon the development of the society's import trade while exports were actively encouraged. Where imports of strategic materials were unavoidable, sources other than potential adversaries were to be sought with speed and energy. Where others proved reluctant to accept strategic materials and products from one's own state they might, in extreme cases, have to be 'persuaded' to open their frontiers to such trade.

Within early modern Europe, the domestic objectives of mercantilism were pursued through the development and extension of such medieval institutions as guilds. Mercantilism's external objectives were promoted through the proliferation of the state's regulative and enforcement organizations and the granting of official monopolies to state-approved trading companies, corporations and associations.

The free-trade agitation of the mid-nineteenth century, and the progressive prosperity of the Edwardian 'summer', did much to displace mercantilist notions. Many of the pressures for a mercantilist revival were, however, persistent and growing during this period. The turmoils, both economic and political, of the years between the two world wars demonstrated many of these bases of neo-mercantilism and prompted its emergence. Two general features of modern, developed societies form the bedrock of neo-mercantilism: popular political pressures and the imperatives of complex and sensitive national economic systems.[34] No longer can the governments of most advanced industrial societies ignore, for long, the demands of the populace, however those 'demands' be habitually expressed. The populations of the advanced industrial societies are, moreover, increasingly aware of the many ways in which general economic developments impact upon their day-to-day lives. For good or ill, then, popular sentiments for the desirability of measures of protection, support for domestic enterprises, and allied practices, ultimately exert a compelling influence upon governments.

The economies over which the governments of advanced industrial societies preside are also extremely complex and often extremely sensitive to disruptive influences. Governments, of whatever persuasion, are thus forced to go far beyond the minimalist role envisaged by Adam Smith (or latter day ultra-liberals) and interest themselves in a wide range of developments in the domestic economy and its relationships with the global system. Few but the most ideologically blinkered of governments now believe that the advanced capitalist economy can, if left entirely to its own devices, maintain such a pattern of employment and production as to ensure the economic well-being and, hence, political quiescence of the greater part of the population. 'Externalities' of one sort or another would, indeed, prove so great as to threaten the very social and political harmony of a 'freed' capitalist economic system.

The role of governments in preserving economic well-being and, hence, political stability is one, extremely powerful motive for neo-mercantilism. The vulnerability of the modern industrial economy to disruption is a further consideration. The economies of modern advanced states are vitally dependent upon the continued availability of a profusion of energy sources, raw materials, components and services. Interference with the inflow, or circulation, of these may bring entire industries or, indeed, the whole economy to a halt, with clear and drastic social, economic and political consequences. The neo-mercantilist's concern to minimize the national economy's dependence upon foreign sources of such vital imports thus reflects the classical mercantilist's doctrine of maximizing the dependence of others while minimizing one's own. The utility of asymmetrical patterns of dependence when making threats, at times of conflicts of interest, or when actually engaged in confrontations will be immediately apparent to observers of recent developments in international relations.

Economic security, both for economic and politico-military ends, is thus a major, defensive motive for neo-mercantilism. Increasing the dependence of others upon one's own society is a further politico-military advantage.

The range of policies, actions, organizations and instruments which governments may direct towards neo-mercantilist ends is considerable. All measures of domestic economic protection—tariffs, quotas on imports and non-tariff barriers to entry—may be so directed. Subsidies, of all manner, to domestic producers may be similarly intended. However, a considerable range of domestic social, health, educational, and research policies and programmes may also have neo-mercantilist implications. Providing mass education will, for instance, furnish a more sophisticated and skilful work-force for industry. Advanced education will equally facilitate the development of new technology, superior products and improved services.

Neo-mercantilist practices are thus ubiquitous in the modern world and may well assume a momentum of their own as one area of action, or intervention, requires further action to make it fully effective. This characteristic of the modern neo-mercantilist state is precisely that to which its critics direct their greatest attention. Such a state is deemed to be excessively meddlesome in the economy. An ever-expanding bureaucracy encroaches steadily upon the work of economic entrepreneurs, making it less effective and generally more costly, and then attempts to take over the task of managing economic production and distribution once the efforts of the private entrepreneurs have been undermined.

Creeping bureaucratization of, and state control over, most aspects of a nation's economic life is thus the implication of neo-mercantilism to its critics. All the efficient, dynamic and constructive features of the free-enterprise system are negated. Personal freedom is subsequently diminished as opportunities for entrepreneurs and consumers alike are progressively constrained by bureaucrats in one guise or another. Neomercantilism thus unleashes a process which, however well-intended initially, spawns a bureaucracy which meddles increasingly in the lives of others while seeking to preserve the position of itself and its kind.

Neo-mercantilism is thus criticized as being detrimental to domestic economic freedom, efficiency and general vitality. Internationally, it is also held to disrupt those patterns of trade that encourage a specialization in production which, in turn, reflects an optimal allocation of the world's productive resources and hence ensures the maximum satisfaction of consumers' wants. To those who see the development of international trade as a source of increasing global integration and harmony, a neo-mercantilism that impeded such a development would be further viewed as a regressive political influence.

The perspectives on the international political economy outlined thus far, while indicating the major strands of thought and analysis, do not exhaust the realm of possibilities. R. Dan Walleri has rightly highlighted the variety of approaches that fall under the general Marxist umbrella.[35] His additional category of internationalist[36] is also reflected in the identification of a *structuralist* approach, by D. H. Blake and R. S. Walters,[37] and a perspective linked to the work of Raul Prebisch, by Joan Spero.[38] This structuralist approach has been reflected in recent 'Southern' proposals and arguments in various 'North–South' conferences and therefore warrants further attention.

The structuralist perspective

Abjuring the extremes of Marxist doctrine or the platitudes of liberal neo-classicism, the structuralists paint a picture of structured asymmetry in the patterns of economic relations between the advanced capitalist nations of the North and the less developed countries of the South. The empirical manifestations of this structured asymmetry are to be seen in developments in the terms of trade of the 'Southern' countries (developments in the ratio of the unit value of their exports to the unit costs of their imports), in patterns of revenue earnings from the production and export of primary commodities, and, finally, in the general failure to secure extensive and rapid development of much of the less developed world.

The structured asymmetry between North and South is held to rest upon the contrasting conditions within the two sets of economies. In the North a well-organized and unionized workforce produces an extremely wide range of goods and services; goods and services, moreover, which have a high income elasticity of demand (as general wealth increases, demand for these goods and services increases proportionally to the demands for other types of goods and services).

The conditions of supply for many Northern products are also, effectively, oligopolistic. A *relatively* few firms, from a *relatively* few northern countries, supply the greatest portion of those goods and services which are characteristically northern. This situation permits tacit coordination, price fixing, and other forms of restraint upon real, though mutually detrimental, competition: arrangements which while neither universal nor constant are, nevertheless, the norm.

A unionized workforce in oligopolistic industries which supply goods and services that have a high income elasticity of demand ensures that most of the benefits of improvements in productivity are retained in the North. Workers receive higher wages. Shareholders obtain increased dividends. Revenues are retained for the expansion of, or innovation within, the firms. Rarely do consumers in the South share the benefit in the form of reduced prices (modern electronics mark, perhaps, *the* exception to this general rule).

The situation of Southern countries could hardly be more of a contrast. An overlarge, disorganized and generally ununionized workforce generates products that have a low (or even negative) income elasticity of demand. The supplying firms and nations are numerous, heterogenous and generally difficult to coordinate. Substantial movements in the prices (and wages) for the South's basic products result as market conditions or supply conditions (harvest failures, gluts, innovations that improve productivity) change. When demand drops for a commodity, prices may follow suit and wages will eventually have to be lowered. If supply suddenly increases, while demand remains unchanged, then similar results will follow. If productivity improves substantially in some area of primary production it is likely that international competition will force prices to fall, thence eliminating any short-term improvements in workers' wages.

Beyond the difficulties created for Southern producers of primary commodities by short-term changes in market or production conditions there is also a longer-term reduction of demand for such products. Consumers are increasingly switching to more 'sophisticated' goods or using synthetics that result from technological innovations made in the North and that are largely produced in the North (the switch from sacks made from natural fibres to plastic bags).

The structural asymmetry between North and South is further evidenced, in the view of analysts like Raul Prebisch, in the long-term deterioration of the South's terms of trade. As the South receives progressively lower prices for its primary exports so it faces steadily rising prices for most of the goods and services it imports from the North. Moreover, not all such imports from the North can be deemed luxuries, as many play a vital role in the development programmes of the LDCs. The steady decline in the South's terms of trade thus threatens the very development upon which its future rests and, incidentally, diminishes global prosperity by reducing the South's capacity to purchase goods and services from the North.

Such a vision of contemporary North–South realities underlies the proposals made in successive conferences of a New International Economic Order (NIEO). A programme of commodity price stabilization, financed by a common fund, was intended to resolve, in part, the terms of trade problem. Substantially improved and extended aid programmes were also envisaged as a supplement to such commodity schemes. Future North–South imbalances were to be guarded against by constraining the current 'brain-drain' from South to North, and through providing the South with easier access to Northern technological innovations. The operations of multinational corporations were to be controlled internationally to ensure that their actions were more consistently beneficial to their Southern hosts. The operations of central agencies within the international monetary system—the International Monetary Fund (IMF), the World Bank and its subsidiary International Development Agency (IDA), were to be modified substantially to secure greater advantage for the less developed countries.

The thrust of the 'structuralist' perspective is thus the reform, rather than the overthrow, of the prevailing international economic order. In this they expose themselves to charges of reformist naïvete by radicals and Marxists, and to accusations of undue meddlesomeness by hard-bitten liberals and neo-classicists. Neo-mercantilists, of all political hues, also dub reformist structuralism as naïve in its advocacy of a philan-thropic internationalism in a world dominated by national self-interest and self-help. Many would also criticize the exaggeration of supposed global interdependencies that is often present in the arguments of structuralists, in general, and reformist proselytizers, like the Brandt Commission in its recurring reference to 'mutual interests'.[39]

On a more technical front, the pioneering structuralist work of Raul Prebisch has also been criticized as misleading. Argu-ments about movements in terms of trade depend, critically, upon the base year from which calculations are made. Choice of a high point for commodity prices will show a subsequent decline in prices and, in all probability, in terms of trade (if, that is, import prices remain stable or actually rise).

Prebisch's work was based upon statistics relating to the trade between Latin America and Great Britain during the late nineteenth century and, moreover, upon prices recorded at the British end of the trade relationship. Two basic problems arise here. First, the neglect of the falling transport costs which occurred during the late nineteenth century and which contri-buted noticeably to the apparent decline in the prices of the Latin American commodities that arrived at British ports of entry (an element which would, of course, have not been reflected in the receipts of exporters at their ports of ship-ment). The second difficulty is that Britain was, at this time, already becoming decreasingly competitive with her new industrial competitors in Europe and North America. British prices, therefore, were decreasingly representative of the general level of prices for Northern industrial goods.[40]

Similar difficulties of base date and unrepresentative statistics, or of ignored but salient complicating factors, affect most terms of trade arguments. What is rarely disputed, however, is that many LDCs do continue to face a serious problem of fluctuating revenues resulting from over-reliance upon the sales of commodities, the production of which is vulnerable to disruption or the market prices for which are liable to rapid and substantial fluctuation.[41] This problem of fluctuating commodity earnings is a matter of extreme seriousness for many LDCs and one on which such schemes as the Integrated Programme on Commodities offer merely a partial solution.

A 'multi-model' approach

An alternative to that of viewing the international political economy through the lenses of only one perspective is to investigate defined issues through the explicit use of more than one analytical approach. This is the procedure adopted by Robert Keohane and Joseph Nye in the influential *Power and Interdependence*,[42] the focus of which is the attempt to 'explain' basic changes in the governing arrangements—regimes —in given areas of activity—the issue areas—within the contemporary global political economy.

Despite the reservations that have been expressed about Keohane and Nye's usage of the concepts of regime and issue area,[43] their study serves some extremely useful purposes. By drawing out two pure models—the economic processes model (broadly neo-classical) and the overall power model (broadly corresponding to a 'realist' view of international relations)—they reveal how limited such perspectives are when trying to account for real world developments. More discriminating perspectives are called for, particularly the issue-area power model, which references the actual patterns of power and influence within any area of activity, and, on occasion, an international organizational model which may illuminate developments within a few arenas. The force of this is to encourage flexibility in the employment of analytical perspectives and modesty in the claims that are made for those that are adopted.

The second significance of Keohane and Nye's work for students of the international political economy is the emphasis that it gives to the role of 'power', by one definition or another. While there are many difficulties surrounding the definition and use of the concept of power, its consideration is likely to be central to any student of the international political economy who wishes to reconsider the established perspectives and evaluate their contribution, potential or actual, to realistic and effective analysis.

TOWARDS AN INTEGRATED INTERNATIONAL POLITICAL ECONOMY

In addition to the perspectives considered thus far, some of the bases for a more effective approach to the analysis of domestic, comparative and international political economy reside in the writings of a body of economists grouping under such titles as *institutionalists*, the *'Cambridge'* school, *post-Keynesians* and, even, *ultra-Keynesians*.[44] The international dimension of this burgeoning approach remains relatively underdeveloped, greater strength thus far existing in empirical investigation[45] rather than theoretical elaboration.

Institutionalists and post-Keynesians counter the neo-classicists/liberals by arguing that monopoly, oligopoly and generally uneven distributions of power and influence are prevalent within any modern economy. Such phenomena, and their many implications, cannot be treated as mere aberrations by a sound economic theory for they arise out of the basic workings of the economy itself.

This view can be extended into a general statement about the human condition: a statement which constitutes a basis for a genuinely *political economy*. Beyond the obvious advantages that power and influence impart, possession of these attributes can furnish protection against much that would otherwise prove troubling.

Most troubling in the modern world is the characteristic change and uncertainty: change that is often sharp and dramatic; and uncertainty that goes beyond mere alternatives bearing variable probabilities. Change in human affairs confronts the analyst with formidable problems of definition, identification and explanation.[46] The possibility of changes, both surprising and qualitatively significant, lies at the heart of the *profound* uncertainty[47] that confronts both analysts and real world actors. Indeed, the possibilities of such change, and the pre-valence of such uncertainties, are such as to evoke feelings of considerable insecurity in decision-makers and to render their decision-making tasks unmanageably complex. While some small measure of risk and novelty may be stimulating to most human beings, such chronic uncertainty is so disturbing and disruptive as to warrant strenuous efforts to secure its reduction, if not total elimination.

Uncertainty can be eliminated by acquiring the capacity to control the pertinent environment—natural or human: by developing power over man or nature. Such control, when over other human beings, may, however, be exerted in a number of ways and it is this variety that has engendered a measure of confusion, and even controversy, over the use of the term power.

In discussions of power some have identified it with the capabilities that might be employed in an attempt to exert influence over some other. Contrasting arguments have contended that power properly refers only to the resulting influence that is actually exerted by one party over another: the contrast between power seen as capability and power conceived of as a behavioural relationship.[48] An exclusive choice between these two usages need not, however, be made for the most illuminating view of power in human affairs employs both in an integrated approach.

Any consideration of developments over time both invites and calls for an analysis of the dynamic interaction between the distribution of pertinent strengths and capabilities between two or more actors and the patterns of influence actually established between those actors.[49] Indeed, the salience of any capabilities cannot be established without some reference to the issue with which the actors are concerned and in respect of which they seek to establish influence over one another. Furthermore, it is clear that capability distributions have some, though by no means a simple, relationship to the patterns of influence that actually develop between actors.

Capability distributions pose no particular intellectual difficulties, once the pertinent issues have been identified and the salience of various resources established. The behavioural power structure is, however, a slightly more complex analytical matter for patterns of influence do not appear in a vacuum nor do they simply reflect the distributions of pertinent capabilities.

The behavioural power structure, with its patterns of advantage and disadvantage, dominance and submission, or differing roles in critical decision-making, exists within a broader behavioural structure. The broader structure also includes, as central features, the modal tendencies[50] exhibited by all actors —the objectives commonly pursued and the forms of behaviour conventionally adopted in their pursuit.

Any discussion of behavioural power is further complicated by the question of intentionality.[51] It may be argued that the existence of power between two or more actors depends, critically, upon the intention of the wielder of such power to exert influence over the other(s). In contrast, many significant forms of power may be seen to exist in the clear absence of any such intention and, indeed, in the absence of any recognition by the 'powerful' that it holds any particular advantage.

A significant area of such unintended power is that of concession by actors who 'imagine' capabilities possessed, or threats made, by other actors. A further, and equally interesting, form of unintended power is that of the impersonal influence that some actors are able to exert in such spheres of interaction as markets for goods and services. Such structural strength or structural weight may provide its possessor with a considerable resource once it is acknowledged and exploited intentionally. Such phenomena are also of central importance to the analysis of the international political economy.

Wherever power is pertinent, the complex equation between capability and behavioural outcome turns, centrally, upon the perceptions of the involved actors. The submissive may, as aforementioned, imagine the capabilities of the powerful. In contrast, the possessor of structural weight may not recognize this asset and fail to exploit its full potential.

The views and responses of participants are also central to the dynamic quality of power relationships. Dissatisfaction with the existing power structure, or some of its consequences, may prompt efforts to acquire greater capabilities. Power tomorrow may thus be pursued as a response to adverse experiences of power today. Indeed, the vision of others' adverse experiences of power may encourage the wise to acquire the means to power on a precautionary basis. Such a dynamic form of power analysis, when introduced into the study of international political economy, contrasts clearly with the static vision provided by the liberal or neo-classical perspective upon economic matters.

Many, then, are the inducements for the acquisition of the capabilities upon which power might be based and for the exercise of power once conditions are suitable. Inequalities of power and influence do not, therefore, arise as anomalies but as natural responses to experiences of both other actors and the natural environment. There should be nothing surprising, therefore, in the discovery that firms frequently seek to increase their size and strength, eliminate their competitors, control sources of important supplies, exert influence over potential purchasers or, ultimately, dominate entire industries. Equally unsurprising would be the identification of efforts by workers to protect themselves by organization and the exercise of pressure upon their employers.

Nation states, too, will have experience of the power realities inherent in their international relationships, both political and economic. The effect of such experiences, in a world that remains an arena of self-help, will be to sustain a neo-mercantilist undercurrent in the thinking and policy dispositions of governments for much of the time: an undercurrent that will surface more clearly as greater international and economic difficulties are encountered. Even the most idealistic of internationally minded governments will feel compelled to place their own neo-mercantilist house in order before embarking upon altruistic ventures in the international community.

The perspective being developed in this section underlies an expectation of much that actually characterizes the contemporary international political economy. These characteristics can be grouped into two, albeit empirically related, models: the first of the politico-economic realities within, and amongst, the advanced capitalist societies; and, the second concerning the realities of economic relations between advanced capitalist states and the less developed countries.[52]

The economies of advanced capitalist societies are now largely dominated by huge companies and corporations. The power of such firms is considerable and allows them to determine many developments at their own behest and to their own advantage. Many innovations are controlled by such corporations, and investment largely provided from retained profits. Given the oligopolistic framework within which most such companies operate, they are able to determine their own pricing through tacit agreements and understanding with others. Indeed, conditions generally permit administered pricing for the products of such enterprises:[53] a process in which prices are determined by adding a chosen level of profits to the established costs of production rather than by accepting the price produced in a free market. Imbalances between supply and demand are dealt with, in a world of administered pricing, by adjusting the volume of production and sales rather than by altering prices substantially.

The partial counterbalancing of the corporations' power by strong trade unions has resulted in increased resistance to downward movements of prices.

Governments constitute the third side of the triangular structure of power in the modern capitalist economy. Political considerations, and economic imperatives, sometimes occasion attempts to moderate the influence of the large corporations or the trade unions. General political constraints, however, impel governments towards a number of responses to the prevailing politico-economic conditions. The desiderata of trade unions must be satisfied, in part at least, as the price of politico-economic harmony. The needs of large corporations must be met if they are to continue to contribute to the economic well-being of society. A range of services and facilities must be sustained if social harmony and economic viability are to be preserved.

Of particular pertinence are two pressures to which governments of advanced capitalist societies have felt particularly exposed. The first is that of unresolved, and fundamental, distributional issues within their societies. The need to modernize, coupled with the liquidity requirements of expanding economies, have, it is argued, fuelled inflationary tendencies and pressures.[54] The second pressure, that of the need to maintain a high level of employment while avoiding serious balance-of-payments difficulties, has motivated governmental pursuit of export-led growth throughout the advanced capitalist world[55]—a clear encouragement towards neo-mercantilism, however disguised or vigorously denied.[56]

The paradox of government in advanced capitalist society is that it is constantly pushed into an attempt to resolve distributional issues in a way that is ultimately inflationary and into an effort to secure export-led growth that, by being neo-mercantilist, inevitably induces 'zero-sum' competition with other advanced capitalist societies.

Paradox is also, however, inherent in the relations between advanced capitalist societies and the less developed countries. A basic asymmetry afflicts this pattern of relationships with the administered price goods of the North being exchanged with the South's goods, with their demand-determined prices[57] (as was discussed in the earlier consideration of the structuralist perspective). The cruel paradox from the South's point of view, here, is that when economic buoyancy in the North does stimulate an increase in the prices of basic commodities, the North's 'reluctance' to share its gains with the South manifests itself in the form of higher prices for Northern exports. The South, therefore, is rarely a beneficiary from world economic growth except in the short term, for not only does Northern inflation cancel out the gains from increased commodity prices but, ultimately, encourages Northern governments to adopt counter-inflationary, and recession inducing, policies which eventually dampen demand for, and hence the prices of, the South's primary commodity exports.

A major contrast between the intra-advanced capitalist country model and the North–South scenario is revealed by the role and position of the multi- or transnational corporation. This analysis also reveals the MNCs as major wielders of power within the global economy: indeed, to be a phenomenon that cannot properly be understood without reference to a discriminating power analysis.[58]

Multinational corporations derive considerable potential power from their size and wealth. Even more significant capabilities are, however, furnished by their transnational mode of operation. While they are not automatically translated into attempts to create power, these capabilities are numerous and allow MNCs to play national governments off against one another on such issues as taxation and general operational conditions. MNCs are, here, particularly advantaged by their ability to determine substantial patterns of investment and to undertake extensive exploration for natural resources and development of various facilities. The pricing of components for shipment across national frontiers, but between subsidiaries of the same firm—transfer pricing—also gives the MNC an invaluable ability to avoid taxes, evade exchange controls and other currency restrictions, and to shift investments or otherwise syphon funds across frontiers.

The advances that MNCs obtain from their transnational mode of operation illustrate a basic paradox of the current situation. It is the very concern of governments to preserve national autonomy that runs counter to efforts to secure international collaboration on effective regulation of MNCs. The absence of effective international control then gives MNCs that freedom of manoeuvre that allows them to evade national regulation and, thereby, reduce the effective sovereignty of nation states.

Internally, MNCs also illustrate the prevalence of power and allied phenomena for they are, in effect, massive bureaucracies. Decision-making and the pursuit of internal promotion constitute 'games' of bureaucratic politics in which individuals and groups manoeuvre for position and influence.[59] Power, in many senses, plays a far more central role in such bureaucratic politics and bureaucratic decision-making than does the rational analysis so beloved of liberal economists.

While the power of MNCs is considerable, most advanced industrial countries are sufficiently strong to offer effective resistance, once their governments are so determined. Such countries are usually able to dispense with the services of any MNC or group of MNCs, as alternative sources of production or technical capacity will be available locally. Investment can also be generated locally. Moreover, the advanced industrial country is likely to constitute a vital market for the MNC, from which it could be excluded by a determined government. Indeed, it is this latter capacity that has given the governments of Eastern Bloc countries the ability to strike advantageous deals with Western MNCs, despite their lack of many of the other advantages available to Western governments.

The potentialities of government-MNC relations in the advanced industrial countries are not, however, generally realized for the Western governments are ideologically constrained from exploiting many of their opportunities for pressure and control. This well illustrates the general point that the possession of capabilities in no way ensures a corresponding pattern of power relationships.

The less developed country is generally lacking in most of the capabilities available to advanced industrial countries. In vital need of investment and technical competence, the LDC is often vulnerable to adverse agreements with incoming MNCs. Only when the MNC has accumulated costly investments with the LDC can its government seek to modify the relationship in a more advantageous direction. However, the LDC's government takes this course only at its peril, risking international pressure—economic or financial—or even political destabiliza-tion.[60]

It is of more than passing interest that the MNCs are also highly involved in the pattern of technological superiority-inferiority that so characterizes, and helps to sustain, the asymmetrical structure of North–South relations. The Northern MNCs are heavily involved in the research and development that contributes much of the innovation within the advanced industrial countries. Once introduced, such innovations are often retained by the MNCs through patents and other, less formal, measures of protection.

CONCLUSIONS

The picture of the international political economy that emerges is one in which power is central and deemed to be empirically ubiquitous. The distribution of capabilities, and the resultant power structures, is such as to establish an empirical world far removed from the vision of the liberal and neo-classical economists. Where markets exist they do so only because of a favourable disposition of power. The manner in which markets operate further reflects the prevailing distribution of power. Genuinely free and competitive markets, with mobile prices, certainly exist but by no means constitute the norm within the contemporary political economy—domestic or international. Indeed, where competitive markets do exist, as they do for some primary commodities, they often create considerable difficulties for at least some of the major participants.

The global political economy thus envisaged is a *political economy* in two central respects. First, power is manifest in most of its central features and the exercise of that power is beset by all the indeterminacies of general power politics —unpredictable calculations of potential advantage, uncertain choices, efforts at image manipulation and the posing of threats.

The second intrinsically political feature of the contemporary international political economy derives from the extensive opportunities that exist for linkages across, and transfers of capabilities between, issues and contexts. Outcomes in one area can be linked to, or made conditional upon, outcomes elsewhere: a decision on military procurements from another country, for instance, being made conditional upon some new trade concession from that country. Moreover, a capability, such as the ability to withold a vital resource like oil, can be employed in the pursuit of an essentially political objective, such as international acceptance of the Palestinian cause in the Middle Eastern conflict. The possibilities of such linkage are endless in a world of such complexity as today's and render international relationships intrinsically a matter of political economy.

In establishing the bases of a more fruitful approach to the analysis of the global political economy a number of points will have become apparent. The perspective lacks much of the deductive rigour and theoretical elaboration of the liberal or neo-classical approach. While this might seem to be a shortcoming of the approach it might be viewed as a virtue given the complexities and inherent indeterminacies of a changing, and often turbulent, world.

The approach does not deny market processes but, rather, locates them within a broader structural analysis which identifies their role and significance rather more effectively than does the liberal perspective. While the approach accepts insights into market processes, contributed by liberal theory, it is much informed by, indeed often converges with, features of both the structuralist and the Marxist perspectives.

Finally, the perspective leads to an expectation of strong neo-mercantilist dispositions within governments in the contemporary world. This expectation is based upon an acknowledgement of the powerful imperatives inherent both within the international system and domestic political, and economic, systems. A form of economic internationalism may still offer the path to a golden future but naïve idealists or obdurate liberals, who contend that such can materialize without profound prior changes, do such aspirations no real service. Real progress towards a sane global political economy must rest upon a firm grasp of prevailing realities allied to an unremitting determination to deploy such knowledge and understanding in the pursuit of necessary change.

NOTES AND REFERENCES

1. R. O. Keohane and J. S. Nye, *Power and Interdependence: World Politics in Transition* (Boston, Little, Brown, 1977).
2. See especially Bruce M. Russett, *Economic Theories of International Politics* (Chicago, Markham, 1968).

3. Robert Gilpin, *U.S. Power and the Multinational Corporation: The Political Economy of Foreign Direct Investment* (London, Macmillan, 1976).
4. For a more technical account see my textbook on basic economic theory or international economics, for example, C. P. Kindleberger, *International Economics*, 5th ed. (Homewood, Illinois, Irwin, 1973).
5. For another outline of the principle of comparative advantage see: R. J. Barry Jones, 'International political economy: perspectives and prospects—Part II', *Review of International Studies*, 8 (1982), esp. pp. 40-3.
6. See the arguments of E. H. Phelps Brown, 'The underdevelopment of economics', *Economic Journal*, 82 (1972), 1-10, esp. pp. 3-5.
7. C. P. Kindleberger, *Power and Money: The Politics of International Economics and the Economics of International Politics* (London, Macmillan, 1970), p. 19.
8. Fred Hirsch, *Social Limits to Growth* (London, Routledge & Kegan Paul, 1977), esp. Chs. 3, 4, 5 and 6.
9. See in particular: Mancur Olson Jr., *The Logic of Collective Action: Public Goods and the Theory of Groups* (Cambridge, Cambridge University Press, 1965); N. Frohlich and J. A. Oppenheimer, 'I get by with a little help from my friends', *World Politics*, 20 (1970), 104-20; N. Frohlich, J. A. Oppenheimer and O. R. Young, *Political Leadership and Collective Goods* (Princeton, Princeton University Press, 1971); and N. Frohlich and J. A. Oppenheimer, *Modern Political Economy* (Englewood Cliffs, Prentice-Hall, 1978).
10. Despite a somewhat desperate and confused attempt to wish the problem away by Richard Kimber, 'Collective action and the fallacy of the liberal fallacy', *World Politics*, 33 (1981), 178-96.
11. See A. S. Eichner, ed., *A Guide to Post-Keynesian Economics* (London, Macmillan, 1979); W. J. Samuels, ed., *The Economy as a System of Power,* Vols. I and II (New Brunswick, Transaction Books, 1979); and R. Tooze, 'Economics, international political economy and change in the international system', in Barry Buzan and R. J. Barry Jones, eds, *Change and the Study of International Relations: The Evaded Dimension* (London, Frances Pinter, 1981).
12. For introductions to basic Marxism see: D. McLellan, *Marx* (London, Fontana Books, 1975); R. Milliband, *The State in Capitalist Society: The Analysis of the Western System of Power* (London, Weidenfeld & Nicholson, 1969); A. Bose, *Marxian and Post-Marxian Political Economy* (Harmondsworth, Penguin Books, 1975); M. C. Howard and J. E. King, *The Political Economy of Marx* (Burnt Mill, Longman, 1975); and M. Barratt Brown, *The Economics of Imperialism* (Harmondsworth, Penguin Books, 1975).
13. See, in particular, Howard and King, *The Political Economy of Marx*, op. cit., esp. pp. 203-10.

14. V. I. Lenin, *Imperialism: The Highest Stage of Capitalism* (1916), various editions, including *Collected Works, Vol. 22* (Moscow, Progress Publishers). See also, V. G. Kiernan, *Marxism and Imperialism* (London, Edward Arnold, 1974).
15. See Barratt Brown, op. cit.
16. Lenin, op. cit.
17. See Jack Woodis, *Introduction to Neo-Colonialism* (London, Lawrence & Wishart, 1967); S. Amin, *Neo-Colonialism in West Africa*, trans. F. McDonagh (London, Penguin Books, 1973) and, Barratt Brown, op. cit., esp. Ch. 11.
18. On 'informal empire' see H. Magdoff, 'Imperialism without colonies', pp. 144–70 in R. Owen and Bob Sutcliffe, eds, *Studies in the Theory of Imperialism* (London, Longman, 1972).
19. See, especially, Immanuel Wallerstein, ed., *World Inequality* (Montreal, Black Rose Books, 1973); S. Amin, *Accumulation on a World Scale*, 2 vols, trans. B. Pearce (Hassocks, Harvester Press, 1974); Andre Gunder Frank, *On Capitalist Underdevelopment* (Bombay, Oxford University Press, 1975); and Andre Gunder Frank, *Dependent Accumulation and Under-Development* (London, Macmillan, 1978).
20. On such 'realism' see John Maclean, 'Marxist epistemology, explanations of "change" and the study of international relations', pp. 46–67 in Buzan and Jones, op. cit.; and Karl Marx, *Grundrisse*, trans. M. Nicolaus (Harmondsworth, Penguin Books, 1973).
21. See F. G. Castles, *Politics and Social Insight* (London, Routledge & Kegan Paul, 1971).
22. See part 3 of D. K. Fieldhouse, ed., *The Theory of Capitalist Imperialism* (London, Longman, 1967).
23. See W. Arthur Lewis, 'Evolution of the international economic order', *Economic Impact*, 31 (1980), 37–43 (reprinted from his *Evolution of the International Economic Order* (Princeton, Princeton University Press, 1978).
24. See, in particular, J. H. Dunning, ed., *The Multinational Corporation* (London, Allen & Unwin, 1972).
25. See Andrew Gamble's contribution to this volume.
26. See Ian Steedman *et al.*, *The Value Controversy* (London, Verso, 1981).
27. See J. Holloway and Sol Picciotto, eds, *State and Capital: A Marxist Debate* (London, Edward Arnold, 1978).
28. See Robin Murray, *Multinational Companies and Nation States* (London, Spokesman Books, 1975).
29. See, for a broad outline, D. H. Blake and R. S. Walters, *The Politics of Global Economic Relations* (Englewood Cliffs, Prentice-Hall, 1976); E. K. Hunt, *Property and Prophets: The Evolution of Economic Institutions and Ideologies* (New York, Harper & Row, 1981); Eric Roll, *A History of Economic Thought* (London, Faber & Faber,

1973), esp. Ch. II; and P. T. Ellsworth, *The International Economy* (New York, Collier Macmillan, 3rd ed., 1964), esp. Ch. 2.

30. Hans J. Morgenthau, *Politics Among Nations: The Struggle for Power and Peace* (New York, Alfred Knopf, numerous editions).

31. Adam Smith, *The Wealth of Nations* (1776).

32. See especially, W. E. Minchinson's introduction to W. E. Minchinson, ed., *Mercantilism: System or Expediency* (Lexington, D. C. Heath, 1969); and D. C. Coleman, ed., *Revision in Mercantilism* (London, Methuen, 1969).

33. See E. F. Heckscher, *Mercantilism*, Vol. 2, trans. M. Shapiro (London, George Allen & Unwin, 1935).

34. On neo-mercantilism see Joan Robinson, 'The new mercantilism', in Joan Robinson, *Contributions to Modern Economics* (Oxford, Basil Blackwell, 1978), Ch. 18; H. G. Johnson, ed., *The New Mercantilism: Some Problems in International Trade, Money and Investment* (Oxford, Basil Blackwell, 1974); and, D. P. Calleo and B. J. Rowland, *America and the World Political Economy: Atlantic Dreams and National Realities* (Bloomington, Indiana University Press, 1973).

35. R. Dan Walleri, 'The political economy literature on North–South relations: alternative approaches and empirical evidence', *International Studies Quarterly*, 22 (1978), 587–624.

36. Ibid., esp. pp. 599–604.

37. Blake and Walters, op. cit., esp. pp. 31–6.

38. J. E. Spero, *The Politics of International Economic Relations* (London, George Allen & Unwin, 1977), esp. pp. 124–9.

39. The 'Brandt Report', *North–South: A Programme for Survival* (London, Pan Books, 1980).

40. See John P. Powelson, 'The LDCs and the terms of trade', *Economic Impact*, 22 (1978), 33–7.

41. See Michael Michaely, *Concentration in International Trade* (Amsterdam, North Holland Publishing Co., 1962).

42. Keohane and Nye, op. cit.

43. See in particular Susan Strange, review in *International Affairs*, 51 (1977), 270–3.

44. See Eichner, op. cit.; Samuels, op. cit.; Robinson, op. cit.; and John Knapp, 'Economics or Political Economy', *Lloyds Bank Review* (January, 1973), 19–43.

45. See, particularly, R. E. Mueller and R. J. Barnet, *Global Reach: The Power of the Multinational Corporation*, New York (Simon & Schuster, 1974).

46. See Buzan and Jones, op. cit.

47. An uncertainty that reflects, but goes beyond, its treatment by Shackle; see G. L. S. Shackle, *Uncertainty in Economics and other Reflections* (Cambridge, Cambridge University Press, 1955).

48. See Klaus Knorr's distinction between putative power and actualized

power in K. Knorr, *Power and Wealth: The Political Economy of International Power* (London, Macmillan, 1973), esp. Ch. 1. On related issues see D. Wrong, *Power: Its Forms, Bases and Uses* (Oxford, Basil Blackwell, 1979), esp. Ch. 1.

49. See the structural analysis suggested in R. J. Barry Jones, 'Concepts and models of change in international relations', in Buzan and Jones, op. cit., pp. 15-16.

50. On such a use of the notion of modal tendencies see R. O. Keohane, 'The study of transnational relations reconsidered', paper given to the annual conference of the British International Studies Association, Warwick University, 16 December, 1976.

51. See Wrong, op. cit., pp. 3-5, 68-9, and 251-4.

52. See J. B. Burbridge, 'The international dimension', in Eichner, op. cit., pp. 139-50.

53. See Eichner, op. cit.; and C. G. Means, 'The problems and prospects of contemporary capitalism', in Samuels, op. cit., Vol. 1, pp. 124-37.

54. Joan Robinson, 'The second crisis of economic theory', pp. 1-13 in Robinson, op. cit.; P. Kenyon, 'Pricing', pp. 34-45 in Eichner, op. cit.

55. Joan Robinson, 'The need for a reconsideration of the theory of international trade', pp. 212-22 in Robinson, op. cit., esp. p. 219.

56. Joan Robinson, 'The new mercantilism', op. cit.

57. Burbridge, op. cit., esp. pp. 144-6.

58. Samuels, op. cit., Vol. II, Part 5.

59. See H. A. Simon, *Administrative Behavior: A Study of Decision-Making Processes in Administrative Organization* (New York, Free Press, 2nd ed., 1957); and G. T. Allison, *Essence of Decision: Explaining the Cuban Missile Crisis* (Boston, Little, Brown, 1971).

60. For example, recent IMF pressure on M. Manley's Jamaican government after the pressure it exerted on international bauxite mining companies. Also Allende's Chile and the role of ITT in its destabilization. See A. Sampson, *The Sovereign State: The Secret History of ITT* (London, Hodder & Stoughton, 1973).

8 Structures, Values and Risk in the Study of the International Political Economy

SUSAN STRANGE

INTRODUCTION

I have three suggestions to make for the consideration of scholars who are interested, as I am, in ways of looking at world politics which comprehend both the traditional issues of war and peace familiar in the study of international relations and the new-old issues of political economy that now arise globally rather than—or as well as—locally and nationally. I make them in the hope that they might be of interest and possibly of use to men and women of all political persuasions and predilections, whether realist and traditional or radical and neo-Marxist. I do not claim that any of these three ideas are wholly novel. Indeed, two of them in some form or other have already gained fairly wide acceptance and are the subject of ongoing debates. They concern first, the notion of structures and second, the place of values in the study of international political economy. On both these I therefore propose to be fairly brief. The third concerns the concept of risk as a unifying and also an indispensable component in any realistic approach to the subject. Though familiar enough in other contexts, the idea of risk in the context of world politics is comparatively novel and perhaps therefore deserves somewhat lengthier examination. However, since my ideas about risk relate somewhat to what I have to say about structures and values I shall deal with these first, and come to the concept of risk afterwards.

VALUES

The belief that we should firmly and unequivocally bring values back into the analysis of international political economy is now shared by many scholars in the field. But I would quickly add that I do not, personally, feel that it follows from this belief that international political economists necessarily have a responsibility to preach moralistic sermons or even to advise people (or governments) as to what is the best or ideal solution to any problem, or what is the desirable policy measure in any situation. Rather, I think that a consideration or awareness of values is mainly necessary to avoid the snare of ideology, and to this end, to make one's students and colleagues articulate, to themselves and others, *why* they prefer one kind of arrangement for managing the world economy to another. The main aim, in my opinion, is to make the study of international political economy value-sensitive, not to make it value-laden.

Of course there will always be those who want (or feel they ought) to come up at the end of their analytical work with moral exhortations or with more specific normative prescriptions; and they are perfectly free to do so whether it is more order, more justice, more free trade and efficiency or just more brotherly love that they value and advocate. But there are also those like myself who do not always (or even very often) feel any such compulsion but are mostly motivated by unsatisfied curiosity about the endless whys of the international system. We also need to develop greater sensitivity to hidden or unstated value-preferences in that system. For if and when we do develop that sensitivity, we will find it easier to set out clearly the outcomes—the who-gets-what—of existing arrangements and the policy options—the who-can-do-what—in any given situation in such a way as to clarify which arrangement or which policy is likely to be biased for or against one or more of the fundamental values that are sought through any economic or political organization of society and what allocations of values among stages, groups or individuals follows from such arrangements.

But what are these fundamental values and how do they relate to each other? The basic point here is that the separation of economics and politics in this century has brought about a totally unreal separation in the discussion of these values. Political scientists and theorists have talked and written about freedom, order, and justice; economists have talked about efficiency in the creation and distribution of wealth and welfare. The two only rarely came together. It is as if we have been looking at a picture composed of red lines superimposed on green ones. But without the 3D spectacles of political economy neither can be related to the other and we cannot see the complete three-dimensional picture. In the international political economy we need to look for the provision of each of the four fundamental social values—to wit, the provision of wealth and material needs, the provision of security and order in human life and relations, the provision of justice, and the provision of liberty or freedom of choice. Who gets how much of each of these values and by what means are the basic questions, the starting point of all else. And we can interpret 'who' as referring not only to states or to nations but equally to classes or to more specific social and economic groups—agricultural producers, bankers, state employees, academics, students, pensioners and unborn children—or indeed to individuals.

Commonsense—not to mention a great deal of classical writing about politics—tells us that there is a continuous and inescapable trade-off between the four basic values. Or to put it another way, we may say that in order to have more of any one of them, you may have to sacrifice something of one or more of the others. For instance, it must be obvious that in order to have the most efficient system for creating wealth (whether capitalist and market-oriented or socialist and authority-directed) there is a price to be paid *either* in the equality with which the proceeds are allocated *or* in the freedom of choice of producers or consumers, or perhaps of both.

Similarly, the most orderly, stable and secure system is unlikely also be one in which the greatest liberty is accorded to the individual or to discontented groups in society. And so on; it is hardly necessary to labour the point that political arrangements regarding the system of production, exchange and distribution, regarding the maintenance of order and security in society, and the administration of justice between competing claims and regarding the balance between the interests of the community and those of groups or individuals within it—between the free choice of the state and the free choice of the citizen—all reflect a certain trade-off or preference between the pursuit of basic values for the society as a whole and in the allocation of those values within the society. That is the stuff of politics and of political economy.

In the international system of our times, we can observe a similar trade-off of values, though it is even more evident than in national societies that those who pay the price in loss of one value seldom reap the benefit in another. For example, greater wealth created by accelerated integration of national economies in a world market system has entailed certain restrictions on the freedom of choice available to developing countries, and a certain loss of stability in the world economy and financial system. The non-aligned countries have exercised their freedom of choice to opt out of the respective alliances of the superpowers but have sometimes paid a price in greater insecurity and local conflict. Everything, as the saying goes, has its price.

What is also abundantly clear, I believe, is that the perennial argument about the 'optional' trade-off between values is never conclusive and cannot ever, by its very nature be so. For the choices are subjective. Each individual must decide for himself or herself; and those at the top in any society will seldom agree with those at the bottom of the heap about the most desirable goals, in terms of values, of public policy and social and economic arrangements. Moreover, even the possibility of reaching agreement as a result of logical, rational argument among those who regard themselves as impartial bystanders is an illusion. Argument and reason are not going to settle differences of view. For each of us carries from his or her birth—or rather perhaps from the moment of conception and the fusion of genes—a temperamental predisposition in favour of certain values and a corresponding personal antipathy to certain of their opposites. Culture, education and personal experience may cause us to suppress or to modify—even, very occasionally, to change—our innate predispositions or antipathies. But in my experience argument seldom does. It follows that academics delude themselves when they believe that it is the binding clarity of their rational arguments that influences others and makes disciples of their students. If the one appears to follow the other, it is more likely because in reacting to commonly experienced events, the biases and prejudices of their followers coincide with their own and therefore their chosen proposals or conclusions strike a responsive chord in their readers or listeners. Timing and skill in presentation will help to gain a hearing—but only if the listeners are already predisposed by temperament and perhaps recent experience to listen to the message.

Thus, the main purpose—I repeat—of insisting on the reintroduction of all the fundamental values into discussions of issues of international public policy is not to make converts on moral grounds so much as to illuminate debate by making the protagonists uncover the value-judgements and value-preferences that underlie their reasoning—or at least, if they are not willing to do so, to make sure that someone does it for them.

STRUCTURES

The second set of comments, on the notion of structures, is related to the foregoing stress on analysis in terms of values. It has been customary in the literature of international relations to observe the outcome of events in the international system in terms of the reallocation of values brought about by political and economic change as between states. For example, we are told that World War II increased the security of the Soviet Union, that it added to the wealth of the United States while detracting from that of Britain, that it restored freedom to the countries of Western Europe, and so on. Similarly, we observe that the OPEC price rise of 1973 increased the perceived economic insecurity (in terms of energy supplies) of the United States, while increasing the wealth of the OPEC governments and decreasing that of many oil-importing developing countries. Take any event—the fall of the Shah, the Falklands war, the Polish unrest—and we find that it is analysed in terms of the changes brought about in the allocation of values between states.

But what we are now beginning to do, often without consciously thinking about it—is to think about the outcome of events or of developing trends in terms of the values gained or lost not for individual states but for other groups and for the system as a whole in each of its major structures. For only if we adopt this world system perspective shall we find it natural to relate the values lost in one structure to those gained in another, or to see how changes in structures are likely to affect the allocation of values among social groups within states as well as between states. Only by this means can politics be truly synthesized with economics.

For it seems to me that those engaged in the study of international relations are becoming increasingly divided between those, on the one side, whom I would call the 'Maginot Liners', who adopt a rigidly defensive posture towards 'their' subject, saying in effect to all would-be intruders *'On ne passera pas!'* and those, on the other side, who defend it offensively by carrying with them into the 'foreign' territories of other

disciplines the insights they have gained in studying international relations in order to throw new or additional light on
such fields as international economics or domestic politics and
sociology. My guess is that the 'Maginot Liners' will sooner or
later be over-run while the synthesizers will, by trial and error,
eventually find ways of reuniting their work with that of other
social sciences, as they address problems and issues that have
become global and are no longer either national or simply
inter-national.

The 'Maginot Liners' will see little point in what I have to
say here about structures, but I hope it may make sense to some
of the would-be synthesizers—the development economists,
international historians, students of transnational relations,
environmentalists and those individuals from all disciplines who
are concerned with world problems.

A necessary first step is to clarify what is meant by 'structures'. The dictionary definition says 'a supporting framework'
and that suggests the idea that a structure is something *within
which* things happen and changes take place without affecting
the structure itself. It is a framework within which participating
organs or units function and relate to one another. Thus the
international political system can be designated as a structure—
as Bruce Miller calls it, a 'world of states'—which has developed
certain customs and institutions that favour the state as a
political organism over all other kinds of political organization
and thus make inter-state relations a source of much significant
change within the structure.

Those who have written about transnational relations and
so-called 'interdependence' are familiar with the idea that
within the structure of the international economy, decisions
taken by one political authority sometimes unwittingly affect
outcomes in the domain of another political authority, or
restrict the choices open to other political authorities without
necessarily intending to do so. Some examples would be
decisions taken by states about the price of oil, the taxation of
corporations, the deregulation of banks or the adoption of one
technology for nuclear power production over another.

What the notion of structure is adding is the suggestion that
there is a certain rough predictability about the behaviour of
decision-makers within a certain structure. In the world of
states, the decision-makers will seek to build alliances, negotiate

agreements, emphasize their national identity and jealously defend their right to autonomy. In a market economy, which is another kind of structure, buyers will seek the lowest price for goods or services of the same quality or rarity and sellers will seek the highest price. The whole of liberal economics takes this 'supporting framework' for granted and seeks to discover the laws of behaviour within it. The predictability that is looked for in any structure concerns first the kind of decision — for example, to buy or to sell, to fight or to give in, to be neutral or to seek allies. Secondly, we look in any structure for the likely source of decisions. Who decides, or as international relations parlance has it, who are the actors, and how are foreign policy decisions taken? Thirdly, we look for patterns of cause and effect, for the consequences of the kinds of decisions taken within the supporting framework of the structure, by the kinds of decision-makers given the power to take decisions in that structure and with the probable (or possible) consequences that experience has shown may or might follow from such decisions. As the historians (if they are any good) are well aware, the consequences to be looked for are of three kinds. There are the benefits, both material and in intangible values. There are the costs, including material costs as well as the sacrifice of intangible values; and thirdly and fourthly—the point to which I shall return in the latter part of this chapter—there are the risks run and the opportunities acquired. For the accelerating pace of change in the modern world has undoubtedly alerted us—or should have done—to the advent of many new and sometimes unsuspected risks, some of which may outweigh in our considered perception the benefits and opportunities that accompany them. And there are also new opportunities opened up—by technological advance, for instance, which may outweigh the costs, material or intangible, that accompany them.

At this point, readers may well object that with this use of the word 'structure' the meaning is really no different from that of 'system' in much of the international relations literature. And up to a point the objection is a valid one. But words have shifting nuances according to how they are used and by whom. Moreover, different people 'hear' or feel the nuances of particular words differently, as people hear sounds, see colours or react to weather in different ways. For my part, I 'hear' certain significant differences between a 'system' and a 'structure'. To my ears, a system implies an element of determinism— 'It's the system, comrade!'—whereas a structure can be used for very different purposes and to quite different ends. 'Structure', too, sounds organic and unplanned, whereas a system carries the implication of being designed or planned to some pre-selected end. A structure is organic also in the sense that it is subject to change, to growth and decay, to development and atrophy, whereas the notion of system suggests predictability and is somehow far more static. And finally, a system as it has been used in economics, politics and to some extent in sociology too, carries the implication of being composed of equal or at least comparable units, whether they are citizens, classes, political parties, buyers, monopolists, workers or states. Whereas 'structure' has no such implication and suggests a more vertical, three-dimensional framework within which the units (girders, bones, muscles, connecting joints) may be of very different size and importance and play not the same but quite opposite roles in the functioning of the whole.

Having said what it is we understand by the term 'structure' and what we look for in observing them, the point I want to make is that we should now begin to build on the fundamental point of Marxist structuralism by adding three new—or, at least, hitherto neglected—structures to the structures of production and exchange recognized by Marxist and most neo-Marxist writers.

Their main point in laying stress on the structure of production and exchange is, of course, that political problems and issues must be analysed within this determining structure because the relations between labour and management, or between buyer and seller, can only be understood in the context of the way in which factors of production are brought together for production or in which a market system operates between buyer and seller. It is no less true, I believe, that the relations between participants in the international political economy (states, corporations, non-state political organizations, international institutions, etc.) can only be understood in the context of certain other structures which by their nature exert a generalized influence on behaviour and on relations— including inter-state relations and relations of states with non-state actors.

The first of these added structures is the structure of world credit and money. I would not call it the international monetary system because that is usually taken to mean the rules or customs governing the relations between national currencies; whereas what I have in mind is something rather different, which is the structure within which the big international banks operate and which determines how much credit is created and who gets access to it on what terms. In the dominant world market economy, this highly dynamic and fast-changing monetary structure is the creation partly of market forces and partly of state policies. But whatever form it has taken, it does not deal equally with all and therefore must be regarded as a 'supporting framework' of other government and corporate policy decision-making.[1]

The second is the knowledge structure. This like the monetary structure is now globally integrated where once it was much more fragmented by the barriers of ignorance, language and non-communication which kept people in one country from knowing what went on elsewhere in the world, just as until comparatively recently the conditions governing access to credit were national and local rather than global in character. The knowledge structure is the framework which determines broadly what kind of knowledge is pursued and accumulated and the means by which it is communicated, flowing easily in some directions and with difficulty in others. More simply, it consists of what gets to be known (or believed to be known) and understood, and how and to whom that knowledge is communicated.[2] Current discussions over the transfer of technology by multinational corporations to their hosts in developing countries, or over the pattern of trans-border data flows using computers, satellites and electronics—what the French call *informatiques*—testifies to the acknowledged importance of knowledge as a source both of power (which it always has been) and of wealth.

Thirdly, because it is politically important and sensitive, I would add the structure of welfare. By this I mean the measures taken by all kinds of social organization from the family to the United Nations to provide people with basic values that they would not otherwise have and cannot get by their individual efforts. This includes the making of rules to safeguard people from disease, poverty, violence, hunger and so forth, and the transfer of resources for the same purposes. This structure differs from the other two inasmuch as it is *not* for the most part integrated globally. There is a great deal of talk about a world community and of international provision for basic human needs, but when it comes down to brass tacks, the real welfare systems remain bounded by the frontiers of the nation state, whether one is talking about protective rules or about the transfer of resources through political decisions and organizations. It is the state which, by its provision of security from violence and of some measure of economic security, is the mainstay of the whole structure. And the undeniable fact that there is so large a gap between the welfare provided by rich states and that provided by poor ones itself creates a 'supporting framework' within which international issues are perceived and discussed. Think, for instance, of the arguments about the claims of landlocked developing countries to a 'fair' share of the riches of the seabed as part of the common heritage of mankind. The structure of welfare thus consists of those politically determined arrangements which decide how, and for whom, the main threats to human life and contentment are avoided, averted or compensated.

In addition and alongside these three additional structures, we cannot omit or overlook the new-old structure of security, commonly known in international relations shorthand as the international political system. This is the structure on which, in a sense, all else depends, since all social and economic achievement requires the limitation of violence. A political structure which gives prime authority and legitimacy—the claim to absolute sovereignty is an acknowledged exaggeration—to the governments of each of 150 assorted territorial states inevitably adds an extra special risk of conflict or non-cooperation between those states to the arrangements made within all the other structures. If I have least to say about this new-old structure here it is only for reasons of space and because it would be otiose to remind students of international relations of the importance of issues settled (rather than solved) by the global security structure.

In all this discussion of structures what perhaps needs to be stressed is that each of the structures interacts with the others, so that no analysis of international political economy is complete that ignores any one of these basic structures. The

Marxists, for example, rightly stress the connections between the security structure and the structure of production. They stress that the primacy of the state in the security structure is a necessary aspect of the production structure. In a capitalist society, the market can only function effectively if the state can be used to keep the class struggle from breaking out in violence and if the state provides the other necessary public goods—like a system to administer laws, education, defence and some infrastructure of transport and communications. It is also an important fact often forgotten by development economists that the evolution of production structures has been much affected by the involvement of the state in wars or in the risk of wars, leading to the development of defence industries and the provision (as in India, for example) of rail and road communications.[3]

Similarly, it must not be forgotten that the monetary and credit structure as I have described it reacts strongly to changes —peace, war, revolution—in the security structure, or that the knowledge structure is apt to reflect changes taking place in the production structure—so that Japan, once a voracious consumer of Western knowledge, has become as a result of its successful performance in the production structure an important producer of new knowledge.[4] Or, to take just one more example of the interaction of structures, we have noted that the global welfare structure reflects the primacy of the state which is supported and maintained by the security structure (= international political system) inasmuch as welfare benefits are mainly provided by states to their own nationals, while their capacity to make this provision depends in rather large part on their place in the hierarchy of the production structure, i.e. their GNP and stage of economic development. Thus, one cannot take the issue of global unemployment, say, without reference to both the production structure which creates surplus productive capacity and makes workers redundant, and the security structure which defines the role and responsibility of states—or indeed the welfare structure which in part reflects both. But at this point we can put off no longer a more serious consideration of the question of the nature, incidence and management of risk, which is the subject of the third proposition I wish to put forward.

RISK

The proposition, at its simplest, is that no analysis of international political economy, whether of the world system as
a whole or of particular issues or aspects of it, can be complete that does not ask some basic questions about perceptions of the risk, sources of risk, incidence of risk and the
mitigation, allocation and management of risk. Moreover,
risk is not only an indispensable concept for any student of
international political economy who seeks understanding that
is value-sensitive but not value-laden or biased, it is also a
concept which is essentially unifying when it comes to looking
at political and economic issues and outcomes.

The basic questions concern, first, the nature of risk—what
risks are perceived to individuals, to political entities such as
states or alliances of states or to the system as a whole. Second,
the incidence of risk—how it has changed over time for the
system as a whole or how the incidence has shifted within the
state or within the world system between countries or between
classes or sectoral groups. Third, the source or origin of risk:
more particularly, does it arise from the functioning of market
forces, from change, or from decisions taken by political
authority, and especially by states. For the latter can both
create risk directly and indirectly by their own actions, by
assigning liability. (Product liability is already a major hazard
for manufacturers in America and is becoming so in Europe.)
Fourth, and complementary to the third question, how have
markets or states not only created risks but how have they
acted to mitigate them or to convert a risk into a cost—in
the way, for instance, that national laws convert the risk of
damage to property in the shape of a car into a cost in the
mandatory charge for car insurance.

The trouble that most people encounter when such a proposition is put to them is that the whole concept of risk is
too closely associated in their minds with the study of business
management and insurance, so that they are unused to thinking about risk in terms of a range of values that do not simply
concern profit and loss. One recent exception to this is a book
by Richard B. Bilder on risk and international agreement,[5] in
which the author applies the concept of risk to the analysis
of bargaining between states involved in negotiations and

illustrates his thesis with examples taken from recent international history. Indeed, a moment's thought will show that risk is about the obverse of the opportunity to attain all the values sought by individuals and by society through political and economic organization. The risk of poverty is the converse of the opportunity to acquire wealth. Disorder and uncertainty of all kinds are the converse of security; coercion and tyranny the converse of liberty and free choice; inequality of all kinds, or of some particular perceived kind, the converse of justice. Therefore, to introduce a consideration of values—their interpretation, their distribution and the overall balance maintained between them (what was referred to above as the trade-off in values)—is also by implication to lay an equal and corresponding emphasis on the nature of threats to their enjoyment, and to the manner in which the risk of those threats becoming effective is either avoided, averted, diminished or compensated for in the political economy of a society be it a family, a nation or a world system. It follows that in any analysis of a society or a political economy, we must pay attention not only to the costs of achieving that particular mix of values and that particular pattern of their distribution, but must also consider the nature of the attendant risks, their incidence and their management.

Considered in this way, it is also clear that within each structure, there tends to be strong emphasis on one particular kind of risk—yet because of the interaction of structures already referred to, we can no longer afford to consider their respective risks—any more than their respective values—in isolation from each other.

Specifically, it is obvious that the study of international relations has historically been primarily concerned with the risk of war created by the repartition of political power among a large number of territorial states and their enjoyment of a monopoly of violence within their respective territories. As a field of study, international relations has therefore been rather good at analysing the kind of perceived risks to state security that lay behind such international conflicts as, for instance, the Berlin blockade, the Korean War or the Falklands conflict. It has been less clear or coherent when it comes to dealing with the different kinds of risk—for example, with the risks to economic security, or to financial stability that were perceived on either side (i.e., by producers and consumers) at the time of the OPEC oil price rise, or are now perceived in relation to the question of LDC (less developed countries) indebtedness.

The 'Maginot Liners', no doubt, would like to preserve this rather limited concern with one kind of risk. But it is obvious to a growing number of political economists, I believe, that— as happened in 1974 and could happen again—the risk of war could arise out of a risk of deprivation of energy supplies, and that the repartition of power among 'sovereign' states, most of which are inextricably involved now in an integrated trade and financial system, creates risks of another but also very serious kind—of the anarchy and breakdown that occur not through conflict of governments but through an absence of government and authority to control and counterbalance forces of the market.

The study of liberal economics for the most part has also had a rather constricted, even crippling approach to the concept of risk. First of all, it has considered risk primarily in relation to the creation or enjoyment of wealth—and hardly at all in relation to other values sought by organized society. And for historical reasons to which I shall return later, it has drawn an artificial distinction between conditional risk (i.e., 'accidental' risk as of death, illness, burglary, etc.) and entrepreneurial risk. The first is left to the state to avert or to mitigate and the insurance industry to compensate, while the second provided the justification for the notion of profit over and above the rate of interest to be paid on capital to equalize the satisfactions of saving and spending (i.e., the 'price' of money).

Thus it is to the sociologists we have to turn to appreciate that much can be learnt about a society by asking the sort of questions I have listed above, about the way in which risk is perceived, created, managed and distributed. Knowing how the society creates and distributes its wealth—the production structure—is important, as is knowing how it manages conflict to create a structure of security. But knowing how a society perceives and manages different kinds of risk may sometimes tell us more than either about the politics of its economy. And it is certainly true that socio-economic systems often differ more on this—the perception and management of risk—than on either the treatment of wealth or the administration of law, order and security.

To illustrate the point, consider the perception of risk in mediaeval Christendom or, for that matter, in Hindu India. The risk of eternal damnation or of almost interminable purgatory for the soul—or for the Hindus of being born again as a rat—was thought to be at least as much to be feared as being miserable, murdered or starved on earth. The priest or the guru who would rid you of this risk, or at least mitigate your liability to it, was accorded power, prestige and often (if they wanted it) wealth as well. The rules governing behaviour similarly reflected both the perception of risk and the appreciation of groups and institutions with power to deal with it. Authority was therefore divided between the Church with power against the long-term risks and the state, prince or ruler, with power against the short-term ones.

The example of the priest and the guru, moreover, leads us to another important general point. For both acquired authority not only negatively by their claim to avert a serious personal risk, but also positively by holding out the promise of a great opportunity—to get to heaven or paradise or to achieve nirvana or a state of divine detachment. As with most forms of authority, theirs rested on fear and on hope—fear of the risks perceived and hope of benefit from the perceived opportunities. So perhaps I should amend the earlier statement that risk is about the converse of all the values sought by individuals and by organized societies. It might be more correct to say that attention to values sought by individuals and organized societies implies attention to the distribution both of the risks of losing such values and to the opportunities of achieving them.

The generalization can be applied quite usefully to the political and economic history of our own society or world system. For one of the characteristics of the advent of capitalism and the so-called industrial revolution was the change brought about in the nature and incidence of perceived risk and perceived opportunity. Note that (as with Rawls's concept of justice), it is the perception more than the objective reality (even if that exists) which really matters.

In Western Europe, from the sixteenth century onwards, a whole new class, the bourgeoisie, began to perceive that new opportunities were opening to them to mitigate the risk of poverty by means other than by acquiring power—that is, other than by acquiring the direct power to coerce and exact services and goods that had been exercised in earlier times by feudal lords. This new class, by accumulating capital, could reap profits from organizing production or trade. Conversely, the organization of production for expanding markets meant that the poor risked starvation not only when the harvest failed, as under feudalism, but also when the factory closed or they were unemployed. All sorts of individual risks—of death, disease, want of all kinds—consequently became much more unevenly distributed among society. The rich lived longer, ate better and were cleaner, therefore avoided many of the diseases which afflicted and killed off the poor. At the same time, opportunities multiplied for the able and enterprising, creating a social safety valve in the hope of success in seizing them.

For this was by no means certain. To acquire the wealth, entrepreneurs had to take new kinds of 'entrepreneurial' risk. To help them assume this risk, two things happened, both with the aid and support of the state. For the ruler soon perceived a close connection between its own chances of enhancing the power of the state and the chances open to the bourgeoisie to generate wealth through capitalist enterprise. All the capitalist states therefore acted very quickly to mitigate the risks to the entrepreneur. One of the best and commonest ways to do this was to limit legal liability to the extent of the original financial investment in the enterprise. If a venture failed, the entrepreneur lost his enterprise and his investment—but not his house or his land or other possessions.

Another important political decision was to translate into law the conceptual separation already referred to between entrepreneurial risk and conditional or actuarial risk—and thus to promote the use of insurance as an indispensable adjunct first to trade (and especially sea trade because of the serious risks of shipwreck or piracy) and then to production. And a corollary of legalizing and encouraging insurance—which involved also legalizing usury because insurers can only operate profitably if they invest the premiums they collect for insurers —was that the state then had to guard the entrepreneurs and indeed the whole economic fabric against the risks of failure, bankruptcy or fraud run by the banks and the insurers. Rules had to be made and institutions developed both to govern and to restrict the uses made of funds collected, or to prescribe the amount of capital and reserves necessary for a given type and volume of loans made on policies underwritten. Restrictions had to be made on access to the business, limiting it to specific kinds of company or individual. Insurance, then, is as inseparable as banking from the capitalist structure of production and exchange, based as it is on the private assumption of (limited, manageable and shared) economic risks.

The alternative path to economic development and industrialization—that of authoritarian economic planning by the state—can be seen as either centralizing economic risks in the hands of the state or, since the state in this sense is a fiction, of generalizing almost all economic risks to the whole society. Thus, if the state as entrepreneur fails to provide enough toilet paper (as apparently if often does in the Soviet Union), then everyone carries the risk of making do without it. But in this sort of system, while the individual as producer or worker is largely relieved of the burden of economic risk, he or she has to live with much greater burdens of political risk— to social status, livelihood, liberty and even life. For in order to organize production and extract surplus value from it for investment and growth, the state must be able to coerce labour and suppress dissidence. Hence the perceived threat to the very heart of the system of the Polish workers' demands for free labour unions.

Alternatively, looking at the opportunity side of the risk coin, one could say that the difference between a liberal democratic political system and an authoritarian one lies in the distribution between government and opposition of the value of liberty—of the opportunity to choose. In authoritarian political systems, governments are freer and less constrained, and have more choice of policies. Conversely, dissenters opposing governments have much less freedom because they run the risk of imprisonment, exile or in extreme cases, death. Governments, therefore, enjoy greater freedom and greater security from popular discontent; dissenters have less freedom and less security. And the real difference between an economic system based on the market and one based on direction of resources has as much to do with the structure of distribution as it has with the production of structure. The market system where it exists—which of course is by no means everywhere even in the so-called world market economy—offers greater opportunity and freedom to choose, not only to consumers but also to workers in the choice of jobs and to managers in the choice of technologies and markets. Opportunities are more restricted in the directed system, but so are risks—or at least economic risks of bankruptcy or redundancy for managers or workers.

Reality, however, is far less black and white, not so either-or, as this. It is not only that in some important respects the two contrasted systems are converging so that planned or socialist states, including the Soviet Union, make increasing use of profit motives and insurance systems as capitalist states become increasingly involved in the hazards of industrial enterprise or lack of it. It is also that both kinds of national system are— as everyone continues to point out—increasingly involved and integrated into a single world economic system in which the perceived distribution of risks and opportunities seems characterized by a good deal of the worst of both worlds.

Reasons of space oblige me to be rather brief in explaining that last remark, but the grounds for making it are surely familiar to everyone. The integration of national economies, at an accelerating pace over the last ten or fifteen years, into one world economy, appears to have added greatly to the production of quantifiable output in agriculture, mining, industry and services. But within the total of world GNP in the 1980s, there are included many trivial and frivolous quantifiables (pet foods, potted plants, television games, 'brand' advertisements, junk foods), which accepted methods of accounting weight heavier than the loss of certain basic and valued unquantifiables (subsistence crops, plentiful fish stocks, timber reserves, water tables, clean air, job satisfaction, confidence in the future).

The achievement of increased wealth in the system, however measured, therefore, must be set against the accompanying increase in inequity and in insecurity—as documented in the Brandt Report and the Annual Reports of the last two years of all the major international economic organizations—the World Bank, the International Monetary Fund, the Organization for Economic Cooperation and Development, UNCTAD and even the Bank for International Settlements. This is where the value of the concept of risk can be appreciated. For the 'costs' of increased wealth are seen first in the increased *systemic* risks that have been incurred; and secondly in the increased inequity in the distribution of risk and opportunity as well as the distribution of benefits in the form of income, health care, education, housing, etc., etc.

The increased systemic risks are both political and economic. The main systemic risks of a vertical nature arise not from the economy *per se* but from the states' participation in the integrated world market for elements and for nuclear power. This has led to situations of increasing insecurity, both internal and international. The risks of a mainly economic nature concern the financial stability of the entire Western economy, resting as it does on an international banking system that is without constraints or a sure lender of last resort; yet whose credit-creating institutions now begin to fear for their own security. It is significant that warnings of financial collapse from almost all the noted experts, academics and practitioners, have never been so numerous or so insistent as they have been in the past year.

The increased risks have not, on the whole, been accompanied by a corresponding increase in the opportunities for development of new forms of collective government, primarily because the international political system has been frozen, to all intents and purposes, by the need to win consent from 'independent' states for the collective action which intellectually and as individuals, those concerned may concede to be necessary for survival—or at any rate for a reasonable measure of security. All this is fairly familiar ground to students of international political economy.

The increased inequity in the distribution of risks and opportunities is comparatively ill-favoured by academic research. I have already noted the disparity between national welfare systems and the consequent disparity between principles underlying United States', Japanese and European policy-making towards commodity stabilization for primary producers at home and towards the very same issue in the world at large. More evidence of the same inequity is to be found in the data concerning world insurance—scanty and incomplete as it is. There is an enormous disparity between the expenditure of the rich and poor countries of the world on insurance against risk, whether personal (life and health insurance) or corporate (damage by fire, flood, robbery or negligence). In constant dollars, the world total spent on insurance went from $20

billion in 1950 to over $100 billion in 1980. As a percentage
of world GNP, this represented a rise from 3.61 per cent of
world GNP to 4.78 per cent. And within the total, the disparity grew between America, where 7.06 per cent of a very
high GNP was spent on compensation for risk, and Africa,
where only 1.5 per cent of a small GNP went on insurance.[6]
During this time moreover, it is generally accepted that
several factors have combined to increase the general incidence
of risk. Probably the most important one is technology. By
increasing capital costs in every sector from agriculture to data
retrieval, technology has increased the cost of accidents,
whether a fire, crime or malfunction. (In Europe today, for
instance, 1 per cent of GNP is lost by fires, many of them
associated with chemicals and synthetic fibres.) Another factor
is the proliferation of weak states supposedly in charge of
pieces of the world economy which nevertheless are considered
important enough to be integrated, through trade and investment, into the financial and trade system. 'Sovereign risk'
is a recurrent nightmare for many international bankers. The
third factor is the resistance of those with political power to
economic change. The failure of American and European
steel and textile producers, for example, to adjust to Japanese
and NIC low-cost competitors increases the risk of eventual
breakdown.[7] It is no accident that in the business world, corporate risk management is the one professional field with real
prospects of growth and personal advancement.

CONCLUSION

The conclusion to be drawn, however, is not simply that we
should include insurance and banking as politically important
sectors for study by international political economists. It goes,
I think, rather further. For attention to increasing risk and
to the widening rich/poor gap in both the incidence and the
capacity to cope with risk, points to a major feature of the
world system, and one which currently fashionable approaches
to international political economy totally fail, in my opinion,
to comprehend. This feature is the changing balance between
authority and markets, between government and entrepreneurs.
From 1932 to 1945, it can generally be agreed that there was
a steady shift in the other direction—toward government

control and toward collective responsibility for welfare and the redressing of economic inequity within states, and towards management to eliminate or offset, so far as possible, the mercurial rise and fall of the business cycle. From 1968 until the present, the tide has been going exactly the other way. Yet the academic study of international political economy in these same years has perversely focused on a concept of international regimes, despite the evident fact that in most aspects and structures, from Strategic Arms Limitation Talks (SALT) to United Nations Conference on the Law of the Sea (UNCLOS), from Non-Tariff Barriers against imports (NTBs) to debt-rescheduling, the trend has been towards deregulation, de-control and non-regimes—with the attendant probability of increased risks to political as well as economic security in the system.

It seems to me that the clear implication is that this self-deluding concern with 'regimes' that often prove to be non-regimes urgently needs to be checked. Professor Bilder, in the book already quoted, is indeed quite right in directing attention to the processes of bargaining, and of bargaining exchanges, which take into account not only costs and benefits but also the balance between different kinds of risks and different assortments of opportunities.

NOTES AND REFERENCES

1. For a more extended explanation of this alternative concept of the monetary structure, see my article, 'The world's money—an agenda for research', *International Journal*, 36 (1981), 691–712.
2. The best general descriptive work is still the late Colin Cherry's book *World Communications*, now being revised and updated at the Hubert Humphries Institute, University of Minneapolis.
3. Besides the well-known work of Braudel (*The Mediterranean in the Age of Philip II: Capitalism and Material Life 1400–1800*, trans. by Sian Reynolds (London, Collins, 1972)), there are some interesting recent developments in research on this theme. For example, W. Macneill, 'The industrialisation of war', *Review of International Studies*, 8 (1982), 203–13, and an unpublished thesis by Gautam Sen of the London School of Economics.
4. But at some social cost—well argued in M. Morishima's recent, *Why Japan Succeeded* (Cambridge, Cambridge University Press, 1982).
5. Richard B. Bilder, *Managing the Risks of International Agreement*,

reviewed by D. Dunn in *Millennium: Journal of International Studies*, 11 (1982), 90-1.

6. Orio Gianni, 'Development economique et croissance des risques', *Geneva Papers on Risk and Insurance*, 7 (1982). Also SIGMA 1981 'Croissance et structure de l'assurance dans le monde', *Etudes Economiques de la Compagnie Suisse de Reassurances* (July 1981). The International Institute for Applied Systems Analysis, Laxenbourg, Austria, which is the only research institution which is supported by both the United States and the Soviet Union, initiated jointly with IAEA in Vienna in 1974 a study of survey technologies that might reveal factors affecting the perceptions of risk and social attitudes to risk with the purpose of reducing uncertainties in the general policy-making process. The IAEA interest in this project derived from understandable conern with risks connected with nuclear power plants and the use of nuclear fuels. See H. Otway and P. Pahner, 'Risk assessment', in J. Dowie and P. Lefrere, *Risk and Chance: Selected Readings* (Milton Keynes, Open University Press, 1980).

7. GATT Annual Report, 1982, *International Trade, 1981/82*.

ROGER TOOZE

INTRODUCTION

This chapter suggests a partial framework for the analysis of problems and outcomes in the international political economy. It does not put forward an all-embracing theory, nor does it offer a deliberation of the traditional liberal v. Marxist interpretations of the nature of the international political economy. What is suggested here does, however, provide new and useful insights and gets us out of some of the theoretical problems created by both the substantive development and the academic study of the international political economy (IPE).

Before we delve into the 'sectoral' it is necessary to clear the intellectual ground a little and lay out a few basic working assumptions. First, that part of social reality we call 'the international political economy' is much more than the aggregate of the external policies of national political economies. That is, in a theoretical sense, it is not epiphenomenal. Many of the outcomes which are problematic to national governments, and other social groups, can only be explained through the postulated existence of an intervening structure which influences and affects 'who gets what' in the global system. A simple and traditional model of exchange relationships between national political economies[1] can certainly illuminate certain aspects of some problems, but its explanatory power is severely limited once we attempt an explanation of, say, international monetary instability[2] or the distribution of economic power within the global system.[3]

The precise nature and status of such an international political economy is clearly debatable, although the world systems theorists and Marxist scholars contend that national and international political economy form an ontological whole,[4] thus negating any distinction between national and international political economy. The position taken here is that the ideological delimitation of areas of social enquiry which produced the academic distinction between politics and international relations[5] and the separation of economics and politics merely

serves to obfuscate, maintain and justify present power structures. Hence, understanding the international political economy
now demands more than a synthesis of existing (and therefore
limited) politics, economics and international relations theory.
It demands that we examine the ontological and epistemological
bases of the methodologies and concepts we use before we
proceed with the construction of new, and more relevant,
explanations.[6]

However, and third, we are not yet at the stage of a 'satisfactory' theory of IPE. We are still developing, but now in a
more productive dialectical fashion, theories and criteria for
theory evaluation, which may mean stepping out of long
cherished 'social scientific' methodologies. But, perhaps more
important, we do not yet have sufficient appropriate knowledge
for even an adequate analytical description of the IPE. In this
age of information overload our understanding is still confined
by the concepts and models upon which we base our categories
and questions. And these categories and questions in the main
continue to refer to a world which is often incongruent with
the complex and dynamic global structures we are seeking to
describe and explain.

The predominant image of political-economic relations
within the international relations literature is still (with notable
exceptions) one of interaction between territorially bounded
national economies. Even when concepts that go beyond
a national actor perspective are introduced, such as Waltz's
'structure',[7] they are ultimately reductionist, in that international relations is essentially seen as international politics
and the 'state-as-actor' model is implicit.[8] This national actor
perspective is ideologically based and is too narrow for IPE.
'Actor' based models, in conjunction with empirical social-
science methodologies, have no room for broader 'structural'
analyses, particularly of power. A focus upon actors and institutions cannot encompass the totality of relationships that
frames the parameters for action, that gives direction and
meaning to ideology and that rationalizes and justifies the
exercise and distribution of power and wealth. Moreover,
an actor focus ignores structural power, i.e. the structural
determination of an entity's requirements/wants by the system
within which that entity functions. And these requirements
are not universal givens, but are determined over time by a

sequence of decisions, values and relationships which are incorporated into the structure itself, and which can change as well as change the structure. Historical, structural models of IPE are consequently likely to be more rewarding, and we need, therefore, to fit our empirical enquiries to revised conceptions. But which conceptions?

In the search for a coherent analytical description of the contemporary IPE much current work is of limited scope and applicability. For example 'issue-area' and 'regime' analysis both seem to offer convenient and useful ways of understanding IPE,[9] but both are grounded within a particular and ideological problematic which takes its structural parameters as given.[10] 'Issue area' analysis breaks down complexity and is part of an essential process of theoretical disaggregation, but used on its own it is fundamentally flawed because it fails to take account of the power structures by which issues become issues. If these structural parameters are either not acknowledged or change, 'problem solving theory', such as issue-area and regime analysis, is in trouble.

What seems to be required is a range of complementary analytical frameworks which can account for the development of historical structures, through their critical nature, as well as the bewildering diversity of contemporary IPE at all levels. One of the weaknesses of the world systems work, notwithstanding its many strengths, is its fuzziness when explaining developments and problems in particular sectors and subnational levels of economic activity. Other analytical frameworks, more limited but still with a critical awareness of historical structure, can be used to illuminate this level of diversity and complexity. The key is the link between 'micro' and 'macro' levels.

SECTORAL ANALYSIS AND WORLD ECONOMY

Sectoral analysis attempts to link these levels. Sectoral analysis is simply 'any study of the political economy of a specific industry in its world context, or of specific markets for goods or services'.[11] The purpose served by such studies is left open: all that is required is that sectoral studies are centred on a product or a service which forms part of an integrated world economy, either because it is traded across frontiers, or because its production involves the use of finance, labour, land or knowledge drawn from two or more national economies.

An important structural change within IPE has been the emergence of a 'world economy', which coexists with the older 'international economy'.[12] The international economy is based on nation states with territorially defined national economies in a system of exchange relationships. The world economy is that which defines space in terms of production and service systems which extend beyond national territorial boundaries. Where the world economy interacts and combines with the territorial systems of political economy outcomes are modified. But the assimilation of international into world economy is not uniform—it clearly varies by national economy and by sector. To the extent that certain sectors, such as petrochemicals, are part of the world economy, behaviour and outcomes in these sectors differ from those that are still predominantly within the international economy. Moreover, a world economy, as opposed to a purely international economy, is composed of a variety of functional sub-structures which articulate certain parameters of action e.g. the international monetary structure. And each of these functional structures influences different sectors in different ways. Steel, because of its importance within national structures, presents different problems of economic adjustment from, say, textiles, and has, in effect, *a different political economy*. Or, from the focus of public policy, problems of protectionism can be more easily explained by looking at sector behaviour rather than only national or international structures.[13] The differences do not relate solely to positions within, and the nature of, national structures, they reflect within each sector different technology market and production structures and a myriad of different bargains struck at every stage of investment, production, exchange and distribution.

What is envisaged is a range of frameworks, each vested within or linked to the other. These would include analyses of the particular structures of the world political economy—security, production, money and credit, etc.—and the relationship of these within the whole, and analysis of the various sectors that make up the totality of activity. In effect a 'sector' exhibits similar defining characteristics as a 'structure'; that is, it sets the terms in which problems are formulated and the options available for their resolution. On this reasoning different sectors could be expected to produce different structural constraints and initiatives. In practice these differing constraints have been shown to account for more behaviour than incorporation within a national economy. For example, the capability to react successfully to surplus capacity problems is more a sector characteristic than a national unit characteristic.[14] The simple aggregation of sectors into their respective national unit, regardless of their technological and market dynamics and their level of assimilation into the world economy, is no longer sufficient. Internal sector dynamics, throughout all levels of activity, can have greater explanatory power than factors relating to national or international structures. This means disaggregating national political economies and then linking the sector studies to an analysis of the whole. Only if the analysis links the sector to a wider framework can disaggregation do more than illuminate differences between units and outcomes within each (although this is important in itself). Recent innovative work to explain long-wave economic fluctuations could only succeed by disaggregating macro (i.e. national) economic behaviour into a series of detailed sectoral models and interpreting the sector results within the theoretical literature on the Kondratieff cycle.[15] It is then extremely difficult to explain change at the macro level without investigating sectoral conditions.

Sectoral analysis can also obviate the problems caused by the separation of national and international politics. Analysis of a sector reintegrates four levels of political economy—subnational, national, international and world. We do not assume that activity at any one level is *inherently* distinct from any other level, although in practice differences may occur according to the characteristics of the sector. We can, on this assumption, revise the basis for the study of IPE because there is, for sector political economy, no *a prior* separation between the 'domestic' and the 'foreign' (nor between economics and politics).

SECTORAL ANALYSIS

From the foregoing argument sectors are highly relevant, but necessarily limited, theoretical domains of contemporary IPE:

they link different levels of political economy, focus on factors that would otherwise be discounted and make us look at IPE in a non-territorial organizational way. But how do we now analyse sectors? Once we have acknowledged the legitimacy of a sectoral approach—and its costs as well as benefits—the content of such an approach becomes important.

There is no one way of analysing sectors. Much depends on the individual's purpose and predilections. What is absolutely necessary, however, is a *real* political economy analysis, which takes nothing for granted and is concerned with evaluating technological as well as political and economic influences. The problem has been succinctly put by John Zysman in his excellent pioneering analysis of the French political economy:

The analytic approaches of the political scientist and the economist may be valuable for the particular range of problems they chose to attack; the difficulty is that many important questions fall into the chasm between them.[16]

One way of avoiding this problem, apart from the method developed by Zysman, is through the notion of economic power[17] and the focus, therefore, on all the different sources of bargaining power and influence over outcomes within a sector—whether this is from world, international, national or market structures and is exercised by governments or corporations, by buyers or sellers or middlemen, by labour or by management or by some other sector.

However, to get this far is not sufficient. Much work seems to be going on at the moment looking at various sectors. If this work is to be of maximum value it should be broadly comparable over a wide range of sectors—energy and resources, primary products, manufacturing and services. This does not mean generating a rigid 'comparative' framework and then filling in the requisite boxes—that would probably do us more harm than good at the moment! What it does mean though, is some broad agreement on the general attributes of a sectoral approach and the major questions to be asked.

With this in mind, it is more appropriate to indicate potential areas of enquiry rather than develop a particular analysis in depth. It would seem that there are at least four major areas of enquiry necessary for a thorough sectoral analysis:

The nature of the production process.

The nature and structure of the market.

The nature of sub-national, national, international and world structures.

The specific authority/market bargains that condition sector behaviour.

Each area is complementary and overlapping, one influencing the other, rather than exclusive. Technological change in the production process can suddenly involve a particular sector in a new authority/market bargain (fish), whilst a particular international structure may involve more (or less) state control, and, of course, different state structures vary enormously in the direct political salience they give to different sectors (and, because structures are not immutable, salience varies over time).

The nature of the production process

The power to influence outcomes in the production process is a critical factor in IPE—whether you have it or not, whether you are a small company or a large country, or whether you are a redundant steel worker or an overworked software consultant.

Four sources of power over the production process have been identified and these provide the framework for this area of enquiry:[18]

  (i) *Purchasing power*—seen as the primary determinant of the production structure.

 (ii) *Designing power*—the capacity to develop a technology; but technological development by itself is not sufficient to ensure continuing influence (computers, aircraft).

(iii) *Financial power*—the ability to provide capital for investment: who provides finance and what are the financial reserves of bargaining partners, unions or management, buyers or sellers? Becoming increasingly important in sectors of high risk.

(iv) *Production power*—limited (or enhanced) by barriers restraining others from joining, by substitution of alternatives, stockholding, market swings and political power.

The nature and structure of the market

How are agreements that result in price (and other terms which govern exchange) reached between buyers and sellers and what factors influence these? Enormous variations are found depending on the nature of the market—whether it is stable or volatile, or if it is declining, static or expanding and how it is arranged: managed or not, and, if managed, by whom? A whole host of factors influence market bargains, some very clear (number, size and extent of vertical integration of producers), some not so clear (sudden government intervention to restrict previously open markets, as in automobiles), but it is difficult, if not impossible, to generalize. What is not questionable, however, is the importance of ascertaining the market structure and its impact.

The nature of sub-national, national, international and world structures

These structures provide the context for the development and direction of each sector, and they change over time as a result of other influences (including the impact of particular sectors themselves). National structures may not involve the state at all in a particular sector, but increasingly it is political salience which is the key (although authority can be derived from sources other than the state), if only because the state is a major influence over outcomes in the IPE. The perceived importance of a sector to the basic economic and political strategies of the state, sub-nationally, nationally and internationally, is the crucial factor in deciding the degree and nature of government involvement with the sector, and, hence, the decisive patterns of relationships within it. What makes a sector 'important' varies with the sector and the structure and, again, generalization seems impossible: salience varies over time as well, and at any given time what is important (strategic as opposed to non-strategic?) is arbitrary. The micro-electronic sector is clearly attaining the level of political saliency in OECD countries that was once solely held by steel and shipbuilding. Even in those sectors perceived as always salient (defence, energy) the limits are far from clear.

International structures, whether resulting from a broad historical process, a hegemonic system or just plain negotiated, are an important consideration. What international rules, institutions, norms and agreements exist and what effect do they have on sector behaviour? In this context regimes may be seen as specific instances of structure. However defined, international regimes and, more importantly, non-regimes mediate between the market and the state, collectively and individually, either to protect industry within the state from market and production power or to enhance domestic industry through the creation of a 'favourable regime'. Whatever the case, the influence over outcomes can be decisive.

World structures are distinct from international structures in the same way that the international economy differs from the world economy. They are the overarching, historical structures that condition values and ideologies and set the total context of political economy. In many cases they are not articulated, and in some cases (such as the development of the Euro money markets)[19] the emergence of 'new' processes and institutions is only symptomatic of deeper underlying change stemming from tension between the different structures of IPE. The effect of these structures on sectors and the way we analyse sectors is great and we have, at least, to acknowledge this influence.

Authority/market bargains

A final area of enquiry is the nature of the authority/market bargains that exist within the sector. This is obviously related to the other three areas but catches some questions that the others miss out. Since there is no market or enterprise anywhere totally unaffected by authority, the question of how authority is exercised and by whom is essential. And the 'by whom' is important because authority can have diverse sources. It may come from an explicitly organized public political institution or from some private body, like a labour union, a professional association or a cartel of corporations. In some important cases the market itself acts as a source of authority. As the sources of authority are multiple so are the consequences of its impact upon production and exchange, and therefore the outcomes of these processes, not only in terms of the benefits but the costs and risks of economic activity as well. Whose interest is legitimated by authority if, say, authority intervenes to maintain, or suppress, competition? And who decides the share of the costs for necessary public goods (infrastructure) for a sector, and who bears the brunt of any public 'bads' on an international and world as well as national level?

CONCLUSIONS?

The only conclusion is that there are no 'conclusions'! We have yet to map out the changes currently happening in the IPE, particularly in patterns and processes of industrialization.[20] It is the contention of this chapter that to the extent that the international economy becomes an integrated world economy our problems of understanding and explaining the IPE will grow and to that extent, a sectoral approach, broadly along the lines suggested here, will help. Only by standing outside of the comfortable concepts and frameworks that we are used to, can we expect to understand and achieve change.

NOTES AND REFERENCES

1. This is the conventional notion of the international economy embodied in the majority of books on international relations and international economics.
2. See particularly E. L. Versluyen, *The Political Economy of International Finance* (Aldershot, Gower, 1981); and D. T. Llewellyn, *International Financial Integration* (London, Macmillan, 1981).
3. See W. Ladd Hollist and J. N. Rosenau, eds, *World Systems Structure* (Beverly Hills, Sage, 1981); and T. L. Hopkins and I. Wallerstein, eds, *World Systems Analysis: Theory and Methodology* (Beverly Hills, Sage, 1982).
4. Here ontology is used in the sense developed by Quine, i.e., to the existence of what kind of thing does belief in a given theory commit us? Willard van Orman Quine, *From a Logical Point of View* (Oxford, Oxford University Press, 1953).
5. See the discussion on this point in Susan Strange and Roger Tooze, eds, *The International Political Economy of Surplus Capacity* (London, George Allen & Unwin, 1981), Ch. 1.
6. For an excellent example of an attempt to do just this see Richard K. Ashley, *The Political Economy of War and Peace* (London, Frances Pinter, 1980), particularly Appendix A.
7. K. N. Waltz, *Theory of International Politics* (New York, Addison-Wesley, 1979).
8. See particularly John Maclean, 'Political theory, international theory

and problems of ideology', *Millennium: Journal of International Studies*, 10 (1981), 102-25.

9. See *International Organization*, 36 (1982), a special issue on 'Regimes'.
10. This is what Robert Cox calls 'problem solving theory' (R. W. Cox, 'Production, hegemony and the future', *American Political Science Association* (Washington, 1980), mimeo).
11. This is the concept used in Strange and Tooze, op. cit.
12. For a pioneering theoretical discussion see Charles Albert Michaelet, *Le Capitalisme Mondial* (Paris, Presses Universitaires de France, 1976) and Charles Albert Michaelet, 'From international trade to world economy', in H. Makler and N. Smelser, eds, *The New International Economy* (Beverly Hills, Sage, 1982).
13. For the notion of sectoral protectionism see S. D. Cohen, 'Coping with the new protectionism', *National Westminster Bank Review* (November, 1978), 3-15.
14. See the sector studies in Strange and Tooze, op. cit.
15. Cf. the discussion by Manfred Bienefeld in Strange and Tooze, ibid. Bienefeld draws attention to the work of the Systems Dynamics Group of the Alfred P. Sloane School of Management at MIT.
16. John Zysman, *Political Strategies for Industrial Order* (Berkeley, University of California Press, 1977), p. 10.
17. See Susan Strange, 'What is economic power and who has it?', *International Journal*, 30 (1975), 207-24 for an analysis of the content of the concept.
18. Strange, ibid.
19. See R. B. Johnston, *The Euromarkets: History, Theory and Policy* (London, Macmillan, 1982).
20. See R. H. Ballance and S. W. Sinclair, *World Industry in Transition* (London, George Allen & Unwin, forthcoming).

Notes on Contributors

Colin Crouch is Reader in Sociology at the London School of Economics and Political Science. He is the author of *The Student Revolt* (1970), *Class Conflict and the Industrial Relations Crisis* (1977), *The Politics of Industrial Relations* (1979 and 1982), and *Trade Unions: the Logic of Collective Action* (1982). He is the editor of *Stress and Contradiction in Modern Capitalism* (1975, with L. N. Lindberg and others), *British Political Sociology Yearbook*, Vol. III: *Participation in Politics* (1977), *The Resurgence of Class Conflict in Western Europe since 1968*, two volumes (1978, with A. Pizzorno), and *State and Economy in Contemporary Capitalism* (1979). He has also written several articles in the fields of social stratification, industrial relations and social policy. He is a member of the editorial boards of *Political Quarterly, New Universities Quarterly, Survey* and *Stato e Mercato*, and is a former chairman of the Fabian Society.

Andrew Gamble is Reader in Political Theory and Institutions at the University of Sheffield. His books include *The Conservative Nation* (1974) and *Britain in Decline* (1981). In cooperation with P. Walton he has published *From Alienation to Surplus Value* (1972) and *Capitalism in Crisis: Inflation and the State* (1976). He has also written several articles and papers on political economy.

Wyn Grant is Senior Lecturer in Politics at the University of Warwick. He is co-author of *The Confederation of British Industry* and author of *The Political Economy of Industrial Policy* (1982).

R. J. Barry Jones lectures on politics and international relations in the Department of Politics, University of Reading. He co-edited *Change and the Study of International Relations: The Evaded Dimension* (1981) and has written a number of papers and articles on international relations' theory, 'appeasement', and international political economy. He helped found the British International Studies Association and is a member of the editorial board of the *Review of International Studies* (formerly the *British Journal of International Studies*). Since 1975 he has convened the SSRC-supported International Relations Theory Research Group.

David McKay lectures in the Department of Government at the University of Essex. He is also the Director of the ECPR/ Essex University Summer School in Social Science Data Analysis and Collection. He is joint editor, with Wyn Grant, of *Industrial Policies in OECD Countries* (special edition of the *Journal of Public Policy*, vol. 3, February 1982).

Charles K. Rowley is Professor of Economics at the University of Newcastle upon Tyne and Director of its Centre for Research in Public and Industrial Economics. His publications include *The British Monopolies Commission* (1966), *Steel and Public Policy* (1971), *Antitrust and Economic Efficiency* (1972), and, with A. T. Peacock, *Welfare Economics: A Liberal Restatement* (1975).

Susan Strange has been Professor of International Relations at the London School of Economics and Political Science since 1978 and was previously Senior Research Fellow at the Royal Institute of International Affairs, Chatham House. She is married to Clifford Selly, lives in Buckinghamshire and has six children. Among many publications are *Sterling and British Policy: A Political Study of an International Currency in Decline* (1971) and, with Roger Tooze, *The International Political Economy of Surplus Capacity* (1981).

Roger Tooze is Senior Lecturer in the Department of International Relations and Politics, North Staffordshire Polytechnic. He is co-editor of *The International Political Economy of Surplus Capacity* (1981) and has written articles on international political economy. He has convened the international political economy group.

Name Index

Subject Index